D1560645

Microsoft®
Systems
Management
Server
Resource Guide

Microsoft Press

PUBLISHED BY
Microsoft Press
A Division of Microsoft Corporation
One Microsoft Way
Redmond, Washington 98052-6399

Library of Congress Cataloging-in-Publication Data pending.

Printed and bound in the United States of America.

1 2 3 4 5 6 7 8 9   QMQM   1 0 9 8 7 6

Distributed to the book trade in Canada by Macmillan of Canada, a division of Canada Publishing Corporation.

A CIP catalogue record for this book is available from the British Library.

Microsoft Press books are available through booksellers and distributors worldwide. For further information about international editions, contact your local Microsoft Corporation office. Or contact Microsoft Press International directly at fax (206) 936-7329.

Microsoft, the Microsoft logo, Microsoft Press, the Microsoft Press logo, MS-DOS, PowerPoint, Visual C++, Win32, Windows, and Windows NT are registered trademarks and BackOffice is a trademark of Microsoft Corporation in the United States and/or other countries.

Other product and company names herein may be the trademarks of their respective owners.

Part Number: 097-0001677 (Systems Management Server Resource Guide)

Acquisitions Editor: Casey Doyle
Project Editor: Stuart J. Stuple

Contributors

Technical Writers:

Tami Beutel, Steve Kahn, Bill Muse, Candy Paape, Tim Toyoshima

Technical Consultants:

Bruce Copeland, Doyle Cronk, Mike Davis, Ben Gamble, Rick Hantz, Jennifer Harrison, Anat Kerry, Wally Mead, Oscar Newkerk, Yvette O'Meally, Roger Padvorac, Ken Pan, Michael Poling, Louise Rudnicki, Luis Salazar, Rob Wickham, David Wohlferd, Jeff Young

Technical Editor:

Marian Ranum

Production:

David Oxley, Erin Pearson

Indexer:

Julie Hatley

Graphic Designers:

Flora Goldthwaite, Sue Wyble

Graphic Artist:

Johnni Cutler

Contents

Introduction

Welcome to the *Microsoft® Systems Management Server Resource Guide*. This guide is designed for people who are, or who want to become, expert users of Microsoft Systems Management Server (SMS). The *Microsoft Systems Management Server Resource Guide* is a technical supplement to the documentation included as part of the SMS product and does not replace that information as the source for learning how to use SMS.

This guide is included in the *Microsoft BackOffice™ Resource Kit*. The *Microsoft BackOffice Resource Kit* also includes many tools that you can use to support your SMS implementation. For more information about the SMS tools, see the SMSTOOLS.HLP file on the *Microsoft BackOffice Resource Kit* compact disc.

About the Resource Guide

This guide includes the following chapters.

Chapter 1, "Server Reference" Describes the different types of servers used in SMS, and the components, shares, directories, and files used on those servers.

Chapter 2, "Client Reference" Describes the components used on SMS clients, and the files installed on the clients.

Chapter 3, "System Flow" Describes in detail how SMS performs its primary functions. Includes detailed system flow diagrams that illustrate how the components interact.

Chapter 4, "File Formats" Describes the text-based files that SMS uses to maintain system performance.

Chapter 5, "Working with Systems Management Server" Describes a variety of tips for working with SMS. Includes information on working with package definition files (PDFs), Network Monitor, and SNMP traps.

Chapter 6, "Tuning" Describes how to find and fix bottlenecks in an SMS system.

Chapter 7, "Troubleshooting" Provides information about troubleshooting an SMS system.

This guide also includes a glossary and an index.

Conventions in the Resource Guide

The following table summarizes the typographic conventions used in this book.

Convention	Description
bold	Command-line commands, options, and portions of syntax that must be typed exactly as shown.
italic	Information you provide, terms that are being introduced, and book titles.
KEY+KEY	Key combinations in which you press and hold down one key and then press another.
`Monospace`	Examples, sample command lines, program code, and program output.
SMALL CAPITALS	Names of keys on the keyboard.

Where to Look for More Information

You can find additional information about SMS version 1.2 product documentation and on the SMS Web sites, described in the following sections.

SMS version 1.2 Product Documentation

SMS version 1.2 ships with the following four books:

Getting Started
This book presents the basic information needed for new users to evaluate and quickly become familiar with the main features of SMS.

Concepts and Planning
This book describes the components that make up the product, and provides information on how to design and plan a successful implementation of SMS. This book is essential reading when you come to fully deploy SMS across your organization.

Installation and Configuration
> This book explains the SMS installation options, how to create an SMS site hierarchy, and how to configure this infrastructure.

Administrator's Guide
> This book provides detailed information on how to use all of the SMS features, and provides a glossary of SMS terms.

All four books are provided online. *Getting Started* is also included as a printed book with the SMS product. All four books can be ordered in print form by contacting Microsoft and ordering the "SMS 1.2 EN Doc Set" (SKU 271-00100).

SMS Web Sites

Visit the following Web sites for up-to-date information about SMS:

http://www.microsoft.com/smsmgmt   The SMS Web site contains up-to-date information about SMS, and links to other Microsoft BackOffice™ products.

http://www.microsoft.com/support/products/backoffice/sms.htm   The SMS Technical Support Web site gives you access to the SMS knowledge base, support information, and frequently-asked questions.

http://www.microsoft.com/TechNet/   The Microsoft TechNet Web site contains information about subscribing to the Microsoft TechNet, which provides in-depth technical information about Microsoft's business products, including SMS and other Microsoft BackOffice products.

http://www.microsoft.com/train_cert/   The Microsoft Training and Certification Web site provides information about training options and the Microsoft Certified Professional Program.

C H A P T E R   1

Server Reference

This chapter describes the components, directories, and shares that are installed for the Microsoft® Systems Management Server (SMS) system.

Site Server

SMS has individual components and services that maintain the system at the site level. The SMS site components are the SMS services, shares, and site server directories. By default, all site-level components and directories are installed on the server for that site. All site component directories (except outboxes) must be on the site server.

Site Server Services

There are several SMS services that can use Windows NT® user accounts and passwords and can be managed through the Windows NT Control Panel. By default, the following services run on all SMS site servers:

- Hierarchy Manager
- Site Configuration Manager
- Inventory Agent
- Package Command Manager for Windows NT
- Client Configuration Manager
- SMS Executive

Other SMS services include Bootstrap, SNA Receiver, SNMP Trap Receiver, and Inventory Agent for OS/2. Bootstrap runs temporarily on the secondary site servers during SMS installation. The Inventory Agent for OS/2 runs on LAN Manager for OS/2 logon servers.

Hierarchy Manager

The Hierarchy Manager monitors the site database for changes to the configuration for a site or any of its subsites. If the Hierarchy Manager detects a change in a site's proposed configuration, it creates a site control file that contains all proposed configurations for a site and sends it to the site. If you make site configuration changes using the SMS Administrator, the Hierarchy Manager must be running so it can create a site control file to make changes to that site. The Hierarchy Manager exists only in primary sites.

If changes are proposed at the primary site, its control file passes directly to the Site Configuration Manager for that site, to record the changes.

The Hierarchy Manager includes several commands for diagnosing and fixing sites. You can use PREINST.EXE, in the SMS\SITE.SRV*platform*.BIN directory, to pass commands to the Hierarchy Manager while it is running. The syntax for PREINST.EXE is as follows:

preinst *options*

Where *options* are:

/DUMP
Writes site control images for all sites to the SMS\SITE.SRV\SITECFG.BOX directory.

/SYNCPARENT
Forces all site control images in the site database simultaneously up to the parent for the current site and all its subsites. Use this option when sites are out of synchronization due to time lags or job failures.

/DELSITE:{*sitecode, parentsite*}
Deletes incorrectly removed sites. Use this option if you removed a site before detaching it from its parent site. Note that the braces are required.

The *sitecode* parameter specifies the site to delete, and *parentsite* is the site code of the parent site for the site you are deleting. When you specify *parentsite*, it prevents unwanted deletion of a site previously relocated under a different parent site in another part of the site tree. For example, typing **preinst /DELSITE:**{CHL,PAR} deletes CHL only if it has a parent site of PAR. This transaction proceeds up the site hierarchy to all parent sites for the current site.

Note This instruction does not send a remove job to the target site. It merely removes the site and its SMS domains from the local site database and propagates the change up the site hierarchy.

/DEINSTALL:{*sitecode*}

Sends a job to remove a specific secondary site. The *sitecode* parameter specifies the site to remove from the site hierarchy. Note that the braces are required.

If you want to remove a secondary site from the hierarchy, you should first try to remove it using the SMS Administrator. If that fails for any reason, use this option.

/UPGRADE:{*sitecode*}

Selectively upgrades a specific secondary site. The *sitecode* parameter specifies the site to upgrade. If a global upgrade fails after specifying a system upgrade, use this option for the failed sites. Note that the curly braces are required.

Site Configuration Manager

The Site Configuration Manager monitors and controls the configuration of the site. The Site Configuration Manager uses the site configuration parameters in the site control files created by the Hierarchy Manager. If the site's configuration control file contains changes, the Site Configuration Manager implements the changes.

The Site Configuration Manager exists in both primary and secondary sites. It automatically restarts after the site server restarts, and it starts all other services.

When you add a Windows NT or LAN Manager domain to the site, the Site Configuration Manager:

- Detects all logon servers (if appropriate) and verifies that each server is active and part of a supported network operating system for the domain.
- Creates the SMS root directory (and shares it as SMS_SHR*x*) and the SMS_SHR share on the NTFS drive with the most free space on all logon servers. If no NTFS drive exists, it chooses the drive with the most available space even if it is a FAT drive.
- Installs and starts the Inventory Agent to collect inventory for servers running Windows NT and LAN Manager. It also installs and starts the Package Command Manager on domain controllers.
- Installs and starts the SMS Executive on helper servers.

- In LAN Manager and Windows NT domains, when you select the Automatically Configure Workstation Logon Scripts option, the script files (SMSLS batch file and SETLS program files) are sent to the REPL$\SCRIPTS directory on the primary domain controller. If a user has an existing logon script, (text or ASCII script in a *.BAT or *.CMD file), the Site Configuration Manager adds the SMSLS command to the script. If a user has no logon script, it adds the script to the user's profile.

- If you add a NetWare domain, the Site Configuration Manager creates an SMS directory on the volume with the most disk space. When you select the Automatically Configure Workstation Logon Scripts option, the system logon script for each logon server is modified. Once the system logon scripts are modified, the Site Configuration Manager installs the SMS client software in the SMS directory. The Maintenance Manager collects inventory information for the NetWare servers.

If you make site configuration changes using the SMS Administrator, the Site Configuration Manager must be running to implement the changes to the site.

Setting Monitoring Intervals for the Site Configuration Manager

The Site Configuration Manager uses values set in the Windows NT registry to determine how frequently to monitor parts of the site. You can modify these values directly in the Windows NT registry using the Windows NT Registry Editor. These values are located in the HKEY_LOCAL_MACHINE\SOFTWARE \Microsoft\SMS\Components\SMS_SITE_CONFIG_MANAGER registry key. You can set the following values:

Logon Script Configuration Interval
The frequency (in minutes) that the Site Configuration Manager checks the logon script configuration for all SMS domains in the site. By default, the interval is 1440 minutes (24 hours). This interval is checked only during the processing of a site control file or at the start of the next watchdog cycle.

Restart After Shutdown Delay
Determines the duration (in minutes) that the Site Configuration Manager waits before restarting SMS services at a site after the site server and the SMS system have been restarted. The startup delay is five minutes. This is the length of time that the Site Configuration Manager waits before activating the first cycle. Subsequent cycles work from the watchdog interval.

Site Configuration Reporting Interval

The frequency (in minutes) that the Site Configuration Manager writes a new site control file to report its current configuration. By default, the interval is 1440 minutes (24 hours). Note that this interval is checked only during the processing of a site control file or at the start of the next watchdog cycle.

User Group Reporting Interval

The frequency (in minutes) that the Site Configuration Manager retrieves the list of user groups from all SMS domains in the site and writes a management information format (MIF) file to report the user groups to the site database. By default, the interval is 1440 minutes (24 hours). This interval is checked only during the processing of a site control file or at the start of the next watchdog cycle.

Watchdogging Interval

The frequency (in minutes) that the Site Configuration Manager checks for new SMS logon servers, stopped services or components, or if any of the preceding reporting or configuration intervals are up. By default, the interval is 120 minutes (2 hours). This interval resets itself to be 24 times the service response polling interval whenever the service's response rate is changed. The response polling intervals are set by the Service Response rates for the Maintenance Manager, Site Configuration Manager, and Despooler. For more information, see SMS version 1.2 *Installation and Configuration*, Chapter 5.

Triggering a Specific Site Configuration Manager Task

You can trigger a specific task by sending a service control code to the Site Configuration Manager using the SMS utility program SENDCODE.EXE. The syntax for SENDCODE.EXE is as follows:

sendcode sms_site_config_manager *svccode*

The following table lists the values for *svccode* supported by the Site Configuration Manager.

Name	*svccode*	Description
Memtrack_on	128	Starts memory allocation tracking.
Memtrack_off	129	Stops memory allocation tracking.
Memtrack_dump	130	Dumps the memory allocation data to ALERTER.MEM, APPMGR.MEM, HMAN.MEM, SCMANMEM.LOG, SCHED.MEM, and SMSEXEC.MEM in the root directory.

(continued)

Name	*svccode*	Description
"Net pause" toggle	132	Toggles the **net pause** support on and off for the Site Configuration Manager.
Watchdog	192	Initiates a normal watchdog cycle (verifies current installation, checks for new SMS logon servers, restarts any stopped components, and so on).
Status	193	Initiates a watchdog cycle then writes a status file (.CT2).
Upgrade	194	Initiates a watchdog cycle but treats it as an upgrade. To be most effective, this should be preceded by **shutdown**.
Usergroups	195	Initiates a watchdog cycle and writes a user group MIF file.
Scripts	196	Initiates a watchdog cycle and modifies logon scripts only if the Automatically Configure Workstation Logon Scripts and the Use All Detected Servers options are enabled.
Shutdown	234	Stops and removes services in the site (on the site server and all SMS logon and helper servers).
Deinstall	255	Initiates a site removal (this removes all components, as well as files and shares, from the site server and all SMS logon and helper servers).

Inventory Agent

The Inventory Agent runs on OS/2 and Windows NT-based servers. The Inventory Agent performs software and hardware inventory on the server, except NetWare servers (Maintenance Manager performs inventory on NetWare logon servers).

The Inventory Agent is started by the Site Configuration Manager during SMS installation on domain controllers for domains which SMS controls. The Inventory Agent wakes up at an interval specified by the Inventory Agent Service Interval in the HKEY_LOCAL_MACHINE\SOFTWARE\Microsoft\SMS\Components \SMS_MAINTENANCE_MANAGER registry key. The default wake-up interval is 24 hours (1440 minutes). When it wakes up, the Inventory Agent checks software and hardware scan interval settings from the local DOMAIN.INI file. By default, scan interval settings for both hardware and software are 7 (days), indicating that inventory should once every seven days. To change the software and hardware scan interval settings, use the Site Properties dialog box in the SMS Administrator.

Package Command Manager for Windows NT

The Package Command Manager is installed on all Windows NT-based servers (site and SMS logon servers) in an SMS hierarchy. The Package Command Manager service (PCMSVC32.EXE) provides unattended package installation—a user does not have to be logged on to a server running Windows NT for package installation to occur. However, the package must be configured for automated installation in background mode.

If a package arrives at a server running Windows NT that is also running the Package Command Manager (PCMWIN32.EXE file), the package is handled by the Package Command Manager.

The Package Command Manager initially wakes up once every 60 seconds to check the package polling interval. You set the polling interval in the Site Properties dialog box (under Clients) in the SMS Administrator. The default is 60 minutes. If the polling interval has elapsed, the Package Command Manager checks the package instruction file to see if the time and date have changed. If the polling interval has changed, the Package Command Manager resets the polling interval counter to the new value, and waits until that many minutes have passed before polling again. The Package Command Manager Service is limited to package installations that do not require user input and do not display windows on the server. The polling interval is set in the SMS.INI file.

Bootstrap

The Bootstrap sets up a Windows NT-based server as a secondary site. After the Hierarchy Manager at the primary site detects the request to add a secondary site, it initiates a job to the site to install the SMS installation directory on the secondary site server. It also tells the senders (LAN or RAS) to install and start the Bootstrap from that directory.

When the primary site sends a package containing site components to the secondary site, the Bootstrap:

- Decompresses the package.
- Creates the site directory structure, and then places components in the appropriate directories on the site server.
- Starts the Site Configuration Manager when it detects the site control file sent by the primary site. The Site Configuration Manager then removes the Bootstrap.

SNA Receiver

After you add an SNA Sender to a site using the SMS Administrator, the SNA Receiver is activated by the Site Configuration Manager (the SNA Sender is started as part of the SMS Executive). The SNA Receiver processes information that has been sent from an SNA Sender at a remote site.

Client Configuration Manager

The Client Configuration Manager exists in both primary and secondary sites and is used by SMS Client Setup to install, upgrade, and remove SMS service components on computers running Windows NT. When SMS Client Setup needs to perform actions that may require special access on a computer running Windows NT, it posts a client configuration request to the Client Configuration Manager. The Client Configuration Manager then carries out the request. The Client Configuration Manager runs on all SMS logon servers running Windows NT Server.

The Client Configuration Manager configures the following components on Windows NT-based computers running as SMS clients:

- SMS Client Inventory Service
- SMS Remote Control Agent
- SNMP Event to Trap Translator

Note The Client Configuration Manager uses the SMS Service Account to install these components on computers running the Windows NT operating system. The service account must have administrative privileges on the computers or Client Configuration Manager will not be able to install the components. To grant administrative privileges on clients running Windows NT, do *one* of the following:

- Make the SMS Service Account on the site server a member of the client's Administrators local group (directly or through other groups).
- Have a local account on the client with the same name and password as the SMS Service Account. This account must have administrative privileges.
- In the SMS domain where the client is a member, have an account with same name and password as the SMS Service Account.

Setting Parameters for the Client Configuration Manager

The following Client Configuration Manager parameters are maintained in the site server registry, in the HKEY_LOCAL_MACHINE\SOFTWARE\Microsoft\SMS \Components\SMS_CLIENT_CONFIG_MANAGER registry key.

Deinstall All Client Services

When this value is set to **Yes**, it specifies that each client configuration request (CCR) be treated as a request to remove all of the SMS service-based client components. The default value is **No**.

Prompt for Restart

When this value is set to 0, the Client Monitor does not prompt the user at the client to restart the computer after installing software. The default value is 1, and it is not recommended that you change this value.

Ignore These Event IDs

Values specified in this parameter represent SMS event IDs that should not be reported to the Windows NT Event Manager. You can specify the following values:

402

Event that occurs when the Client Configuration Manager is unable to connect to a client. This event occurs when the SMS service account does not have administrative rights on the client, and when the client cannot be found (because it is turned off for more than seven consecutive days, it no longer exists, or its computer name has changed).

403

Event that occurs when the Client Configuration Manager succeeded in connecting to the client but encountered an error while attempting to install the client components.

When you encounter many of these events, increase the **Error Reporting Delay** and **Retry Duration** values in the site server registry (under the Retry queue) to allow the Client Configuration Manager to retry the client for longer than the default 24 hours before reporting the problem.

404

Event that appears when an excessive number of CCRs (as defined by the **Machine Count Warning** key in the Retry queue) appear in either the incoming or retry queues on each logon server. This event appears the first time the queue rises above the threshold number of events, and when the number of CCRs drops back below the threshold numbers.

These events indicate a backlog of clients to process. If you see an event for the incoming queue, the Client Configuration Managers running on the logon servers are not keeping up with the demand, and you need to consider performance and tuning issues for the site.

Only Report These Event IDs When Fatal

Values specified in this parameter represent SMS event IDs that should be reported to the Windows NT Event Manager only after they are "fatal," which means that the Client Configuration has stopped retrying to connect to the client and install or maintain client components. This value can be 402 or 403.

SNMP Trap Receiver

The SNMP Trap Receiver makes simple network management protocol (SNMP) trap information available to SMS. The SNMP Trap Receiver is disabled (no traps are received by or stored in the database) by default. You configure the SNMP Trap Receiver using the Site Properties dialog box (under SNMP Traps) in the SMS Administrator.

The SNMP Trap Receiver filters traps according to conditions you set. You can set trap filters based on the trap IP address, enterprise ID, Windows NT event source (for traps generated by the Event to Trap Translator), generic trap type, or specific trap ID. Filtered traps are either written to the database or discarded.

If a trap meets the filter conditions, SMS writes the trap data to the database. However, to minimize the impact on the database, SMS only writes the first 25 **varbinds** in the trap to the database. SMS also limits the size of each **varbind**. If any of the **varbinds** exceed the limit, SMS rejects the trap data. The data is not written to the database; a Windows NT event is created to log the failure instead.

The SNMP Trap Receiver can receive traps from any suitable SNMP source, including (but not limited to) the Event to Trap Translator. Traps generated by the Event to Trap Translator display the Windows NT event source name for the event that triggered the trap.

The SNMP Trap Receiver runs at all primary sites. It stores SNMP trap data in the database as a new architecture. This means that trap data can be viewed, queried against, and used to generate SMS alerts.

SMS Executive

The SMS Executive serves as a master controller of several SMS components. The SMS Executive is started by the Site Configuration Manager, during SMS services startup and any other time that the SMS Executive is not running.

The SMS Executive reads the Windows NT registry to determine which components to start on SMS site, logon, and helper servers. By default, it starts the following components on the site server:

- Maintenance Manager
- Inventory Processor
- Site Reporter
- Scheduler
- Despooler
- Inventory Data Loader
- Senders
- Applications Manager
- Alerter

Each of these components is discussed in the following sections.

Maintenance Manager

The Maintenance Manager installs and maintains the SMS client components on the SMS logon servers in a site. It replicates client components and configuration information to SMS logon servers within the site and retrieves inventory and status files. The Maintenance Manager is installed in every primary and secondary site server. The Site Configuration Manager sets up the registry information and necessary directory structures that the Maintenance Manager needs to run properly.

When a logon server is added to the SMS system, the Maintenance Manager replicates client files, such as the Inventory Agent, Program Group Control, and Package Command Manager programs, to the logon server. The Maintenance Manager also monitors the site server for any changes in configuration. If a change is detected, the Maintenance Manager replicates these changes to all of the SMS logon servers within the site. The Maintenance Manager also periodically scans all the logon servers and updates missing files.

In addition, the Maintenance Manager:

- Monitors the package rule file for changes and replicates it as necessary.
- Passes files back and forth between the site server and SMS logon servers according to the polling interval. For example, it moves RAW files from each SMS logon server to the site server and replicates Package Command Manager instruction files and SMS network applications from the site server to all SMS logon servers.
- Collects inventory from NetWare servers and creates a corresponding MIF file.
- Reads the SYSTEM.MAP file and creates copy lists for the SMS Client Setup program. A copy list tells SMS Client Setup where to place files on the client.
- Creates the unique identifier (*.UID) file. The *.UID file name prefix represents the next available SMS ID number for an SMS logon server.
- Detects when the Despooler has distributed the package, then creates and sends package location MIF files.

Inventory Processor

The Inventory Processor exists in both primary and secondary site servers. It creates the MIF files from the raw binary inventory information returned by the Inventory Agents for Windows NT and MS-DOS® and reads the MIF files returned by the Inventory Agents for OS/2 and Macintosh clients. The Inventory Processor creates a history file for the Windows NT, Apple Macintosh, and OS/2 platforms. MIF files also track history, unless they are created with an NHM extension. When a new MIF file is received, the Inventory Processor compares it with the history file and writes changes to an inventory file called a Binary MIF file. (If this is the first MIF file, the Inventory Processor writes a complete Binary MIF inventory file.)

The Inventory Processor also converts MIF files in the ISVMIF directory into Binary MIF files. ISVMIFs are files generated by independent software vendors (ISVs), which report objects such as computers that have custom architectures. The ISVMIF directory also contains MIF files from OS/2 and Macintosh clients.

Site Reporter

The Site Reporter maintains a queue of MIF files containing inventory, job status, or event information. At child sites, the Site Reporter periodically creates a system job to send these files to the parent site. The queue length that triggers when the files are sent is determined by various registry settings. The Site Reporter keeps track of the different categories of MIF files that arrive for it and compares the category with a registry entry that indicates how long that type of MIF file should be allowed to wait. When any MIF file reaches its maximum wait time, all MIF files for that site are bundled and sent. The registry entries for the Site Reporter are under the HKEY_LOCAL_MACHINE\SOFTWARE\Microsoft\SMS \Components\SMS_SITE_REPORTER key and are maintained by the Site Configuration Manager.

The Site Reporter also deletes MIF files that are not reported to parent sites, either because there is no parent site or because the MIF file is normally not reported to a parent site (such as a job detail MIF file).

The Site Reporter exists in both primary and secondary sites.

Scheduler

The Scheduler detects pending jobs and creates auxiliary files that enable jobs to be processed. This includes jobs that an administrator starts, such as a Run Command On Workstation job, as well as system jobs from system processes such as the Site Reporter.

When the Scheduler detects a job, it:

- Compresses the relevant files (such as all files in a package source directory or all inventory MIF files) into a single file.

- Creates a despooler file, in the SMS\LOGON.SRV\DESPOOLER.BOX directory, with instructions for completing the job at the receiving site.

- Creates a send request file (*.SRQ) with instructions for sending the compressed files and the despooler instructions to the target site, in the corresponding sender outbox.

The Scheduler also manages send requests. It examines send requests for a specific sender's outbox and schedules them on a priority basis. For example, it might suspend a low priority job in progress and substitute a higher priority send request. After the higher priority job runs, it restarts the previous job.

The Scheduler runs on the site server, but you can use the Services button in the Site Properties dialog box in the SMS Administrator to move it to a helper server. The Scheduler exists in both primary and secondary sites.

Despooler

The Despooler watches the SITE.SRV\DESPOOLR.BOX\RECEIVE directory for despooler instruction files and compressed packages created by the Scheduler. The instructions and packages can come from the local site or from another site. The Despooler reads the instruction file and uses the instructions to decompress the package files and determine how to process them. For example, it decompresses inventory files and moves them to the SMS\SITE.SRV \DATALOAD.BOX\DELTAMIF.COL directory so they can be processed by the Inventory Data Loader, which then updates the site database.

Note Specify the drive that the Despooler will use for temporary files in the Preferred Drive For Temp Directory setting for the Despooler registry key. This value is blank by default, which directs SMS to use its drive. The SMS Drive Minimum Free Space in Mbytes option specifies that SMS look for a drive of the configured value (default value is 100 MB). If the free disk space on the SMS drive is less than 100 MB, the Despooler will start looking for other drives on which to place the package.

If there are two package shares, the Despooler will pick the drive (share) with the most free disk space until both of them have less than 100 MB of free space. Then it attempts to find a third drive with more free disk space. The Despooler will never place the same package on two shares even if they came in different jobs. To determine where packages are stored, look under the SMS\Components\SMS_Despooler\Transfer Package registry key.

For Run Command On Workstation jobs, the Despooler updates the Package
Command Manager instruction files for all target computers in the site. After the
package has been installed, the Despooler reports the job's status to the site where
the job was created. It also logs an event to the site server's Windows NT event
log if there is a failure.

The Despooler initially runs on the site server but can be moved to a helper
server. The Despooler exists in both primary and secondary sites.

Inventory Data Loader

The Inventory Data Loader updates computer inventory, events, job location, and
user group and job status information in the database. When an inventory MIF file
arrives from a computer, the Inventory Data Loader attempts to locate the
computer in the site database based on its SMS ID and key attributes in its
identification group. If the MIF file contains instructions to update an object, such
as a client's identification group that is missing from the database, the Inventory
Data Loader initiates a **resync** command to update the database. The Inventory
Data Loader processes job status, user group, event, and package location
information, and then updates the database directly (no **resync** is necessary).

In SMS version 1.2, each of the main architectures creates MIF files with different
extensions, as shown in the following table:

MIF file name extension	Contains
.EMF	Event data
.JMF	Job status data
.UMF	User group data
.PMF	Package location data

All other MIF files are processed by the 'misc' processing thread, including MIF
files from sites that are running earlier versions of SMS. The Inventory Data
Loader processes the different MIF files in parallel.

The Inventory Data Loader:

- Monitors the DELTAMIF.COL directory for MIF files.
- When it finds a file, it moves the file to the DELTAMIF.COL\PROCESS directory.
- Starts the appropriate thread to process the file.
- Copies the file to the SITEREF.BOX directory.

Note If the Inventory Data Loader is stopped before it has finished processing a MIF file, that file is renamed with an X at the beginning of the file name (for example, X0712.EMF). When the file has three X's at the beginning of the file name, it is considered a corrupt MIF file and is moved to the DELTAMIF.COL\BADMIFS directory.

If you stop and restart SMS Executive often, you might end up with many files in the DELTAMIF.COL\BADMIFS directory that would otherwise process normally.

The Inventory Data Loader is also responsible for:

- Transferring the inventory from a child site to the Site Reporter, which uses a sender to deliver the information to a parent site after the parent/child hierarchy is first established.
- Forwarding Binary MIF files to the Site Reporter after processing them. The Site Reporter creates a job to send Binary MIF files to a parent site if it exists.

The Inventory Data Loader initially runs on the site server but can be moved to a helper server. The Inventory Data Loader exists only in primary sites.

Senders

To enable each site to communicate with its parent sites and child sites, every site must have one or more senders. A sender is an SMS component used to transmit instructions and data from one site to another (such as reporting inventory information or installing software on clients in another site).

There are six types of SMS senders:

- One LAN Sender
- Three RAS Senders (ISDN, X.25, and ASYNC)
- Two SNA Senders (batch and interactive)

Each type of sender uses a specific type of communications link. The RAS Senders require a Remote Access Service (RAS) server, and the SNA Senders require the SNA Server communications service.

The sender monitors its outbox directory (the location for files waiting to be sent to another site) for a valid send request. When it detects a valid request, the sender connects to the target site and transfers the compressed files and its despooler instruction file to the destination site.

The LAN Sender runs on the site server but can be moved to a helper server. Use the SMS Administrator to add other senders. The sender exists in both primary and secondary sites.

Applications Manager

The Applications Manager copies package and program group configuration information from the site database to other components in the site and to the sites beneath it in the site hierarchy.

When you create, modify, or delete packages or program groups using the SMS Administrator, the changes are added to the site database. When the Applications Manager detects a change to a package or program group, the new configuration information is updated in the Program Group Control database for the site. The Program Group Control database is a set of configuration files used by the Applications Control program for each SMS Windows®-based client.

The Applications Manager uses a system job to replicate package and program group data to child sites. Each child site then generates its own copy of the Program Group Control database. The Applications Manager also uses a system job to add data to the database from parent sites.

The Applications Manager exists in both primary and secondary sites.

Alerter

The Alerter monitors the database for new alerts and any changes to existing alerts. It runs queries associated with alerts and compares query results with alert criteria.

If an alert's trigger condition becomes true, the Alerter performs any or all of the following actions:

- Logs an SMS event and a Windows NT event.
- Runs a command line from the system path of the computer where the Alerter is installed.

Note The Alerter cannot run a command that writes to a window.

- Sends a message to a computer or user on the local network.

The Alerter exists only in primary sites.

SMS Services Memory Requirements

SMS services require approximately 19 MB of memory on primary site servers. The following tables lists the service or service thread RAM requirements.

SMS service or service thread	Memory requirement
APPCTL32	999 K
CLICFG	623 K
INVWIN32	602 K
PCMSVC32	500 K
PCMWIN32	549 K
PREINST (primary site only)	1,466 K
SITEINS	1,671 K
SMS	2,625 K
SMSEXEC	2,338 K
Subtotal	11,373 K
Overhead	7,336 K (5,012 K on SMS logon servers)
Total for primary site	18,709 K

Site Server Shares

During installation, the Site Configuration Manager creates the shares shown in the following table.

Share name	Used by	Description
SMS_SHR*x*	SMS services	Represents the SMS root directory, where *x* is the drive where SMS is installed. It exists on all site, logon, and helper servers running Windows NT or LAN Manager.
SMS_SHR	Inventory Agent, SMS Client Setup, Program Group Control, Package Command Manager, and MIF Entry	Created on the site server and all SMS logon servers running Windows NT or LAN Manager. It represents the LOGON.SRV directory, which is a subdirectory of the SMS root directory. This share contains all SMS logon server components and serves as the collection point for inventory files.
SMS_SITE	Bootstrap, Despooler, and sender	Exists only on site servers. It represents the SMS\SITE.SRV \DESPOOLR.BOX\RECEIVE directory and is the location where remote site senders place despooler instruction files and compressed packages that are targeted for the site.

Important Do not modify share comments! These are read by services and will cause errors if they are altered.

Site Server Directories

When you set up a site, directories are created on the site server (for a primary or secondary site). For primary sites, the drive and SMS root directory name are the ones specified when you created the site using the SMS Setup program. For secondary sites, the drive and the SMS root directory name are the ones you specified when you created the site using the SMS Administrator.

In general, the directory names follow this naming scheme:

- The first level directory name (such as SITE.SRV and LOGON.SRV) indicates the server's role and contains the directories for those components. For example, the site components use SITE.SRV directories.

- The second level directories (such as DESPOOLR.BOX) are named for the components that monitor or use the directory. For example, the Despooler monitors the DESPOOLR.BOX\RECEIVE directory for new packages and instructions from other sites.

- The third level directories normally contain specific types of files. For example, the MAINCFG.BOX\PKGRULE directory contains the master copy of the package rules used for software inventory at the site.

A site server contains the following directories:

```
drive:\SMSroot
    LOGS
    SITE.SRV
        APPMGR.BOX
        DATALOAD.BOX
            DELTAMIF.COL
                BADMIFS
                PROCESS
            FILES.COL
        DESPOOLR.BOX
            RECEIVE
            STORE
        INVENTRY.BOX
            BADRAWS
            HISTORY
        ISVMIF.BOX
```

```
MAINCFG.BOX
    APPCTL.SRC
        DATABASE
        INIFILES
        SCRIPTS
    CLIENT.SRC
        platform.BIN
            language
    INVDOM.BOX
        domainname.000
    MSTEST
        platform.BIN
            language
    PCMDOM.BOX
        domainname.000
    PKGRULE
SCHEDULE.BOX
SENDER.BOX
    TOSEND
    REQUESTS
SITECFG.BOX
SITEREP.BOX
platform.BIN
    language
    ERRORHIS
```

A primary site also contains the following directories, which provide the sample scripts (for package installation and SMS network application configuration) and secondary site configuration information:

```
drive:\SMSroot
    PRIMSITE.SRV
        AUDIT
            PACKAGE
                platform.BIN
                    language
        IMPORT.SRC
            language
        RMOTECFG.BOX
        RMOTESRC.BOX
```

Both site and SMS logon servers also contain the following directories for desktop services such as the Package Command Manager and the Inventory Agent for Windows NT:

```
drive:\SMSroot
    HELPER.SRV
        platform.BIN
            language
            ERRORHIS
```

If an SMS component, such as the Scheduler, is moved to an SMS logon server to reduce site server load, the files required to run the component are also placed in the HELPER.SRV directory. For more information about the SMS logon server directories, see "SMS Logon Server Directories" later in this chapter. The site server directories are described in the following table.

Directory	Description
SITE.SRV	Contains the site server directories.
APPMGR.BOX	The location for secondary sites where the Applications Manager stores package and program group information.
DATALOAD.BOX	Stores decompressed inventory files.
…\DELTAMIF.COL	The location at primary sites where the job status MIF files (*.JMF) are placed.
	The Inventory Data Loader monitors this directory and uses the job status MIF file to update the site's database (if the site is a primary site) and then forwards the job status MIF file to its parent site.
…\…\BADMIFS	Contains MIF files that could not be processed by the Inventory Data Loader.
…\…\PROCESS	Contains MIF files that the Inventory Data Loader recognized and has started to process.
…\FILES.COL	Contains collected files for the current site and all subsites.
DESPOOLR.BOX	Contains Package Command Manager job status MIF files, placed by the Maintenance Manager, for the Despooler to examine.
…\RECEIVE	The location where the sender places despooler instruction files and compressed packages that are targeted for the site.
	The Despooler monitors this directory and processes any instruction files found.
…\STORE	The location where the Despooler stores compressed packages sent to the site from its own site or another site.

(continued)

Directory	Description
INVENTRY.BOX	The location where Maintenance Manager puts client inventory files (*.RAW files) that it collects from SMS logon servers. The Inventory Processor monitors this directory.
…\BADRAWS	Contains client inventory files (*.RAW) that could not be processed by the Inventory Processor.
…\HISTORY	The location where the Inventory Processor maintains a record (history) of the last inventory for each SMS client.
ISVMIF.BOX	Contains MIF files generated by ISVs.
MAINCFG.BOX	Contains SMS directories used by the Applications Manager and the Maintenance Manager.
…\APPCTL.SRC	Contains directories used by the Application Control program for SMS network applications.
…\…\DATABASE	The location where the Applications Manager places the network application database for SMS network applications at the site.
	The Maintenance Manager replicates these files to the SMS\LOGON.SRV\APPCTL.BOX directory for each SMS logon server for every SMS domain in the site.
…\…\INIFILES	The location of initialization files for SMS network applications at the site.
…\…\SCRIPTS	The location of script files for SMS network applications at the site.
…\CLIENT.SRC	The location where the SMS client components are placed as source for configuration and replication to the site's logon servers.
	The Maintenance Manager uses this directory to generate configuration files for SMS Client Setup and the Inventory Agent service on each SMS logon server. The configuration files and the SMS client components are replicated to the SMS\LOGON.SRV*platform*.BIN directory on each SMS logon server for every SMS domain in the site.
…\INVDOM.BOX	The location of the master inventory command file (RESYNC.CFG) for each SMS domain. The Maintenance Manager replicates RESYNC.CFG to the SMS\LOGON.SRV directory for each SMS logon server for every SMS domain in the site.

(continued)

Directory	Description
MSTEST	The location where the run-time version of Microsoft Test is placed as a source for replication to the site's logon servers. The directory also contains utilities used in the operating system installation jobs.
	The Maintenance Manager replicates these files to the SMS\LOGON.SRV\MSTEST directory for each SMS logon server for every SMS domain in the site.
PCMDOM.BOX	The location where the Despooler places instructions for target clients of Run Command On Workstation jobs in each SMS domain.
	The Maintenance Manager replicates the instruction files to the SMS logon servers in the SMS domains that contain the target clients.
...\PKGRULE	The location where the Applications Manager places the PACKAGE.RUL file, which contain rules for inventorying packages at the site.
	The Maintenance Manager uses the PACKAGE.RUL file to generate the configuration file for the Inventory Agent. This configuration file (PKG_16.CFG) is replicated to the SMS\LOGON.SRV directory on each SMS logon server for every SMS domain in the site.
SCHEDULE.BOX	The location where SMS services can leave instructions for system jobs.
	The Scheduler monitors this directory and uses the instructions to start the specified system jobs.
SENDER.BOX	The location where all senders installed in a site are stored.
...\TOSEND	The location where the Scheduler places compressed packages and despooler instruction files to be sent to target sites.
	When the sender processes a send request for a job, it sends the job's files from this directory to the target site.
REQUESTS	The location where the Scheduler places send request files for the sender. The specific sender assigned to each subdirectory (outbox) monitors its directory and processes the requests.

(continued)

Directory	Description
SITECFG.BOX	The location where SMS places site control files used by the Site Configuration Manager to configure the site.
SITEREP.BOX	The location at secondary sites where the job status MIF files (*.JMF) are placed.
	When the Site Reporter detects a queue of job status MIF files, it creates a system job that sends these MIF files to the parent site.
…*platform*.BIN	The location where all the SMS server components (the SMS Administrator, services, and dynamic-link libraries [DLLs]) are installed. This directory appears as X86.BIN on Intel-based systems, as ALPHA.BIN on Alpha-based systems, and as MIPS.BIN on MIPS-based systems. By default, this is the location for the Package Command Manager and Inventory Agent service executables.
	This directory contains a language ID subdirectory (for example, 00000409 for English), which contains language specific files. The name used is the Win32® locale identifier.
…\ERRORHIS	The location where SMS components write event history files to prevent frequently occurring events from flooding the Windows NT event log and the SMS event log in the SMS database.
PRIMSITE.SRV	Contains directories installed on and used by primary sites.
…\AUDIT	The location of inventory code for the Software Audit program that runs as a Package Command Manager job.
…\…\PACKAGE	The location of inventory code for software inventory.
…\IMPORT.SRC	The location of the sample configuration scripts provided with SMS.
…\…*Language*	The location of the supplied package definition files (PDFs). For example, when you install U.S. English, the PDFs are located in this directory: PRIMSITE.SRV\IMPORT.SRC\ENU
…\RMOTECFG.BOX	The location where the Site Hierarchy Manager puts packages containing site control files for secondary sites.

(continued)

Directory	Description
…\RMOTESRC.BOX	The location that the Site Hierarchy Manager uses to build a complete directory tree when a job is sent to install a secondary site.
HELPER.SRV	Contains directories associated with desktop services (Inventory Agent, Package Command Manager) installed on all SMS servers. The files that are required to run components that have been moved from the site server are also placed here.

Note The location of the PDFs has changed from version 1.0 of SMS. These files were directly under the IMPORT.SRC directory. Now, they are in a language-specific subdirectory under the IMPORT.SRC directory. If you upgrade from version 1.0, the new directories will be added to the old directory structure, but will not overwrite custom changes made in the IMPORT.SRC directory. You should move any files you need from IMPORT.SRC to the appropriate language subdirectory, and then delete the duplicate files in IMPORT.SRC. The PDF files have changed, so be sure to use the new PDF files when you import packages.

Network Monitor Directories

If you install Network Monitor with SMS Setup, the SMS site server will contain the following directories:

```
drive:\SMSroot
    NETMON
        platform
            CAPTURES
            PARSERS
```

These directories are described in the following table.

Directory	Description
platform	Contains initialization files, help files, and the NMAPI.DLL, which defines the Network Monitor API.
…\CAPTURES	The location of the default filters that accompany Network Monitor (DEFAULT.CF, DEFAULT.DF, NOBROAD.CF, and NOBROAD.DF).
…\PARSERS	The location of Network Monitor protocol parsers. These parsers are DLLs that distinguish one protocol from another and copy frames to the Network Monitor capture buffer. To capture frames sent in a particular protocol, a corresponding parser must exist in this directory and must be enabled. In addition, this directory contains SMB.HLP, an online version of the Server Message Block (SMB) Protocol specification.

Site Server Default Permissions

The following table lists the default permissions for shares and directories on
SMS site servers. For a description of Windows NT file and special permissions,
see your Windows NT documentation.

Share	Directory	Permissions
SMS_SHR*x*		Administrator's local group has full control; Everyone has Read capabilities.
	SMSroot	Administrator's local group has full control; Everyone has Read capabilities.
	SITE.SRV and all subdirectories	Administrator's local group has full control.
	HELPER.SRV and all subdirectories	Administrator's local group has full control.
	LOGS	Inherits permissions from the drive where SMS is installed. Defaults to Everyone has full control.
	PRIMSITE.SRV and all subdirectories	Inherits permissions from the drive where SMS is installed.
	NETMON and all subdirectories	Inherits permissions from the drive where SMS is installed.
SMS_SHR		Administrator's local group and Everyone have full control.
	(Windows NT and LAN Manager)	Administrator's local group has full control; Everyone has Read capabilities.
	DESPOOLER.BOX INVENTRY.BOX ISVMIF.BOX PCMPKG.SRC SMSID*.UID (file)	Administrator's local group has full control; Everyone has Change capabilities.
	platform.BIN *platform*.BIN*language*	Administrator's local group has full control; Everyone has Read capabilities.

(continued)

Share	Directory	Permissions
SMS_SHR *(cont.)*	MSTEST PCMINS.BOX INVENCFG.BOX APPCTL.SRC and all subdirectories	Administrator's local group has full control; Everyone has Read capabilities.
	PCMPKG.SRC*packageID* CCR.BOX	Administrator's local group has full control; Everyone has Change capabilities. (Read and Write permissions for Users and Guests can be modified through the user interface. By default, Users and Guests have Read and Write permissions.)

SMS Logon Servers

Every site has one or more SMS domains and each domain has at least one SMS logon server. From the site server, the following SMS components maintain SMS on every SMS logon server in an SMS-supported domain:

- Site Configuration Manager
- Maintenance Manager
- Despooler

If you move an SMS component from the site server to another SMS logon server, you create an SMS helper server. This configuration reduces the load on site servers.

Helper servers must be logon servers running Windows NT that are in one of the site's domains, and the HELPER.SRV directory must be on an NTFS partition. If the SMS domain containing a helper server is configured with the Use Specified Servers option in the Domains dialog box (under Site Properties), the helper server must be one of these servers. You can allow an unlimited number of helper servers.

When you move a component to another server, files required to run the specific SMS components are placed in the server's HELPER.SRV*platform*.BIN directory. The Site Configuration Manager creates the SMS_SHR*x* share on that drive and copies the required component files to the HELPER.SRV*platform*.BIN directory.

SMS_SHR*x* also contains desktop services (the Package Command Manager and Inventory Agent), which are automatically installed on all SMS logon servers by the Site Configuration Manager.

SMS Logon Server Shares

During installation, the Site Configuration Manager creates the SMS_SHR*x* and SMS_SHR shares. SMS logon servers also use a NETLOGON share. The SMS logon server shares are described in the following table.

Share name	Used by	Description
SMS_SHR*x*	SMS services	Represents the SMS root directory where *x* is the drive on which SMS is installed. It exists on all site, SMS logon, and helper servers running Windows NT or LAN Manager.
SMS_SHR	Inventory Agent, SMS Client Setup, Program Group Control, Package Command Manager, and MIF Entry	Created on the site server and all SMS logon servers running Windows NT or LAN Manager. It represents the LOGON.SRV directory, which is a subdirectory of the SMS root directory. SMS_SHR contains all SMS logon server components and serves as the collection point for inventory files.
NETLOGON	SMS logon servers	If you enable the Automatically Configure Workstation Logon Scripts option, the Site Configuration Manager automatically copies the files needed to use the SMSLS batch file as a logon script to the REPL$ share on servers running Windows NT or LAN Manager. These files are then replicated to the NETLOGON share of domain logon servers by the LAN Manager Replicator service or the Windows NT Directory Replicator service.

Important Do not modify share comments! These are read by services and will cause errors if they are altered.

Note The SMSLS.BAT file from version 1.0 has been split into two files that initiate SMS inventory and client setup. The new version of SMSLS.BAT is used for logon scripts and is located in the NETLOGON share. The old version of SMSLS.BAT will remain under SMS_SHR to allow you to copy any custom changes from that file to the new SMSLS.BAT file in the NETLOGON share. You should delete the old SMSLS.BAT file after the changes are copied. Use the new RUNSMS.BAT file when manually running from SMS_SHR. There are also two command (.CMD) files to support OS/2 clients.

The Site Configuration Manager copies the files into a domain set to enumerate all servers added to SMS. The following table lists the components required by the SMS logon script.

Component	Description
CLRLEVEL.COM	Resets the error level to 0 before the script quits.
DOSVER.COM	Verifies if the client is running an SMS-supported version of MS-DOS.
NLSMSG16.EXE	Used by clients running MS-DOS, Windows version 3.1, Windows for Workgroups, and Windows 95 as a NLS-enabled version of CHOICE.COM. It is used when user input is required.
NLSMSG32.EXE	Used by clients running Windows NT as an NLS-enabled version of CHOICE.COM. It is used when user input is required.
NLSMSGO2.EXE	Used by OS/2 clients as an NLS-enabled version of CHOICE.COM. It is used when user input is required.
NLSRES.INI	Used by NLSMSG*x*.EXE as a language mapping file to relate country codes or language IDs to the appropriate NLS_LS.DLL file.
NETSPEED.COM	Detects a slow network.
SMSLS.BAT	Logon script file (except for OS/2 clients).
SMSLS.CMD	Logon script file for OS/2 clients.
SETLS16.EXE	Finds SMS logon servers and launches CLI_DOS and INVDOS.
SETLS32.EXE	Used by clients running Windows NT to find SMS logon servers and launch CLI_NT and INVWIN32.
SETLSOS.EXE	Used by OS/2 clients to find SMS logon servers and launch CLI_DOS and INVOS2.
SMSLS.INI (present when domain mapping is used)	Maps clients to SMS domains.

SMS Logon Server Directories

Each logon server in a SMS domain has the following directories:

```
drive:\SMSroot
    LOGON.SRV
        APPCTL.BOX
            DATABASE
            INIFILES
            SCRIPTS
        CCR.BOX
            RETRY
        DESPOOLR.BOX
        INVENCFG.BOX
        INVENTRY.BOX
        ISVMIF.BOX
        MSTEST
            platform.BIN
        PCMINS.BOX
        PCMPKG.SRC
        SMSID
        platform.BIN
            language
```

The following table shows the SMS logon server directories.

Directory	Description
LOGON.SRV	Stores components for scanning and collecting inventory from clients. Also stores SMS client components for installation on clients running MS-DOS, Windows version 3.1, Windows for Workgroups, Windows 95, and Windows NT.
...\APPCTL.BOX\ DATABASE	The location where the Maintenance Manager places the SMS network application database.
...\CCR.BOX\RETRY	Contains client configuration files (*.CCR) that the Client Configuration Manager could not complete.
...\DESPOOLR.BOX	The location where the Package Command Manager writes a despooler instruction file (*.SNI) and application status MIF files after it has completed a package installation. The .SNI file reports status for the Run Command On Workstation job. The Maintenance Manager monitors this directory and moves instruction files to the site server.

(continued)

Directory	Description
…\INVENCFG.BOX	The location where the Maintenance Manager places resync files (*.CFG).
…\INVENTRY.BOX	The location where the Inventory Agent places client inventory files (*.RAW files) collected from clients. The Maintenance Manager monitors this directory and moves the inventory files to the SITE.SRV\INVENTRY.BOX directory on the site server.
ISVMIF.BOX	The location where the Inventory Agent puts MIF files generated by ISVs and inventory files for Macintosh and OS/2 clients. The Maintenance Manager monitors this directory and moves the MIF files to the SITE.SRV\ISVMIF.BOX directory on the site server.
…\MSTEST	The location where Maintenance Manager places the run-time version of Microsoft Test and scripting types of information. It includes common files and applications for client installations using Package Command Manager and Program Group Control and platform-specific subdirectories for X86.BIN, ALPHA.BIN, and MIPS.BIN.
…\PCMINS.BOX	The location where the Maintenance Manager replicates Package Command Manager instruction files (*.INS) from the site server. This directory is monitored by the Package Command Manager.
…\PCMPKG.SRC (NetWare servers)	The location of directories containing decompressed package source files. Each package directory name is the package ID for the package.
…\SMSID	The location of a single file (*.UID), which gives unique SMS IDs to clients that are added to the SMS domain.
…*platform*.BIN*language*	The location of SMS client executables for installation on clients.
	This directory is maintained by the Maintenance Manager.

SMSSVR16.EXE and SMSSVR32.EXE are installed on the SMS logon server for upgrading and removing SMS components. However, to start the SMS Client Setup program for upgrades or removal, the program must be run from the client.

Directory Structure for the NETLOGON Share

The directory structure for the NETLOGON share has changed since SMS version 1.0. The SCRIPTS*platform*.BIN directory for each client platform has been added. The files that are included in this directory, as well as the previous location, are shown in the following table.

File name	Moved from
SETLS32.EXE	SITE.SRV\MAINCFG.BOX\CLIENT.SRC*platform*.BIN
NLSMSG32.EXE	SITE.SRV\MAINCFG.BOX\CLIENT.SRC*platform*.BIN
NLSRES.INI	SITE.SRV\MAINCFG.BOX\CLIENT.SRC*platform*.BIN
SETLS16.EXE	SITE.SRV\MAINCFG.BOX\CLIENT.SRC\X86.BIN
NLSMSG16.EXE	SITE.SRV\MAINCFG.BOX\CLIENT.SRC\X86.BIN
SETLSOS2.EXE	SITE.SRV\MAINCFG.BOX\CLIENT.SRC\X86.BIN
NLSMSGO2.EXE	SITE.SRV\MAINCFG.BOX\CLIENT.SRC\X86.BIN

The SCRIPTS*platform*.BIN*language* directory for each client language has been added.

File name	Moved from
NLS_LS.DLL	SITE.SRV\MAINCFG.BOX\CLIENT.SRC*platform*.BIN\00000409

SMS Logon Server Default Permissions

The following table lists the default permissions for shares and directories on SMS logon servers.

Share/volume	Directory	Permissions
SMS_SHR*x*		Administrator's local group has full control; Everyone has Read capabilities.
	SMSroot	Administrator's local group has full control; Everyone has Read capabilities.
	HELPER.SRV and all subdirectories	Administrator's local group has full control.
	LOGS	Inherits permissions from the drive where SMS is installed. Defaults to Everyone has full control.
NetWare volume		No change from existing.
	SMS\LOGON.SRV (NetWare)	No change from existing.
SMS_SHR		Administrator's local group and Everyone have full control.
	(Windows NT and LAN Manager)	Administrator's local group has full control; Everyone has Read capabilities.
	CCR.BOX DESPOOLER.BOX INVENTRY.BOX ISVMIF.BOX PCMPKG.SRC SMSID*.UID (file)	Administrator's local group has full control; Everyone has Change capabilities.
	platform.BIN *platform*.BIN*language*	Administrator's local group has full control; Everyone has Read capabilities.

(continued)

Share/volume	Directory	Permissions
SMS_SHR (*cont.*)	MSTEST PCMINS.BOX INVENCFG.BOX APPCTL.SRC and all subdirectories	Administrator's local group has full control; Everyone has Read capabilities.
	PCMPKG.SRC*packageID*	Administrator's local group has full control; Everyone has Change capabilities. (Read and Write permissions for Users and Guests can be modified through the user interface. By default, Users and Guests have Read and Write permissions.)

Important Do not modify share comments! These are read by services and will cause errors if they are altered.

Package Distribution Servers

The following table shows default permissions for SMS shares and directories on package distribution servers. For a description of Windows NT file and special permissions, see your Windows NT documentation.

Share	Directory	Permissions
Shared package share	*SharedPackageDirectoryName* (Windows NT and LAN Manager)	Administrator's local group and Everyone have full control.
SMS_PKG*x*	*SharedPackageDirectoryName* *OptionalDirectory* (Windows NT and LAN Manager)	Administrator's local group, Everyone, and users have full control.
	PackageID	Administrator's local group has full control; Everyone and users have Read capabilities.

CHAPTER 2

Client Reference

The Microsoft Systems Management Server (SMS) system supports clients running MS-DOS and Windows version 3.1, Windows for Workgroups version 3.11, Windows 95, Windows NT version 3.51 and later, Macintosh System 7.*x*, OS/2 version 2.11, and OS/2 Warp. Supported protocols include NetBEUI, TCP/IP, IPX, and AppleTalk.

This chapter describes the SMS client components and programs, the client files that are modified by SMS, and provides troubleshooting tips for SMS clients.

Client Components

The first time a client is added to an SMS-supported domain, the SMS system installs and configures the SMS client components on the client, assigns the client a unique SMS ID, and scans the client to collect its inventory.

Each SMS client running Windows NT, Windows 95, Windows version 3.1, Windows for Workgroups, and MS-DOS contains the following directories.

Directory	Contains
MS\SMS\BIN	Executable files for the major SMS components.
MS\SMS\DATA	Files that provide data or input to executable files.
MS\SMS\LOGS	Log files written by SMS client components.
	For version 1.2, several client files have been moved from the MS\SMS\BIN directory to this directory.
MS\SMS\INVDATA	Raw inventory files that are created by the Inventory Agent.
MS\SMS\IDMIFS	Extended client inventory when an IDMIF is placed in the IDMIFS directory on an SMS client.
MS\SMS\NOIDMIFS	Inventory information that contains groups with no ID or architecture.
MS\SMS\TEMP	Files that are created for temporary use.

The following table describes the major SMS components on clients running Windows NT, Windows 95, Windows version 3.1, Windows for Workgroups, and MS-DOS (Macintosh files are listed in a table in the section "Macintosh Components" later in this chapter). For a complete list of SMS files installed on clients, see the CL_*.TXT files in the LOGON.SRV directory on an SMS logon server. There is one file for each type of client supported.

Note If a client component has a 16-bit, a 32-bit, and a Windows 95 version, the following table lists all filenames separated by a slash (/), as in APPCTL16.EXE/APPCTL32.EXE/APPCTL95.EXE. If a file has separate NetBIOS and IPX versions, the IPX version is noted in parentheses, as in USERTSR.EXE (USERIPX.EXE).

Directory	Component	Description
drive:\SMSroot	SMS.INI	Initialization file that contains configuration information for the inventory, Package Command Manager, software auditing, and shared application components on the client. SMS.INI is generated by SMS Client Setup and is updated by several other SMS client components. It contains a unique ID used by SMS to identify the client. SMS.INI is always a hidden file in the root of the first (alphabetical) local hard drive.
Windows	_WCHAT32.DLL	Library used by WCHAT32.EXE for internationalization resources, on clients running Windows NT.
	_WSLAV32.DLL	Library used by WSLAVE32.EXE for internationalization resources, on clients running Windows NT.
	ACMEWKS_.DLL	Library used by the Microsoft Test program.
	ACTDLL16.DLL/ ACTDLL32.DLL/ ACTDLL95.DLL	Library used by the Applications Control program.
	APPSTART.EXE	Shell program that locates and runs SMS shared applications.
	APSRES16.DLL/ APSRES32.DLL/ APSRES95.DLL	Library that contains locale/language-specific strings used by APPSTART.EXE.

(continued)

Directory	Component	Description
Windows (cont.)	CPPS32.DLL	Library used by NADAPI16.DLL for access to classes that work with file enumeration, file information, and directory monitoring on clients running Windows NT.
	DEINSDLL.DLL	Library used by SMS Client Setup.
	IMP.INI	Initialization file that contains settings for IMP16.DLL.
	INV32CLI.EXE	Program for inventorying clients running the Windows NT platform.
	ISMIF16.DLL/ ISMIF32.DLL	Library used for status MIF files.
	MULTPROT.DLL	Library with multi-protocol abstraction layer, used by Remote Control for clients running Windows NT 3.51 and later.
	NADAPI16.DLL/ NADAPI32.DLL/ NADAPI95.DLL	Library used by the Applications Control program (APPCTL*x*.EXE) and APPSTART.EXE to manage SMS network applications.
	QUEUEBUF.DLL	Library used to manage "send buffer" for Remote Control of clients running Windows NT.
	PROXYDLL.DLL	Library used by the Applications Control program (APPCTL*x*.EXE).
	SMS16NET.DLL	Library used by clients running Windows 3.1, Windows for Workgroups, and Windows 95.
	SMS16THK.DLL	Library used by clients running Windows 3.1, Windows for Workgroups, and Windows 95.
	SMS32SHL.DLL/ SMS95SHL.DLL	Library used by clients running Windows NT/Windows 95.
	SMS95LAN.DLL	Library used by Windows 95 clients for networking.
	SMS95NET.DLL	Library used by Windows 95 clients for networking.

(continued)

Directory	Component	Description
Windows (cont.)	SMS95NW.DLL	Library used by Windows 95 clients for networking with NetWare.
	SMSCFG.DLL	Library used by the Applications Control program when running the SMS shared application configuration scripts.
	SMSMS32.DLL	Library used by SMSNET32.DLL for making network calls that are specific to LAN Manager.
	SMSNET.DLL/ SMSNETS32.DLL	Library used by NADAPI16.DLL/ NADAPI32.DLL to make connections and get information such as user group and server names.
	SMSNETMS.DLL (SMSNETNW.DLL)	Library used by SMSNET.DLL for making network calls that are specific to LAN Manager (or NetWare). If NetWare is detected, SMSNET.DLL loads SMSNETNW.DLL. If not, it loads SMSNETMS.DLL.
	SMSNWRES.DLL	Library of resources for SMSNETNW.DLL.
	SMSRUN32.EXE	Program that reads SMSRUN32.INI on clients running Windows NT to create program groups on the client and then launch SMS client programs.
	SMSSETU_.DLL	Library used by SMS Client Setup.
	SMSSU16.DLL/ SMSSU32.DLL	Library used by SMS Client Setup.
	SNMPELEA.DLL	Library that provides an extension to the SNMP Service, for the SNMP trap sender on clients running Windows NT.
	SNMPELMG.DLL	Library that contains the locale and language-specific strings used by the SNMPELEA.DLL on clients running Windows NT.

(continued)

Directory	Component	Description
Windows (cont.)	VUSER.386	Device driver used to view command windows on clients running Windows 3.1, Windows for Workgroups, and Windows 95.
	WCHAT32.EXE	Program used for Remote Chat on clients running Windows NT.
	WSLAVE32.EXE	Program used for specific network operations on clients running Windows NT.
	WUSER32.EXE	Remote Control agent for clients running Windows NT.
	WUSERMSG.DLL	Library used by WUSER32.EXE for error messages.
	_WUSER32.DLL	Library used by WUSER32.EXE.
Windows/SYSTEM	IDIS_NT.DLL	Display driver that works with WUSER32.EXE on clients running Windows NT version 3.51.
	SMSROUTR.VXD	Windows 95 device driver for SMS network applications.
	SNMPAPI.DLL	Library that contains the SNMP management API for Windows NT 3.51.
	VSMSNET.VXD	Device driver for SMS network applications
Windows/SYSTEM /DRIVERS	KBSTUFF.SYS	Driver used to send keystrokes to a client running Windows NT when it is being remotely controlled and no user is logged on.
MS\SMS\BIN	_CLILANG.DLL	Library that contains locale and language-specific strings used by SMSRUN16.EXE.
	_CLMON32.DLL	Library that contains locale and language-specific strings used by the SMS client monitor for Windows NT (CLIMONNT.EXE).

(continued)

Directory	Component	Description
MS\SMS\BIN *(cont.)*	_EDITINI.DLL/ _EDTINNT.DLL	Libraries used for EDITINI.EXE/ EDTININT.EXE, for configuring remote control options from the client.
	_IDISP16.DLL	Library used by IDISP16.DLL for internationalization resources.
	_MIF.DLL/ _MIFDOS.DLL	Library used by the MIF Entry program.
	_WCHAT16.DLL	Library used by WCHAT16.EXE for internationalization resources.
	_WSLAV16.DLL	Library used by WSLAVE16.EXE for internationalization resources.
	_WUSER.DLL	Library used by the Remote Control agent (WUSER.EXE).
	APPCTL16.EXE/ APPCTL32.EXE/ APPCTL95.EXE	Configures SMS shared applications.
	APPRES16.DLL/ APPRES32.DLL/ APPRES95.DLL	Library that contains locale/language specific-strings used by the Applications Control program.
	CLIMONNT.EXE	Program for monitoring and inventory on clients running Windows NT.
	COEXIST.DLL	Library used by IDISP16.DLL to perform function-hooking tasks.
	EDITINI.EXE/ EDITININT.EXE	Program for configuring remote control options from the client.
	HELP.HLP	Help file for clients running MS-DOS.
	IDISP16.DLL	Library used by Remote Control as a display driver to capture screens on clients running Windows 3.1, Windows for Workgroups, and Windows 95.
	IDIS_LM.DLL (IDIS_IPX.DLL)	Library used by WUSER.EXE for network-specific calls.

(continued)

Directory	Component	Description
MS\SMS\BIN *(cont.)*	IMP16.DLL	Library that provides a multi-protocol abstraction layer for Remote Control of clients running Windows 3.1, Windows for Workgroups, and Windows 95.
	IPCONFIG.EXE/ WINIP95.EXE	Program used by clients running Windows for Workgroups/Windows 95 to manipulate and display basic network configuration information, used by the Inventory Agent.
	INV32CLI.EXE	Program for inventorying clients running the Windows NT platform.
	MIFDOS.EXE/ MIFWIN.EXE	MIF Entry program for completing forms that are reported as MIF files.
	NNP.EXE	Program Group Control program for Windows 95.
	PCM16R.DLL/ PCM32R.DLL	Library that contains locale/language-specific strings used by Package Command Manager.
	PCMDOS.EXE	Package Command Manager program for MS-DOS. PCMDOS.EXE calls a series of related programs named PCMDOS_2.EXE, PCMDOS_3.EXE, and PCMDOS_3.EXE.
	PCMDOS_2.EXE	Program that provides network connection code for PCMDOS.EXE.
	PCMDOS_3.EXE	Program that provides status reporting for PCMDOS.EXE.
	PCMDOS_4.EXE	Program that provides the text-based user interface for PCMDOS.EXE.
	PCMWIN16.EXE/ PCMWIN32.EXE	Package Command Manager program for Windows version 3.1, Windows for Workgroups, Windows 95, and Windows NT.

(continued)

Directory	Component	Description
MS\SMS\BIN *(cont.)*	QBASIC.EXE	Program that interprets BASIC programming, used on MS-DOS clients to display help files.
	SIGHT.OVL	Overlay used by USERTSR.EXE and USERIPX.EXE to access data.
	SM16.CNT/ SM32.CNT	Help contents file for SMS clients running Windows 95 or Windows NT.
	SM16.HLP/ SM32.HLP	Help file for SMS clients running Windows.
	SMSOS2AG.EXE	Program that enables Package Command Manager to gain access to SMS logon servers on the network.
	SMSRUN16.EXE	Program that reads SMSRUN16.INI on clients running Windows version 3.1, Windows for Workgroups, Windows 95, or OS/2 to create program groups on the client and then launch SMS client programs.
	SMSWORK.EXE	Program that queues work to be done after a system restart.
	START.EXE	Program required by clients running Windows 95 as part of the operating system.
	UINFO.XNF	Default MIF form for clients.
	USERTSR.EXE (USERIPX.EXE)	As a terminate-and-stay-resident (TSR) program on clients running MS-DOS and Windows version 3.1, this program displays a computer's configuration and provides Help Desk features for the SMS Administrator.
	WCHAT16.EXE	Program used for Remote Chat on clients running Windows 3.1, Windows for Workgroups, and Windows 95.
	WOUDAT16.EXE	Program used for diagnostics on clients running Windows 3.1, Windows for Workgroups, and Windows 95.

(continued)

Directory	Component	Description
MS\SMS\BIN *(cont.)*	WSLAVE16.EXE	Program used for File Transfer on clients running Windows 3.1, Windows for Workgroups, or Windows 95.
	WUSER.EXE	Remote Control agent for clients running Windows 3.1, Windows for Workgroups, and Windows 95.
MS\SMS\DATA	CL_DOS.MOD/ CL_WIN.MOD/ CL_NT.MOD/ CL_OS2.MOD/ CL_W95.MOD	File that lists changes made to the client (not including copying files). Note that this file is *not* an exact copy of the CL_*X*.MOD file on the SMS logon server.
	CL_DOS.TXT/ CL_WIN.TXT/ CL_NT.TXT/ CL_OS2.TXT/ CL_W95.TXT	File that lists changes made to the client (not including copying files). Note that this file is *not* an exact copy of the CL_*X*.TXT file on the SMS logon server.
	CLIENT.BAT	Batch file created by SMS Client Setup and used by clients running MS-DOS, Windows version 3.1, Windows for Workgroups, and Windows 95 to run SMS components at startup.
	CMNDHIS.DOS/ CMNDHIS.WIN/ CMNDHIS.NT	Created on clients when the Inventory Agent is run with a **resync** command. The Inventory Agent reads this file to find out if it has already run a **resync**.
	DOMAIN.INI	Initialization file used by SMS client programs.
	PCMHIST.REG	Registry containing Package Command Manager status information. This file is created on each client that runs the Package Command Manager to store package information. If PCMDOS.EXE and PCMWIN16.EXE both run on the same client, they share access to a single PCMHIST.REG.
	SMSRUN16.INI/ SMSRUN32.INI	Initialization files used by SMSRUN16 and SMSRUN32. This ASCII file tells SMSRUN which program group icons to set up.

(continued)

Directory	Component	Description
MS\SMS\LOGS	AUDIT16.LOG/ AUDIT32.LOG	Log file for software auditing on the client. This file exists only after an audit job has run.
	CLI_X.LOG	Log file for SMS Client Setup.
	CLIMON.LOG	Log file for the Windows NT Client Monitor (CLIMONNT.EXE).
	INV32CLI.LOG	Log file for the Windows NT Inventory Agent.
	NNP.LOG	Log file for Program Group Control for Windows 95 and Windows NT.
	PCMDEBUG.LOG	Log file containing detailed trace information, created when the **/DEBUG** command-line switch is used with PCMDOS.EXE, PCMWIN16.EXE, or PCMWIN32.EXE.
	PCMDOS.LOG	Log file that provides troubleshooting information for Package Command Manager on clients running MS-DOS.
	PCMWIN.LOG	Log file that provides troubleshooting information for Package Command Manager on clients running Windows.
	PGC.LOG	Log file for Program Group Control.
	SMSRUN.LOG	Log file for the SMSRUN program.

Macintosh Components

To start inventory collection for the first time, a user on a Macintosh client must manually connect to the Windows NT Services for Macintosh logon server to run the Installer program. After that, inventory collection is automatic at system startup.

To run Installer, the user selects the Chooser to connect to the SMS_SHR volume on the SMS logon server, to locate the MAC.BIN folder. When Installer is run from the MAC.BIN folder, the SMS files and INVMac program are copied to the client. Restarting the Macintosh then runs INVMac that generates client files, including SMS.INI and all local history files. INVMac also starts the Package Command Manager program (PCMMac) on the Macintosh. When a package is first run from the Package Command Manager, PCMMac generates the PCMHIST.REG file, which contains package status information.

The following table lists SMS components on the Macintosh.

Component	Description
SMS.INI	Initialization file that contains configuration information for inventory and Package Command Manager on the client. This file is located in System Folder:Preferences: Microsoft SMS and contains a unique ID used by SMS to identify the client.
Help on Help	Help file located in System Folder:Extensions: Microsoft:Help.
Microsoft Help	Help file located in System Folder:Extensions: Microsoft:Help that runs the help files.
Foxpro Help	Help file located in System Folder:Extensions:Microsoft: Help that runs Microsoft Help as a standalone application.
DOMAIN.INI	When INVMac runs, it creates a local SMS.INI file as well as two files that store the hardware and software inventory history: InvHWScanResult and InvSWScanResult.
INVMac	Program located in System Folder:Startup Items that generates the SMS.INI file, updates SMS logon server files, performs hardware and software inventory, and starts PCMMac.
InvHWScanResult	Local history file located in System Folder:Preferences: Microsoft SMS for hardware inventory.
InvSWScanResult	Local history file located in System Folder:Preferences: Microsoft SMS for software inventory (not present if no inventory is requested).
PCMHIST.REG	File that contains Package Command Manager package status information. This file is created on each client when the Package Command Manager stores package information (when it is required to run or hide a package).
PCMMac	Package Command Manager program for Macintosh that is launched by INVMac and located in System Folder:Preferences:Microsoft SMS.
Microsoft SMS Client Help	Help file for PCMMac. Located in System Folder:Extensions:Microsoft:Help.
MIFMAC	MIF Entry program for completing forms that are reported as MIFs. Located in System Folder:Preferences: Microsoft SMS:BIN.

SMS Client Setup

There are three versions of the SMS Client Setup program, which support the client operating systems, as shown in the following table.

Client operating system	Client setup file
Windows NT (version 3.1 or later)	LOGON.SRV*platform*.BIN\CLI_NT.EXE
MS-DOS (version 5.0 or later), Windows version 3.1, Windows for Workgroups, and Windows 95	LOGON.SRV\X86.BIN\CLI_DOS.EXE
OS/2 version 2.11 and OS/2 Warp	LOGON.SRV\X86.BIN\CLI_OS2.EXE

Macintosh computers use the Installer program to set up and configure the client.

Caution   SMS Client Setup can fail on computers running the MS-DOS VSAFE utility. VSAFE, which is loaded into memory, is an MS-DOS utility that monitors a computer for viruses.

The SMS Client Setup program performs the following operations on clients running MS-DOS, Windows version 3.1, Windows for Workgroups, OS/2, Windows 95, and Windows NT:

- Analyzes the client to determine whether setup, upgrade, or remove actions are necessary.
- Sets up new clients, copies SMS files, modifies system files, and configures SMS applications to start automatically, if appropriate.
- Updates SMS client files.
- Removes specific SMS programs after an administrator deletes a client program.
- Removes all SMS files, applications, and program groups.

Note   The client DOMAIN.INI file will normally reflect changes faster than the client SMS.INI file, which is only updated when logon scripts are run or the user runs the RUNSMS batch file.

SMS Client Setup uses the [SMS] section of DOMAIN.INI (located in the LOGON.SRV directory on all SMS logon servers) to determine what changes are required on the client. Client configuration changes are made in the Site Properties dialog box. By default, SMS installs and automatically starts all SMS client applications (Package Command Manager, Program Group Control, the remote troubleshooting utilities, and MIF Entry).

SMS Client Setup is called by the SMSLS or RUNSMS batch file (or the system logon script on NetWare clients). The SMSLS batch file runs SMS Client Setup using the **/p:** option, where **/p:** specifies a path to the SMS logon server directory (LOGON.SRV). It contains the copy-list file (CL_*x*.TXT, where *x* represents the client platform).

Note The SMSLS.BAT file has been split into two files. Rather than running as a logon script or running it from SMS_SHR, there are now two batch files that start SMS inventory and SMS Client Setup. Also, two new command (.CMD) files have been added to support OS/2 clients.

SMSLS.BAT is used to generate logon scripts and is located in the NETLOGON share. If you upgraded from SMS version 1.0, the old version of SMSLS.BAT is located in SMS_SHR so you can copy custom changes from an existing SMSLS.BAT file to the new SMSLS.BAT file in the NETLOGON share. Delete the old SMSLS.BAT file after the changes are copied. A new file, RUNSMS.BAT, runs manually from SMS_SHR.

To complete its actions on computers running Windows 3.1, Windows 95, Windows for Workgroups, Windows NT, and OS/2, the SMS Client Setup program uses the SMSRUN (SMSRUN16.EXE and SMSRUN32.EXE) and SMSSVR (SMSSVR16.EXE and SMSSVR32.EXE) programs.

The SMSRUN program reads SMSRUN16.INI/SMSRUN32.INI on computers running Windows version 3.1, Windows for Workgroups, Windows NT, or OS/2 to get the full path for SMS client files, and then it creates program groups on the client. SMSRUN also starts SMS components if the Automatically Start This Component options for the components are set in the Site Properties dialog box.

The SMSSVR program upgrades or removes SMS components from the client. SMSSVR then starts the SMS Client Setup program and upgrades or removes files as selected.

Client Setup Command Line Options

You can run SMS Client Setup manually from the appropriate *.BIN subdirectory of the LOGON.SRV directory (SMS_SHR share) on an SMS logon server. You can run SMS Client Setup with one or more command line options. For example, you can initiate the removal of clients by modifying the SMSLS batch file to run SMS Client Setup with the /r option. Users can initiate removal of their client by connecting to the SMS_SHR on their SMS logon server and running SMS Client Setup manually with the /r option, or they can run DEINSTAL.BAT. The syntax for SMS Client Setup is as follows:

{**cli_dos** | **cli_nt** | **cli_os2**} [**/r** | **/u** | **/f** | **/p:**_path_ | **/d:**_drive_ | **/v** | **/k**]

/r

Removes the SMS client components. With this option, SMS Client Setup must run twice because SMS applications must be stopped before files are removed. This overrides Client settings in the Site Properties dialog box.

/u

Upgrades SMS client components. With this option, SMS Client Setup must run twice because SMS applications must be stopped before files are updated.

/f

Verifies that each SMS client component file is correctly installed and that the client's system files are correctly configured for SMS. With this option, SMS Client Setup must run twice.

/p:_path_

Specifies the path for the SMS\LOGON.SRV directory. For example, at a client running MS-DOS, from the command prompt, type:

cli_dos /p:R:

Where **R:** is the connection to the SMS_SHR on the SMS logon server.

You can also use a UNC path. For example:

cli_dos /p:**_SMS_server_\SMS_SHR**

/d:_drive_

Specifies the installation drive on the client. By default, SMS is installed on the drive with the largest amount of free space.

/v

Sets verbose mode. SMS Client Setup displays status messages on the client desktop as it completes its tasks.

/k

Specifies that SMS components are not running, and they can be overwritten if necessary.

If conflicting options are used (for example, **/r** and **/u**), SMS Client Setup selects the first option.

For information about how SMS Client Setup installs and upgrades SMS components on and removes SMS components from a client, see Chapter 3, "System Flow."

Client Programs

You can use the following programs to configure SMS clients:

- SETLS
- Windows NT Client Monitor
- Inventory Agent
- SMSRUN
- Package Command Manager
- Program Group Control

Each of these programs is described in the following sections.

SETLS Program

The SMS logon script calls the SETLS program to connect to an SMS logon server. SETLS uses information in the SMSLS.INI file to select an SMS logon server from which to run the SMS Client Setup and Inventory Agent programs for a client. SETLS builds a UNC name corresponding to the *platform*.BIN directory on the SMS logon server (*servername*\SMS_SHR*platform*.BIN) and makes the connection. (SETLS will, when necessary, use a path.) Then the client is added to the computer inventory for the SMS logon server's domain. If no SMSLS.INI file is present, SETLS runs SMS programs from the SMS logon server where the SMSLS batch file was run.

SMS uses the Windows NT Directory Replicator service to place SMSLS.BAT, SMSLS.INI, and SETLS on the NETLOGON share of all SMS logon servers running Windows NT and LAN Manager.

Versions of SETLS

To support computers running Windows NT, Windows version 3.1, Windows for Workgroups, Windows 95, MS-DOS, and OS/2, there are three versions of SETLS.

Client operating system	SETLS program	Directory
Windows NT	SETLS32.EXE	LOGON.SRV*platform*.BIN
MS-DOS, Windows version 3.1, Windows for Workgroups, and Windows 95	SETLS16.EXE	LOGON.SRV\X86.BIN
OS/2	SETLSOS2.EXE	LOGON.SRV\X86.BIN

When you select the Automatically Configure Workstation Logon Scripts option in the Clients dialog box in Site Properties, the Site Configuration Manager copies the SETLS programs (and other SMS components) to the SCRIPTS directory in the REPL$ share on the primary domain controllers in LAN Manager and Windows NT domains. Depending on the microprocessor types supported in the site, the SETLS programs for the specific microprocessor types are copied to the corresponding directory: X86.BIN (x86 microprocessors), ALPHA.BIN (Alpha microprocessors), and MIPS.BIN (MIPS microprocessors).

SETLS includes command line options for connecting a logical drive to a network server, deleting an SMS logon server connection, and running a program file located on a network server.

Command Line Options

The SETLS command line options are:

{**setls16** | **setls32** | **setlsos2**} [**/m:C**] [**/d:***drive*] [**/dr:***driverange*] [**/sh:***sharename*] [**/i**[:*inifile*]] [**/v**[:**on**]]

{**setls16** | **setls32** | **setlsos2**} [**/m:D**] [**/d:***drive*] [**/v**[:**on**]]

{**setls16** | **setls32** | **setlsos2**} [**/m:E**] [**/sh:***sharename*] [**/p:***programfile*] [**/pa:***argument* [...]] [**/sn**] [**/v**[:**on**]] [**/i**[:*inifile*]]

/m:C
Makes a network connection using a logical drive letter.

/m:D
Deletes a network connection that uses a logical drive letter.

/m:E
Runs a program file located on a remote server without making a logical drive network connection (the default is to connect).

/**d:***drive*
>Specifies a particular drive letter (the default is the next available drive letter).

/**dr**:*driverange*
>Limits the search for the next available drive.

/**sh**:*sharename*
>Specifies the share to connect to. The default is SMS_SHR.

/**i**:[:*inifile*]
>Names the initialization file to use. The default is SMSLS.INI.

/**v**[:**on**]
>Specifies verbose mode for output messages. The default is off.

/**p**:*programfile*
>Is a file name or relative path to an .EXE or a .COM file.

/**pa**:*argument*
>Passes an argument to the program when it runs. If you want to pass the UNC path of the SMS logon server, specify **%%SMS_unc%%** as the value for this argument. The SETLS program replaces this with the UNC path to the SMS_SHR share of the SMS logon server.

/**sn**
>Indicates that the specified program should not be run on a slow network.

Windows NT Client Monitor

The Windows NT Client Monitor is made up of the CLI_NT.EXE and CLIMONNT.EXE programs. The Windows NT Client Monitor:

- Copies RAW files from the client running Windows NT to the SMS logon server. Whenever CLI_NT.EXE runs, it copies the files that need to be copied, otherwise CLIMONNT.EXE copies the files.

- Monitors changes to clients running Windows NT that require the client to be restarted. (This task is performed only by the CLIMONNT.EXE program.)

CLIMONNT.EXE is started by SMSRUN32.EXE when Windows NT is started and runs in the background as long as the user is logged on. When a directory change notification is received, CLIMONNT.EXE picks up RAW files as soon as they appear and copies them to the SMS logon server. CLIMONNT.EXE uses a polling interval to check whether the files on the SMS logon server (DOMAIN.INI, PKG_16.CFG, RESYNC.CFG) have changed and need to be copied.

CLI_NT.EXE

This program runs from the SMSLS.BAT or RUNSMS.BAT batch file when the user logs on. The CLI_NT.EXE program:

- Copies DOMAIN.INI, PKG_16.CFG, and *smsid*.CFG from the SMS logon server to the client if the versions on the client are not current.
- Checks to see whether a RAW file is present on the client; if so, it copies the file to the SMS logon server and deletes the copy on the client.

CLIMONNT.EXE

This program is started by SMSRUN32.EXE when a user logs on and runs the client continuously. The CLIMONNT.EXE program:

- On a polling interval, copies DOMAIN.INI, PKG_16.CFG, and *smsid*.CFG from the SMS logon server to the client if the versions on the client are not current.
- Checks to see whether a RAW file is present on the client; if so, it copies the file to the SMS logon server and deletes the copy on the client.
- Monitors the registry for configuration changes that require the client to be restarted.

Inventory Agent

Every SMS client has a version of the Inventory Agent program as described in the following table.

Client operating system	Inventory Agent file name
Windows NT	INVWIN32.EXE, INV32CLI.EXE
Windows 95	INVDOS.EXE
Windows for Workgroups	INVDOS.EXE
Windows version 3.1	INVDOS.EXE
MS-DOS (version 5.0 or later)	INVDOS.EXE
Macintosh (version 7.0.0 or later)	INVMac
OS/2 version 2.11 and OS/2 Warp	INVOS2.EXE

Except for Macintosh clients, the Inventory Agent runs when the SMSLS or RUNSMS batch file is called. For clients running NetBIOS protocols, such as NetBEUI and TCP/IP, the Inventory Agent program runs from the SMSLS.BAT logon script. For NetWare IPX-based clients, Inventory Agent runs as part of a NetWare system logon script.

Inventory Agent for Windows version 3.1, Windows for Workgroups, MS-DOS, Windows 95, and Windows NT generates *.RAW files. The Inventory Agent programs for Macintosh and OS/2 clients create ASCII MIF files. Both *.MIF and *.RAW files become binary MIF files after being processed by the Inventory Processor.

On all clients, the Inventory Agent:

- Scans the client for inventory (hardware, software, and ISV MIF files).
- Collects files to include in the inventory.

Inventory on Clients Running Windows NT

The SMS Client Inventory service (INV32CLI.EXE) is installed on Windows NT-based clients by the Client Configuration Manager, if the SMS Inventory Agent (INVWIN32.EXE) is not running. SMS Client Inventory runs under the LocalSystem security context and thus provides a more complete inventory. The SMS Client Inventory:

- Reads DOMAIN.INI, PKG_16.CFG and *smsid*.CFG from MS\SMS\DATA on the client.
- Takes inventory based on the inventory frequency specified by the administrator in the SMS Administrator.
- Places its inventory RAW files locally on the client in the MS\SMS\INVDATA directory.

The inventory RAW file on the client is copied to the SMS logon server by Client Monitor. If no user is logged on to the client when inventory is collected, Client Monitor will not start until the next time a user logs on.

As in previous releases of SMS, INVWIN32.EXE is also an Inventory Agent for Windows NT-based clients. INVWIN32.EXE is launched from SMSLS.BAT or RUNSMS.BAT when the user logs on. The INVWIN32.EXE program:

- Reads input files DOMAIN.INI, PKG_16.CFG, and RESYNC.CFG directly from the SMS logon server.

- Checks whether this is a different site/domain from the site/domain previously established. If the site/domain is different, it checks to see if inventory was collected against this same new site/domain for a specified number of consecutive times (defaults to 3). If not, it prints a message and exits. If so, it changes the site/domain information in SMS.INI and continues.

- Builds (or rebuilds) the list of SMS logon servers in SMS.INI from data in the DOMAIN.INI file.

- Takes inventory based on the inventory frequency specified by the administrator in the SMS Administrator and only if it determines that inventory has not been taken within a reasonable time by the SMS Client Inventory service (INV32CLI.EXE).

- Places its inventory RAW file on an appropriate SMS logon server.

Inventory on Clients Running MS-DOS, Windows 3.1, Windows for Workgroups, and Windows 95

On clients running MS-DOS, Windows version 3.1, Windows for Workgroups, and Windows 95, the Inventory Agent always reports the protocol used while connecting to the SMS logon server. If information about other protocols is available to the Inventory Agent, it will report this also.

On clients running Windows for Workgroups or LAN Manager, you must run the SMSLS.BAT or RUNSMS.BAT file or Inventory Agent using the Full (or Enhanced) Redirector. If you use the Basic Redirector, the Inventory Agent will either not report the inventory or prompt you for an SMS ID. It can also quit the process and display an error. To correct this, start the network software using the Full or Enhanced Redirector.

Inventory Agent Command Line Options

There are four Inventory Agents, each supporting different command line options:

Inventory agent	Client operating system
INV32CLI	Windows NT
INVWIN32	Windows NT
INVDOS	MS-DOS, Windows 3.1, Windows for Workgroups, Windows 95
INVOS2	OS/2

These commands are described in the following sections.

INV32CLI

The syntax for INV32CLI is:

inv32cli /T*minutes*

Where *minutes* sets the sleep interval. Using this option temporarily overwrites the initial 24-hour default value. This setting will last until the service is stopped and restarted.

INVWIN32

To run INVWIN32 as an executable file, the syntax is:

invwin32 /E [/F] [/I] [/V] [/L:*SMS server***\SMS_SHR]**

To run INVWIN32 as a service, the syntax is:

invwin32 [/F] [/I] [/T*minutes***]**

/E
  Causes INVWIN32 to be called as an executable file, rather than a service.

/F
  Forces an immediate hardware and software inventory.

/I
  Performs software and hardware inventory only (does not perform any other task such as downloading or collecting files).

/V

Specifies verbose mode. Displays status messages during execution.

/L:*SMS server***\\SMS_SHR**

Specifies an SMS server to use for inventory input and output files. Overwrites the specified server in SMS.INI.

/T*minutes*

Sets the service sleep interval to *minutes*, temporarily overwriting the default value of 24 hours. This setting will last until the service is stopped, and then restarted.

When running INVWIN32 as a service, specify its switches in the Startup Parameters box in the SMS Service Manager.

INVDOS

The syntax for INVDOS.EXE is:

invdos [**/F**] [**/M**] [**/I**] [**/V**] [**/L:***SMS server***\\SMS_SHR** | **/N***server* **/P***share*]

/F

Forces an immediate hardware and software inventory.

/M

Forces INVDOS to request a unique computer name.

/I

Performs software and hardware inventory only (does not do any other task such as downloading or collecting files).

/V

Specifies verbose mode.

/L:*SMS server***\\SMS_SHR**

Specifies an SMS server to use for the inventory input and output files. Overwrites the specified server in SMS.INI.

/N*server* **/P***share*

Specifies the location for inventory output files. Overwrites the **InventoryCollectionPoint** entry in SMS.INI. These switches will also overwrite the **/L** option.

INVOS2

The syntax for INVOS2.EXE is:

invos2 [**/V**] [**/L:***SMS server***SMS_SHR**]

/V

Specifies verbose mode.

/L:*SMS server***SMS_SHR**

Specifies an SMS server to use for the inventory input and output files. Overwrites the specified server in SMS.INI.

Temporary Files

The SMSSAFE.TMP file is created by the Inventory Agent to record the status of hardware inventory. Every time the Inventory Agent runs, it creates *drive*:\SMSSAFE.TMP. When it successfully finishes, it deletes this file. If the Inventory Agent doesn't complete inventory successfully, the file remains as a signal that something went wrong during the previous inventory collection. When it runs again, the Inventory Agent writes entries to the empty SMSSAFE.TMP for each test it runs. The results are marked COMPLETED after successfully doing each test or CRASHED, if a hardware test fails. The next time the Inventory Agent runs, it reads the file again; all tests marked CRASHED are skipped and their failure is recorded and written to the [WorkstationStatus] section of the SMS.INI file. After moving the failed tests to the SMS.INI file, the SMSSAFE.TMP file is deleted. The next time the Inventory Agent runs, it will detect the failed tests in the SMS.INI file and skip failed hardware tests.

When you troubleshoot a hardware inventory problem, you may need to disable portions of the hardware detection during the SMS inventory on the client. This can be accomplished by creating your own SMSSAFE.TMP file.

To create a SMSSAFE.TMP file, use a text editor to add valid entries of hardware devices or parameters you want the hardware detection to bypass (listed below). For example, if you want to bypass the mouse detection, enter the following in the SMSSAFE.TMP file:

```
MouseInfo=CRASHED
```

The following are valid entries for SMSSAFE.TMP (FailedHardwareChecks):

```
BanyanVines
BiosInfo
CMOSMemory
CommPorts
ComputerConfig
ComputerName
ConventionalMemory
DeviceInfo
Disks
Dma
DPMIMemory
Drive<X>
EMMMemory
EMMMemoryInfo
ExtendedMemory
GamePorts
IRQInfo
Keyboard
Lanman
LanmanInfo
LanManNetcardInfo
Lantastic
LantasticInfo
MouseInfo
MSNet
NetBios
Novell
NovellInfo
NovellNetcardInfo
PrinterPorts
TSRInfo
VCPIMemory
Video
WolverineInfo
XMSMemory
```

When a failed hardware component is fixed or replaced, remove the appropriate FailedHardwareChecks entry from the [WorkstationStatus] section in SMS.INI and remove the SMSSAFE.TMP file (if it only referenced one component). Start the client again and run the Inventory Agent to include the component.

SMSRUN Program

The SMSRUN program (SMSRUN16.EXE and SMSRUN32.EXE) configures SMS program groups and starts SMS applications on clients running OS/2, Windows NT, Windows 95, Windows version 3.1, or Windows for Workgroups.

For clients running OS/2, Windows 95, Windows version 3.1, or Windows for Workgroups, SMS Client Setup modifies the WIN.INI file to load SMSRUN16.EXE each time Windows starts. SMSRUN16 reads SMSRUN16.INI to see which program groups to create and which applications to start.

On clients running Windows NT, SMSRUN32.EXE runs from the Load value in the HKEY_CURRENT_USER\SOFTWARE\Microsoft\Windows NT \CurrentVersion\Windows key in the Windows NT registry, so it runs at startup. SMSRUN32 uses SMSRUN32.INI to create program groups on the desktop and start applications as specified in the [Startup] section.

Package Command Manager

The Package Command Manager program runs on every client and supports the following operating systems.

Client operating system	Package Command Manager file
Windows NT (version 3.1 or later)	PCMWIN32.EXE
Windows version 3.1, Windows for Workgroups, OS/2 version 2.11, OS/2 Warp, and Windows 95	PCMWIN16.EXE
MS-DOS (version 5.0 or later)	PCMDOS.EXE
Macintosh (version 7.0.0 or later)	PCMMac

The Package Command Manager:

- Checks SMS.INI for the location of the PCMHIST.REG registry, specified polling intervals, and other Package Command Manager options.

- Checks the SMS logon server at startup for new or pending packages that have not been run or archived. The service allows automated installation to occur based on the polling interval, unless the user chooses the Package Command Manager icon, which causes an immediate check.

- Displays the Package Command Manager in the foreground whenever a new, visible package is available or whenever the user chooses the Package Command Manager icon.
- Runs the package commands that install packages on an individual client.
- Lets users at client destinations specify which packages to install.
- Stores package information in PCMHIST.REG.
- Returns job status information to the SMS logon servers.

After running a package, the Package Command Manager modifies PCMHIST.REG indicating that the package was run.

Windows NT-based SMS servers also support the Package Command Manager service (PCMSVC32.EXE). This service allows package installation on unattended computers running Windows NT. If a user is not logged on when a package arrives at a target computer running Windows NT, the Package Command Manager service runs packages in the background (if the package supports it); if a user is logged on, the Package Command Manager program installs the package. By default, the PCMSVC32.EXE file is installed only on computers running Windows NT Server that are SMS site, helper, or logon servers.

When SMS installs client components on an OS/2 2.11 client, it also installs the SMSOS2AG.EXE file. SMSOS2AG.EXE enables Package Command Manager to gain access to SMS logon servers on the network. This file monitors the arrival of new packages and reports the package command status to the SMS system and package distribution servers.

Program Group Control

Program Group Control includes two programs (APPSTART and Applications Control [APPCTL]) that manage the environment for SMS network applications on SMS clients running Windows version 3.1, Windows for Workgroups, Windows 95 or Windows NT.

APPCTL manages connections to the SMS network application server and ensures that the assigned SMS network application program groups are built when Windows is started. The user's environment information is obtained from the Program Group Control database. When a user clicks an icon to start an SMS network application, APPSTART retrieves a list of servers from the Program Group Control database and permits access to an available server. After connecting to that server, APPCTL sets up the Windows environment so the application runs correctly, which allows APPSTART to start the application.

APPCTL Command Line Options

{**APPCTL16** | **APPCTL32** | **APPCTL95**} [**/stop**] [**/hide**] [**/deinstall**]
[**/disable:yes**]

/stop

Stops the current APPCTL session.

/hide

Hides the Program Group Control window. By default, this window appears when APPCTL checks for new applications. Before attempting to hide the window, use the **/stop** option to stop APPCTL.

To make the Program Group Control window reappear after hiding it, use the **/stop** option to stop APPCTL, and then choose the Program Group Control icon.

/deinstall

Removes all SMS program groups from the Program Manager and the local registry.

/disable:yes

Disables Program Group Control on the client.

General Guidelines for Program Group Control

Program Group Control can reconfigure an SMS shared application if it determines that its registry entries are corrupted. When the reconfiguration program runs, it selectively removes files from the directory. To prevent deleting user-created files, SMS Setup records the date and time the application was installed and stores this information in the registry. However, if an application is removed, reinstalled, and then removed again, any files modified after the first installation but before the second installation are deleted because its date will not be more recent than the second installation time.

An executable file (DOSETUP.EXE) will run a user-specified installation program under Program Group Control. DOSETUP.EXE allows an arbitrary installation program to be run by Program Group Control. This program would normally be specified as the **ConfigurationScript** entry in the [Program Item Properties i] section of a PDF file. The command-line syntax is:

dosetup *RegName CommandLine*

where *RegName* has the same value as the **RegistryName** entry in the same section of the PDF, and *CommandLine* is any valid command line.

For example, the following command runs the installation program for the Microsoft Access 2.0 Service Pack:

dosetup acs2pak setup.exe

DOSETUP provides a mechanism to run an installation program and sets SMS registry status flags required by Program Group Control.

DOSETUP runs the specified command line and manages the status entry under the program item's registry key (HKEY_CLASSES_ROOT\SMS \APPLICATIONS*regName*\Configuration\Status). The status entry must be set to UNFINISHED, FAIL, or SUCCESS. DOSETUP operates like SMSSETUP in most respects; it displays the SMS Setup screen, reports errors, and does post-processing following a system restart.

Post-processing sets an application's status flag to SUCCESS. DOSETUP initially sets an application's status to FAIL in case anything goes wrong during processing. To handle a possible system restart by an installation program, DOSETUP sets the status to UNFINISHED immediately before running the user's command line. When the installation program ends, or when Program Group Control Start reruns DOSETUP following a system restart, the status is reset to SUCCESS. An installation program cannot pass an error message to DOSETUP.

DOSETUP is installed in the MSTEST directory on the SMS logon server.

Disabling Program Group Control on Clients

When Program Group Control runs on the client, it can take a few minutes to count user groups and set up the Program Group Control environment. This can happen even when Program Group Control has not been set up for that user. If you are using Program Group Control in your site, and users want to disable it, you can use the Registry Editor or a Program Group Control command-line switch.

To disable Program Group Control using the Registry Editor, add the registry key HKEY_CLASSES_ROOT\SMS\DISABLE_PGC. To enable Program Group Control on the computer, remove this key.

To disable Program Group Control from the command line, add the **/DISABLE:YES** switch to the **APPCTL**xx command. For instance, **appctl16 /disable:yes** disables Program Group Control on a client running 16-bit Windows. If an instance of Program Group Control is already running when it is disabled on the computer, Program Group Control will be disabled the next time the user logs on.

Program Group Control Error Messages

After SMS is installed in a site server domain and a client is added, you may see the following message when running Program Group Control:

```
Program Group Control: Could not open the application database because
servers are missing from the SMS.INI. Resolve this problem by rerunning
Client Setup.
```

If you add a client to the site using the SMSLS or RUNSMS batch file (or SMS Client Setup) from an SMS logon server with no servers in the [Servers] section of the DOMAIN.INI file, Program Group Control displays the preceding message.

After SMS is installed in the site server domain, make sure that all SMS logon servers are listed in the [Servers] section of the DOMAIN.INI file on the SMS_SHR share of each SMS logon server in the site server domain. Correct this error by rerunning the SMSLS or RUNSMS batch file or SMS Client Setup when there are one or more servers listed in the [Servers] section of DOMAIN.INI.

A user may see the following message after trying to use an SMS network application:

```
Failed to connect to SMS network server. Cannot determine which groups
the user belongs to. Please contact your administrator.
```

This means the client cannot locate any of the package servers.

To correct this:

1. Examine the PGC.LOG file in the MS\SMS\LOGS directory on the client. This file may contain specific information regarding the failure.
2. Examine the [servers] section of the SMS.INI file on the client.
3. Set up a network connection to the SMS_SHR share for one of the servers listed in this section.
4. Within the SMS_SHR share, connect to the APPCTL.BOX\ DATABASE directory and look for files with .HAF and .HGF extensions. There should be one .HGF file for each program group available to the user, and there should be one .HAF file for each program item in the assigned program groups. If there are no files with these extensions, it can indicate that the program groups for have not been distributed to this site, or that the user at the client does not have permission to view the files in the share.

Client Files Modified by SMS

The following table lists client files that are modified during SMS operations.

File	Modifications
SMS.INI	The first time SMS Client Setup is run, it writes the SMS ID to this file. If SMS.INI is deleted, a new ID is assigned and SMS assumes this is a new computer. Then the SMS.INI file is updated with new information from DOMAIN.INI on the SMS logon server every time the user runs SMS Client Setup.
	When a user chooses the Help Desk Options icon in the SMS Client program group and makes changes to the default remote control settings, the EDITINI.EXE file writes these changes to the [SIGHT] section of SMS.INI. This occurs only on Windows-based clients that support remote control.
	When a user changes settings in the Package Command Manager Options dialog box, the Package Command Manager program writes these changes to the [Package Command Manager] section of SMS.INI.
	The Inventory Agent logs any hardware failures encountered during inventory, and it writes the date and time of the last hardware and software inventories.
SYSTEM.INI	For clients running Windows 95, SMS Client Setup modifies lines in the [386ENH] section as follows:
	`Device=\Windows\vuser.386` `NetHeapSize=48`
	For clients running Windows version 3.1 or Windows for Workgroups, SMS Client Setup modifies lines in the [386ENH] section as follows:
	`Device=\Windows\vuser.386` `NetHeapSize=56`
	VUSER.386 enables the remote troubleshooting utilities to run. Increasing **NetHeapSize** provides more memory for SMS remote troubleshooting utilities. It also adds device drivers (SMSROUTR.VXD and VSMSNET.VXD) for clients running Windows 95.
WIN.INI	For clients running Windows version 3.1, Windows for Workgroups, or Windows 95, SMS Client Setup for Windows modifies the **LOAD=** parameter in the [Windows] section to call SMSRUN16.EXE (**LOAD=C:\MS\SMS\BIN \SMSRUN16.EXE**).

(continued)

File	Modifications
AUTOEXEC.BAT	On clients running MS-DOS, Windows version 3.1, Windows 95, and Windows for Workgroups, SMS Client Setup modifies AUTOEXEC.BAT to call CLIENT.BAT if the remote troubleshooting utilities are installed or if Package Command Manager for MS-DOS is enabled. This modification is inserted before instructions to run Windows because SMS Client Setup looks for strings containing "Win" to determine where to insert the CLIENT.BAT file.
CLIENT.BAT	SMS Client Setup modifies CLIENT.BAT to run the remote support TSR (**usertsr** or **useripx**) on clients running MS-DOS and Windows 3.1, and Package Command Manager for MS-DOS, if appropriate. SMS Client Setup also adds SMSWORK.EXE to all clients except those running Windows NT.
SMSRUNx.INI	For clients running Windows 3.1, Windows 95, and Windows for Workgroups (SMSRUN16.INI), and Windows NT (SMSRUN32.INI), SMS Client Setup modifies this file to define the SMS client program groups and to indicate which SMS applications to load and start automatically.
PCMHIST.REG	This file is generated the first time Package Command Manager runs or archives a package. The file stores information about packages, such as when it was installed or archived.
SMSSAFE.TMP	Inventory Agent creates this file to record hardware inventory status. Every time Inventory Agent runs, it creates *drive*:\SMSSAFE.TMP. Upon successful completion, it deletes the file. If the Inventory Agent does not complete inventory successfully, the file remains as a signal that something went wrong during the previous inventory collection.
	When it runs again, Inventory Agent writes entries to the empty SMSSAFE.TMP file. The status is recorded either as COMPLETED if a test was successful or CRASHED, if a hardware test failed. The next time Inventory Agent runs, it reads the file again. All tests marked CRASHED are skipped and their failed status is written to the [WorkstationStatus] section of SMS.INI.
STARTUP.CMD	Runs the SMSOS2AG.EXE file on OS/2 clients.
Registry database files	On clients running 16-bit Windows, the REG.DAT registry file is modified by SMS Client Setup, SMSRUN16.EXE, and Program Group Control.
	On clients running Windows NT, SMS Client Setup, SMSRUN32.EXE, and Program Group Control modify the Windows NT registry.

Troubleshooting

If you are having trouble installing or running the SMS client software, check the following:

1. Make sure the client has access to the network.

   Use File Manager or command line options to establish a connection to the SMS logon server. If a connection doesn't occur, it can indicate a network problem or that a common protocol has not been established.

2. Verify that the SMS.INI operating system to the network-type keys match the client's operating system and network type.

   If they do not match, rerun RUNSMS.BAT, RUNSMS.CMD, or the logon script.

3. Verify that the appropriate Windows network drivers are installed on clients running Windows 3.1, Windows for Workgroups, or Windows 95.

   Examine the **network.drv =** entry in the Windows SYSTEM.INI file. One of the following entries should be present: LANMAN21.DRV, WFWNET.DRV, MSNET.DRV, or NETWARE.DRV. For Windows 95, this value may be something like "Microsoft Windows Network (version 3.11)." If the appropriate driver is not loaded, Package Command Manager and Program Group Control will not start.

   For clients running Windows 95, look at the Network settings in the Control Panel to verify network support.

4. Verify that the client is running the latest patches of all software.

   Microsoft Operating System patches are available on the Windows NT Server compact disc or from CompuServe. The Windows NT Server version 3.51 compact disc contains updated modules for the following client network operating systems:

   - Network Client version 3.0 for MS-DOS
   - Windows for Workgroups version 3.11
   - LAN Manager version 2.2c
   - TCP/IP-32 for Windows for Workgroups, version 3.11
   - Remoteboot Service for Windows NT Server version 3.51
   - Additional Network Interface Card (NIC) Drivers from the Windows Driver Library (WDL)

5. On the client, ensure that SMS components have not been moved to the Startup group.

   If SMS components are run from the Startup group, SMS upgrades fail. If this happens, you can install or reinstall SMS by removing the SMS component from Startup, restarting Windows, and rerunning SMSLS.BAT or RUNSMS.BAT.

6. Make sure the user logon account for the client has Read permissions for the SMS logon server's SMS_SHR.

7. View the CLI_x.LOG file for reported problems on the client.

8. For Run Command On Workstation packages:

   - Make sure that packages are designated for the appropriate operating systems. For example, if a package is targeted for clients running MS-DOS, it will not appear on clients running Windows version 3.1.

   - The date and time on the client must be consistent with the date and time on the SMS server. If these values are not the same, the package expiration time could possibly occur before the package arrives at the client.

   - Check the event log for failure explanations. Likely problems include insufficient disk space on a client or a network connection failure. In the latter case, try to make the network connection with the **net use** command.

9. Check the **FilesNotDownloaded** entry in SMS.INI. Component problems can sometimes be caused by missing files.

10. For problems with SMS Client Setup:

    - Verify that the path is not too long and the Windows directory is at the beginning.

    - Ensure that WINVER.EXE exists in the Windows directory.

    - Temporarily disable virus protection software.

11. For problems with inventory, restart the client and run inventory again. Then check the **FailedHardwareChecks** entry in SMS.INI.

CHAPTER 3

System Flow

This chapter describes the Microsoft Systems Management Server (SMS) process for the following operations:

- SMS infrastructure management, including how sites, servers, and clients are installed and maintained.
- Inventory collection and maintenance, including how SMS processes the various types of inventory-related files.
- Software Distribution, including how SMS processes jobs, sets up SMS network applications, and selects default distribution servers.
- SMS event collection and reporting.
- Remote troubleshooting.

You can use this information to track the flow of data and control files within and between sites.

SMS Infrastructure

The following sections describe primary and secondary site installation, SMS logon server component installation, and SMS client installation.

Primary Site

A primary site has its own SQL Server database to store the system, package, inventory, and status information for the primary site and the sites beneath it in the hierarchy. It also has administrative tools to directly manage all sites in the site hierarchy.

A primary site must be installed from the SMS Setup program that is included in the Microsoft Systems Management Server version 1.2 compact disc. When a primary site is installed for the first time, it is a standalone central site. Once a primary site is installed, you can use the SMS Administrator to integrate the new site and any of its subsites in the hierarchy of another SMS system.

Installing a Primary Site

When you run the SMS Setup program to install a primary site, it begins by determining the available language and platform included on the Microsoft Systems Management Server version 1.2 compact disc. It then decompresses files and writes them to disk as specified in the SYSTEM.MAP file. SMS Setup reads SYSTEM.MAP directly from the Microsoft Systems Management Server version 1.2 compact disc, and then copies it to your disk for later use by the SMS Administrator and the Hierarchy Manager and Site Configuration Manager services. In order to interact with logon servers and clients running various CPU platforms and languages, SMS Setup downloads binaries for all supported configurations according to the directory structure mapped out in SYSTEM.MAP. The SYSTEM.MAP file is also used to manage client files.

While copying files to the hard disk and creating the directory tree, SMS Setup initiates SQL Server database operations. Once file installation and database operations are complete, SMS Setup starts the Hierarchy Manager and Site Configuration Manager services and writes information to the Windows NT registry under the following key:

HKEY_LOCAL_MACHINE\SOFTWARE\Microsoft\SMS

The Identification, Setup, and SQL Server keys contain information relevant to the setup process:

- The Identification key contains the Windows NT domain and server names for the site server and the name of the SMS installation directory.
- The Setup key records the SMS version and user and organization names.
- The SQL Server key stores database and device names, as well as the encrypted SQL Server password and account.

During the installation process, the Hierarchy Manager service reads and writes information to and from the SQL Server database. The Site Configuration Manager service sets up services, domain management, shares, and so on. As part of the installation process, the Hierarchy Manager creates a temporary site control file (SMS\SITE.SRV\SITECFG.BOX_INIT.CT1), which contains all proposed configurations for a site. The Hierarchy Manager passes this file to the Site Configuration Manager, which carries out the proposed configuration.

After the Site Configuration Manager completes the site configuration instructions, it sends a site control file (*.CT2) back to the Hierarchy Manager. The Hierarchy Manager uses this site control file to write configuration data to the site database. The Site Configuration Manager also copies this file to a permanent text file (SITECTRL.CT0) in the SITE.SRV\SITECFG.BOX directory. Note that this process repeats each time there is a proposed change to the site configuration. Each site has its own SITECTRL.CT0 file.

As part of site configuration, the Site Configuration Manager starts the following services: SMS Executive, Client Configuration Manager, Inventory Agent for Windows NT, and the Package Command Manager for Windows NT. The SMS Executive service, in turn, starts additional SMS components such as the Despooler and Scheduler. The SMS Setup program creates the Systems Management Server program group and icons.

Installation on the site server is now complete. Note that if events or errors occur during setup, they are written to the Windows NT event log. You can also view the SMSSETUP.LOG file to trace the actions and errors logged by the SMS Setup program. SMSSETUP.LOG is located at the root of the first hard disk drive on the computer (usually, this is drive C).

Secondary Site

A secondary site does not have a SQL Server database to store its system, package, inventory, and status information. Instead, it forwards inventory and status information to its primary site for processing and storage. It also does not have administrative tools since a secondary site must be administered through one of its parent sites. You create a secondary site from a primary site using the SMS Administrator. This primary site is known as the parent site for the secondary site. The secondary site appears directly beneath the parent site in the site hierarchy.

To create a secondary site, SMS needs an account that has specific privileges at the secondary site and the primary site must have a valid address for the secondary site. Each site must have a common protocol and connectivity.

A secondary site cannot be a parent site and you cannot attach sites beneath it. You also cannot move a secondary site to another position in the site hierarchy nor can you change its parent site. Once the secondary site is created, you can add new domains and clients to the site. Domains and clients are added to a secondary site the same way they are added to a primary site.

SMS services at the primary site connect to the secondary site and install a Bootstrap service to initiate its setup. When the services are started at the secondary site, they manage the installation of SMS components at that site. You can install a secondary site over a LAN or by using RAS from the primary site, but you cannot create a secondary site across an SNA backbone entirely from the primary site. To complete a secondary site installation over SNA, you must install the SNA Receiver and Bootstrap services on the site server for the secondary site.

Installing a Secondary Site

This section describes what happens after you add a secondary site using the SMS Administrator. This process is summarized in Figure 3.1, Secondary Site Installation.

After you have confirmed the secondary site installation and the Success message box displays the message Site creation has been initiated, the secondary site's configuration is added to the database of the current site (the parent site of the secondary site). The Hierarchy Manager detects the new secondary site in the site database and updates the addressing for the parent site so that the addressing for the new secondary site is available for use by the sender.

The Hierarchy Manager then initiates a special send request, which is sent to the Scheduler. The Scheduler creates a send request file that gives the sender instructions to install the installation directory, to install the Bootstrap service to that directory, and to start the Bootstrap service on the site server for the secondary site. The sender connects to the site server for the secondary site and carries out the actions specified by the send request.

After the Bootstrap service has confirmed that it has started at the secondary site, the Hierarchy Manager at the parent site then creates another job to send the SMS site package, which contains all the SMS site components. This job uses the regular Scheduler/sender mechanism to transfer the package to the secondary site. The Hierarchy Manager uses the SYSTEM.MAP file to determine which files to copy to the secondary site.

When the Bootstrap service receives the package, it places the package in the SMS root directory as BOOTSTRP.PK1.

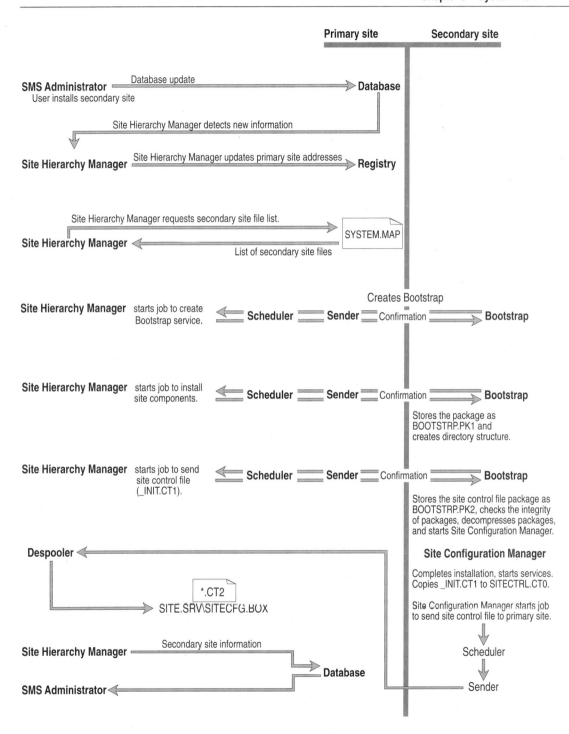

Figure 3.1   Secondary Site Installation

After the Bootstrap service has confirmed that it has started at the secondary site, the Hierarchy Manager at the parent site then creates another job to send the SMS site package, which contains all the SMS site components. This job uses the regular Scheduler/sender mechanism to transfer the package to the secondary site. The Hierarchy Manager uses the SYSTEM.MAP file to determine which files to copy to the secondary site.

When the Bootstrap service receives the package, it places the package in the SMS root directory as BOOTSTRP.PK1.

At the parent site, the Hierarchy Manager creates a job to send a site control file (_INIT.CT1) to the secondary site. The site control file contains the configuration information for the secondary site.

When the Bootstrap service receives the package for the site control file, it places the package in the SMS root directory as BOOTSTRP.PK2. The Bootstrap service then verifies the integrity of the packages.

If the package files are corrupted, the Bootstrap service reports the problem to the trace log and Windows NT event log and then stops the installation process.

If the package files are valid, the Bootstrap service checks to make sure that there is enough free disk space to install the site server components.

If there is not enough disk space, the Bootstrap service reports the problem to the trace log and the Windows NT event log and then stops the installation process.

If there is enough free disk space and the package files are valid, the Bootstrap service decompresses the packages, creates the site directory structure on the site server, and places the components in the appropriate directories

The Bootstrap service then starts the Site Configuration Manager. After the Site Configuration Manager has started, the Bootstrap service stops. The Site Configuration Manager uses the site control file to complete the secondary site's installation and configuration.

As part of site configuration, the Site Configuration Manager starts all SMS services at the site.

After the site services have been started, the Site Configuration Manager creates another temporary site control file (*.CT2) that contains the actual configuration at the secondary site. The Site Configuration Manager creates a job to send the site control file back to the parent site. This job uses the regular Scheduler/sender mechanism to transfer the site control file to the parent site (for more information on how the Scheduler and sender interact, see "Collecting Inventory at a Secondary Site" later in this chapter). This process repeats each time you modify the configuration of a secondary site.

At the parent site, the Despooler places the site control file in the SITE.SRV\SITECFG.BOX directory of the SMS_SHR*x* share on the site server. The Hierarchy Manager at the parent site updates the site database with the actual configuration at the secondary site. When you refresh the SMS Administrator, the secondary site appears as an installed site in the Sites window. Using the Properties command from the File menu, you can view (and modify) the properties for the new secondary site.

Modifying Properties at a Secondary Site

Modifications of the secondary site's properties are initiated from the SMS Administrator and then carried out by the Hierarchy Manager at the parent site and the Site Configuration Manager at the secondary site. The Hierarchy Manager creates a job to send a site control file to the secondary site. This job uses the regular Scheduler/sender mechanism to transfer the site control file package to the secondary site.

At the secondary site, the Site Configuration Manager uses the site control file to update the secondary site's configuration. After the configuration is complete, the Site Configuration Manager creates a site control file that contains the actual configuration at the secondary site. The Site Configuration Manager creates a job to send the site control file back to the parent site. This job uses the regular Scheduler/sender mechanism to transfer the site control file to the parent site. At the parent site, the Hierarchy Manager updates the parent site's database.

Note that during primary and secondary site installation, the Hierarchy Manager and Site Configuration Manager create files called _INIT.CT1 and *.CT2, respectively. When site properties are later modified, these files are recreated using random numerical names.

Installing an SNA-linked Secondary Site

If the secondary site is connected through an SNA link (summarized in Figure 3.2, SNA-linked Secondary Site Installation), installation differs from the regular secondary site installation (summarized in Figure 3.1, Secondary Site installation), as follows:

- You must run the SMS Setup program at the secondary site prior to adding the secondary site to its parent site. SNA Setup starts the Bootstrap and SNA Receiver services at the target site.

- The Hierarchy Manager does not send a job to start the Bootstrap service at the secondary site (because the SNA Setup program starts it).

- Incoming packages at both primary and secondary sites go through the SNA Receiver. The SNA Receiver at the secondary site acknowledges receipt of incoming packages, but does not check to confirm that they have been processed correctly by the Bootstrap service.

Secondary Site Component Upgrade

This section describes what happens after you add a component or upgrade the primary site directly above the secondary site, using the SMS Setup program. This process is summarized in Figure 3.3, Secondary Site Component Upgrade.

After you have confirmed the secondary site update, the SMS Setup program adds an upgrade instruction in the site database for all secondary sites directly beneath the current site. The Hierarchy Manager service detects this instruction and waits for all these secondary sites to be in the active state. The Hierarchy Manager will not begin the upgrade process if any secondary sites are still in the process of being created or deleted.

When all secondary sites are active, the Hierarchy Manager creates a system job for each site. The Hierarchy Manager creates a job (a system job with the comment `Bootstrap Job for <sitecode>` where *sitecode* is the site code for the secondary site to be upgraded) to send to each secondary site to install and start the SMS Upgrade Bootstrap service at each secondary site. The bootstrap job is phase 1 of the upgrade.

Note For a secondary site connected to its parent site using the SNA Sender, the bootstrap job also installs and starts an Upgrade SNA Receiver service. This service is used temporarily so that the primary site can continue to send site upgrade jobs to the site during the removal and upgrade of the existing SNA Receiver service.

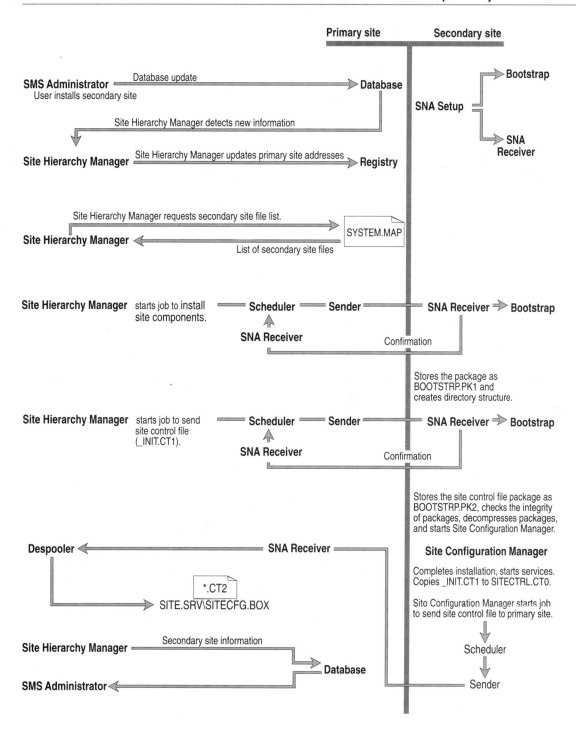

Figure 3.2   SNA-linked Secondary Site Installation

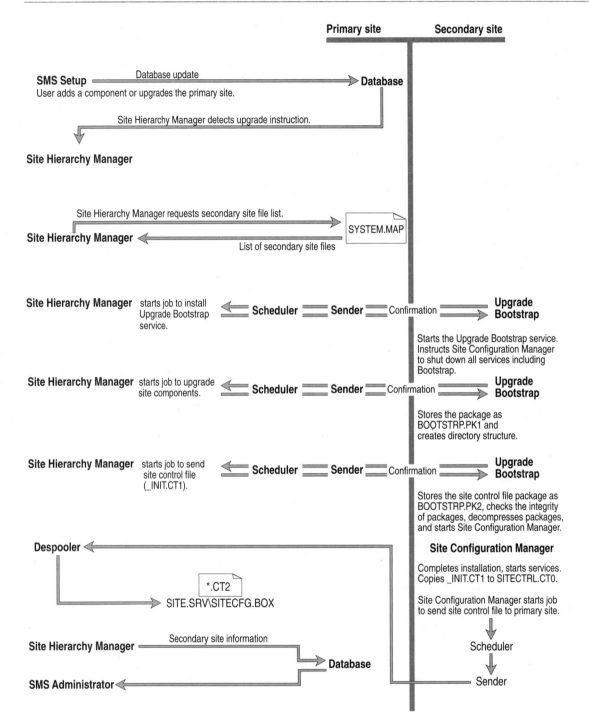

Figure 3.3   Secondary Site Component Upgrade

At each secondary site server, the Upgrade Bootstrap service shuts down the site in preparation for the upgrade. All SMS services are stopped except the Upgrade Bootstrap service. At the primary site, you will not be able to edit Site Properties dialog box for these sites while they are in upgrade status (in the Sites window, the sites will have an under construction icon and their Site Properties dialog boxes will display the site upgrade phase).

After the Upgrade Bootstrap service has confirmed that it has started at the secondary site, the Hierarchy Manager at the parent site then creates another job (a system job with the comment Site Install Job for <sitecode> where *sitecode* is the site code for the secondary site to be upgraded) to send the SMS site package, which contains all the SMS site components. This job uses the regular Scheduler/sender mechanism to transfer the package to the secondary site. The Hierarchy Manager uses the SYSTEM.MAP file to determine which files to copy to the secondary site. The site install job is phase 2 of the upgrade.

When the Upgrade Bootstrap service receives the package, it places the package in the SMS root directory as BOOTSTRP.PK1.

At the parent site, the Hierarchy Manager creates a job (a system job with the comment Site Control Job for <sitecode> where *sitecode* is the site code for the secondary site to be upgraded) to send a site control file (_INIT.CT1) to the secondary site. The site control file contains the configuration information for the secondary site. The site control job is phase 3 of the upgrade.

When the Upgrade Bootstrap service receives the package for the site control file, it places the package in the SMS root directory as BOOTSTRP.PK2. The Upgrade Bootstrap service then verifies the integrity of the packages.

If the package files are corrupted, the Upgrade Bootstrap service reports the problem to the trace log and the Windows NT event log and then stops the installation process.

If the package files are valid, the Upgrade Bootstrap service checks to make sure that there is enough free disk space to install the site server components.

If there is not enough disk space, the Upgrade Bootstrap service reports the problem to the trace log and the Windows NT event log and then stops the installation process.

If there is enough free disk space and the package files are valid, the Upgrade Bootstrap service decompresses the packages, creates the site directory structure on the site server, and places the components in the appropriate directories.

If the Upgrade Bootstrap service does not receive valid packages or cannot decompress the packages within 48 hours, it will attempt to restart the site with the original site components. After the site's SMS services have been restarted, the Hierarchy Manager will report its configuration back to the parent site. If the site upgrade has taken longer than 48 hours, you should verify that the site has been updated or that the components have been added to the site. If the upgrade has failed, you can try again by upgrading the primary site or installing the new software component using the SMS Setup program. You can also use the PREINST program (the executable version of the Hierarchy Manager) to force an upgrade of a specific secondary site.

Then Upgrade Bootstrap service starts the Site Configuration Manager. After the Site Configuration Manager has started, the Upgrade Bootstrap service stops. The Site Configuration Manager uses the site control file to complete the secondary site's installation and configuration.

As part of the site configuration, the Site Configuration Manager starts all SMS services at the site.

After the site services have been started, the Site Configuration Manager creates another temporary site control file (*.CT2) that contains the actual configuration at the secondary site. The Site Configuration Manager creates a job to send the site control file back to the parent site. This job uses the regular Scheduler/sender mechanism to transfer the site control file to the parent site (for more information on how the Scheduler and Sender interact, see "Collecting Inventory at a Secondary Site" later in this chapter). This job is phase 4 of the upgrade.

At the parent site, the Despooler places the site control file in the SITE.SRV\SITECFG.BOX directory of the SMS_SHRx share on the site server. The Hierarchy Manager at the parent site updates the site database with the actual configuration at the secondary site. When you refresh the SMS Administrator, the secondary site appears as an installed site in the Sites window. Using the Properties command from the File menu, you can view (and modify) the properties for the new secondary site.

Secondary Site Removal

This section describes what happens after you delete a secondary site using the SMS Administrator. This process is summarized in Figure 3.4, Secondary Site Removal.

After you have confirmed the secondary site deletion and the Success message box displays the message `Site creation has been initiated`, the SMS Administrator adds a deletion instruction in the site database for the secondary site.

When the Hierarchy Manager detects this instruction, it creates a job (a system job with the comment `Bootstrap Job for <sitecode>` where *sitecode* is the site code for the secondary site to be removed) to send to the secondary site to install and start the Bootstrap service at that secondary site.

At the secondary site, the Site Configuration Manager installs the Bootstrap service, which then takes over removal of the site.

At the primary site, when the bootstrap job has completed, the Hierarchy Manager removes the site from the site database.

The Hierarchy Manager then forwards the site deletion information to its own parent site, which removes the site from its database. The site deletion information is then forwarded to its parent site, and so on. The site deletion is reported all the way up to the central site.

If the secondary site removal has failed, the site may reappear at the parent site, since it may continue reporting. If this happens, you can delete it again. Or you can use the SMS Setup program at the secondary site server.

At the secondary site server, you can view the BOOTSTRP.LOG file (in the root of the drive containing the SMS root directory) for a record of the actions and errors reported by the Bootstrap service.

Note If you delete the site icon twice in the Sites window of the SMS Administrator and the site has already been removed, the second bootstrap job will not be able to complete, because the secondary site no longer exists. If this happens, you can cancel or delete the second bootstrap job and the Hierarchy Manager will remove the site from the site database.

Primary site

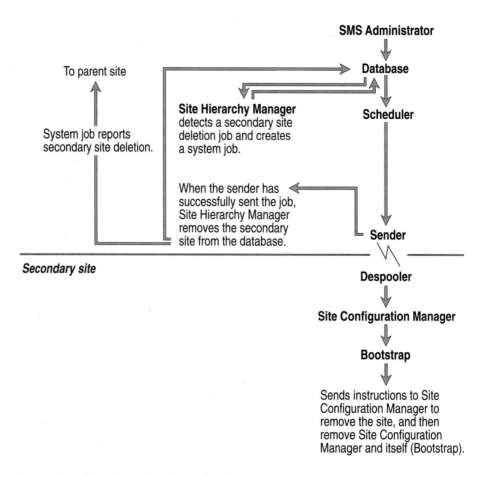

SMS Administrator

To parent site

Database

Scheduler

System job reports
secondary site deletion.

Site Hierarchy Manager
detects a secondary site
deletion job and creates
a system job.

When the sender has
successfully sent the job,
Site Hierarchy Manager
removes the secondary
site from the database.

Sender

Secondary site

Despooler

Site Configuration Manager

Bootstrap

Sends instructions to Site
Configuration Manager to
remove the site, and then
remove Site Configuration
Manager and itself (Bootstrap).

Figure 3.4   Secondary Site Removal

General Management Within a Site

The following section describe how SMS logon servers are installed, how clients are installed, and how SMS identifies and tracks computers.

SMS Logon Server Component Installation

When you add a domain to your SMS site (using the Domains dialog box), the Site Configuration Manager service enumerates all detected (or specified) logon servers in the domain and ensures that the SMS components used to support that domain's clients are installed on each logon server. (Note that the site server's domain is added during primary site installation.)

Windows NT, LAN Manager, and LAN Server Domains

To add a Windows NT, LAN Manager, or LAN Server domain, the Site Configuration Manager:

- Creates the SMS root directory on the logon server NTFS drive with the most available space and shares the SMS root directory as SMS_SHRx (where x is the drive letter where the SMS root directory is installed). If an NTFS drive is not available, the Site Configuration Manager creates SMS_SHRx on the largest non-NTFS drive.

- Creates the LOGON.SRV directory as a subdirectory of the SMS root directory and shares it as SMS_SHR.

- Copies all logon server components to the LOGON.SRV directory.

- On computers running Windows NT Server, installs and starts the Inventory Agent for Windows NT to collect inventory on the logon server. On LAN Manager version 2.x servers, installs and starts the Inventory Agent for OS/2.

- On computers running Windows NT Server, installs and starts the Package Command Manager for Windows NT to collect inventory on the logon server.

- On computers running Windows NT Server, installs and starts the Client Configuration Manager service to process *.CCR files from clients running Windows NT. The Client Configuration Manager uses information in the *.CCR files to configure SMS services on clients running Windows NT.

- Adds the SMSLS batch file to the replication (REPL$) and NETLOGON shares, if the Automatically Configure Workstation Logon Scripts option is enabled. The Site Configuration Manager also adds the SMSLS batch file to all user profiles. If a user has an existing logon script, it adds a call to the SMSLS batch file to the script. If a user has no logon script, it adds the SMSLS batch file to the user's profile.

If the Use All Detected Servers option is enabled, the Site Configuration Manager monitors the domain for any new servers that have been added to the domain, including servers that were temporarily off the network and are now back on. When it detects a new server, the Site Configuration Manager copies files to the new server.

NetWare Domains

In NetWare domains, the Site Configuration Manager installs logon server components on all detected (or specified) logon servers. The Site Configuration Manager places files on the NetWare volume with the most free space. If the Automatically Configure Workstation Logon Scripts option is enabled, it modifies the system logon script for the logon server to run the SMS Client Setup program and the Inventory Agent for MS-DOS.

If the Use All Detected Servers option is enabled, the Site Configuration Manager enumerates all NetWare file servers on the network within 16 router hops and installs the logon server components on these servers. After the initial installation of the domain, the Site Configuration Manager continues to monitor the network for new file servers and adds logon server components to any it detects.

Clients

The following sections describe how clients are installed and how SMS Client Setup works. This section applies to all SMS clients except for SMS logon servers and Macintosh clients. Installation of SMS logon servers is described in "SMS Logon Server Component Installation" earlier in this chapter. Macintosh clients use the Apple® Installer to set up SMS. For more information on how Macintosh clients are installed, see the SMS version 1.2 product documentation.

Client Installation Process

There are three ways that clients are added to an SMS site:

- A user at a client can connect to an SMS logon server in an SMS-enabled domain and run the RUNSMS batch file. This file calls the SMS Client Setup program (CLI_NT.EXE, CLI_OS2.EXE, or CLI_DOS.EXE), which copies SMS files to the client and configures SMS client components. The RUNSMS batch file also calls the Inventory Agent, which collects inventory if the appropriate inventory frequency interval has passed.

- You can use the Automatically Configure Workstation Logon Scripts option to modify logon scripts for all users. This runs the SMSLS.BAT file when a user logs on to the network.

- For Windows NT, LAN Manager, and LAN Server domains, you can manually add the SMSLS batch file to a user's logon script. For NetWare domains, the system login script or individual user login scripts can be modified on NetWare servers to run the SMSLS.SCR script.

When you make a manual connection to the SMS_SHR of an SMS logon server and run the RUNSMS batch file, the client is added to the SMS domain of the SMS logon server where you ran the RUNSMS batch file command.

When you run the SMSLS batch file as part of a logon script, the SETLS program (which is run from within the SMSLS batch file) can read SMSLS.INI to locate a server domain where the client should be added. SMSLS.INI enables you to use existing configurations on a client to map the client to a specific SMS domain and site.

SETLS evaluates SMSLS.INI from top to bottom and uses the first successful match in the mapping list. After it finds a match, it uses the mapped domain as the client's SMS domain and attempts to find a random server within that domain. SETLS then connects to that server and runs SMS Client Setup and the Inventory Agent. If SMSLS.INI is not found, SETLS runs these programs on the current SMS logon server.

How SMS Client Setup Works

The SMS Client Setup program is called by the RUNSMS (or SMSLS) batch file after it determines the client's operating system. There are three versions of the SMS Client Setup program that support computers running Windows NT, Windows 95, Windows version 3.1, Windows for Workgroups 3.11, MS-DOS, and OS/2. Note that Macintosh computers use the Apple Installer program to set up and configure the client.

For computers running Windows NT, the SMS Client Setup program is CLI_NT.EXE. There are three subdirectories beneath the LOGON.SRV directory to support the three microprocessor types supported by SMS for Windows NT: ALPHA.BIN, MIPS.BIN, and X86.BIN. Each subdirectory contains the SMS Client Setup program (CLI_NT.EXE) for each microprocessor type running Windows NT.

For computers running MS-DOS, Windows version 3.1, Windows for Workgroups 3.11, Windows 95, the SMS Client Setup program is CLI_DOS.EXE. The X86.BIN subdirectory beneath the LOGON.SRV directory contains the CLI_DOS.EXE program.

For computers running OS/2, the SMS Client Setup program is CLI_OS2.EXE. The X86.BIN subdirectory beneath the LOGON.SRV directory contains the CLI_OS2.EXE program.

SMS Client Setup General Actions

SMS Client Setup performs the following actions:

1. Determines whether SMS.INI exists on the client.

   If SMS Client Setup cannot find SMS.INI, SMS Client Setup considers this a new installation.

2. Determines the language and operating system.

   The SMS Client Setup program must detect the language used on the computer to install the files appropriate for the language on that computer. SMS Client Setup also needs to know the operating system so that the appropriate copy-list file and modification file are installed and configured properly. On computers running Windows NT, the microprocessor type must also be detected so the files for the appropriate microprocessor type are installed.

   If SMS Client Setup detects a different operating system from the one recorded in the **OS** entry of the [SMS] section in SMS.INI, SMS Client Setup displays a warning message and stops. SMS currently supports one operating system per computer. To force the SMS components to be upgraded to a new operating system, you must run SMS Client Setup in upgrade mode or run UPGRADE.BAT from an SMS logon server.

3. Reads the copy-list file on the SMS logon server for the location of the SMS client component files for the computer's operating system and language.

4. Opens the appropriate language DLL so that messages can be displayed with the language appropriate for the client.

5. Reads DOMAIN.INI (from the SMS logon server) to update information in the SMS.INI file.

6. Performs the required actions depending on the mode that SMS Client Setup is running in.

   For more information, see the following sections.

Installation Mode

If installation is required, SMS Client Setup performs the following steps:

1. Performs the checks listed in the preceding section.

2. Attempts to create a new SMS ID for the computer using the *.UID file in the SMS logon server's LOGON.SRV\SMSID directory.

3. Finds the local drive with the most free disk space.

    SMS client components are installed on this drive if the **/d:***drive* parameter is not specified.

4. Detects the computer's microprocessor type so that the files that are appropriate for the microprocessor type are installed.

5. Determines the network type using the **NetworkType** entry specified in the LOGON.SRV\DOMAIN.INI file on the SMS logon server.

    This entry specifies which network operating system is used by the SMS logon server.

6. Creates the SMS.INI file in the root of the first local hard disk drive (usually, this is drive C).

7. Decides which files to download using the CL_*x*.TXT file and the **Components** entry in the [SMS] section of the DOMAIN.INI file.

    SMS Client Setup tries to copy files to the drive with the most free space, unless you use the **/d:***drive* option to specify another drive. If space is unavailable on the drive you specify, SMS Client Setup will not complete the installation.

    If it cannot copy down one or more files, SMS Client Setup writes the names of these files to the **FilesNotDownloaded** entry in the [Workstation Status] section of the SMS.INI file.

8. Creates a local copy-list file (CL_*x*.TXT).

Copy-list file	Operating system
CL_NT.TXT	Windows NT
CL_W95.TXT	Windows 95
CL_WIN.TXT	Windows 3.1 and Windows for Workgroups 3.11
CL_OS2.TXT	OS/2
CL_DOS.TXT	MS-DOS

9. Uses the [SMS] section in the DOMAIN.INI file as well as the appropriate configuration file (CL_WIN.MOD, CL_DOS.MOD, and so on) to see what modifications it needs to make at the client.

MOD file	Operating system	Logon server location
CL_NT.MOD	Windows NT (Alpha)	LOGON.SRV\ALPHA.BIN*language_id*
CL_NT.MOD	Windows NT (MIPS)	LOGON.SRV\MIPS.BIN*language_id*

    (continued)

MOD file	Operating system	Logon server location
CL_NT.MOD	Windows NT (x86)	LOGON.SRV\X86.BIN*language_id*
CL_W95.MOD	Windows 95	LOGON.SRV\X86.BIN*language_id*
CL_WIN.MOD	Windows 3.1 and Windows for Workgroups 3.11	LOGON.SRV\X86.BIN*language_id*
CL_OS2.MOD	OS/2	LOGON.SRV\X86.BIN*language_id*
CL_DOS.MOD	MS-DOS	LOGON.SRV\X86.BIN*language_id*

10. Modifies the system configuration to add the SMS components. How this is done depends on the type of client.

For clients running Windows NT:

- Uses information in CL_NT.MOD to create SMSRUN32.INI in the MS\SMS\DATA directory. This file specifies which SMS applications to start automatically and which program groups to create.

- Starts SMSRUN32.EXE. SMSRUN32.EXE reads SMSRUN32.INI. SMS Client Setup modifies the HKEY_CURRENT_USER\Software \Microsoft\WindowsNT\CurrentVersion\Windows\Load value in the Windows NT registry to run SMSRUN32.EXE. SMSRUN32.EXE runs the programs listed in the [Startup] section of SMSRUN32.INI. Note that SMSRUN32.EXE is only started by SMS Client Setup when it cannot find SMSRUN32.EXE in the Load value of the HKEY_CURRENT_USER \Software\Microsoft\WindowsNT\CurrentVersion\Windows key.

For clients running Windows 95:

- Uses information in CL_W95.MOD to create SMSRUN16.INI in the MS\SMS\DATA directory. This file specifies which SMS applications to start automatically and which Start menu items to create.

- Modifies WIN.INI to run SMSRUN16.EXE from the **LOAD=** line in the [Windows] section of the WIN.INI file. From then on, when Windows is started, SMSRUN16 runs and uses information in SMSRUN16.INI to decide which applications to start and which Start menu items to set up.

- Creates MS\SMS\DATA\CLIENT.BAT and modifies AUTOEXEC.BAT to run CLIENT.BAT prior to running Windows. The call to CLIENT.BAT is inserted at the end of the AUTOEXEC.BAT file.

- If the client is to be configured for remote troubleshooting, SMS Client Setup modifies these settings in the [386Enh] section of the SYSTEM.INI file: **Device=vuser.386** and **NetHeapSize** (sets it to 48 if the current value is less than 48; keeps the current setting if the value is greater than 48).

- If the client is to be configured for Program Group Control, SMS Client Setup:

  - Modifies these settings in the [386Enh] section of the SYSTEM.INI file: **Device=vsmsnet.vxd** and **Device=smsroutr.vxd**.

  - Installs and configures the SMS Naming Network Provider (NNP) in the registry by adding the entry SMS Naming Network Provider with a value of NNP.EXE to the key HKEY_LOCAL_MACHINE\Software \Microsoft\Windows\CurrentVersion\RunServices.

For clients running Windows version 3.1 and Windows for Workgroups:

- Uses information in CL_WIN.MOD to create SMSRUN16.INI in the MS\SMS\DATA directory. This file specifies which SMS applications to start automatically and which program groups to create.

- Modifies WIN.INI to run SMSRUN16.EXE from the **LOAD=** line in the [Windows] section of the WIN.INI file. From then on, when Windows is started, SMSRUN16 runs and uses information in SMSRUN16.INI to decide which applications to start and which program groups to set up.

- Creates MS\SMS\DATA\CLIENT.BAT and modifies AUTOEXEC.BAT to run CLIENT.BAT prior to running Windows (SMS Client Setup looks for the **win** command on each line).

- If the client is to be configured for remote troubleshooting, SMS Client Setup:

  - Modifies these settings in the [386Enh] section of the SYSTEM.INI file: **Device=vuser.386** and **NetHeapSize** (sets it to 56 if the current value is less than 56; keeps the current setting if the value is greater than 56).

For clients running only MS-DOS (that is, MS-DOS without Windows version 3.1 or Windows for Workgroups installed on the computer):

- Creates MS\SMS\DATA\CLIENT.BAT and modifies AUTOEXEC.BAT to run CLIENT.BAT.

- If remote troubleshooting is to be installed and automatically started, SMS Client Setup modifies CLIENT.BAT to run USERTSR.EXE or USERIPX.EXE, depending on the network type.

- Modifies CLIENT.BAT to automatically start Package Command Manager and the MIF Entry program, if appropriate.

For clients running OS/2:

- Uses information in CL_OS2.MOD to create SMSRUN16.INI in the MS\SMS\DATA directory. This file specifies which SMS applications to start automatically and which program groups to create.

- Modifies WIN.INI to run SMSRUN16.EXE from the **LOAD=** line in the [Windows] section of the WIN.INI file. From then on, when a Windows-based OS/2 session is started, SMSRUN16 runs and uses information in SMSRUN16.INI to decide which applications to start and which program groups to set up.

- Creates MS\SMS\DATA\CLIENT.BAT and modifies AUTOEXEC.BAT to run CLIENT.BAT prior to running a Windows-based OS/2 session (SMS Client Setup looks for the **win** command on each line).

- Adds SMSOS2AG.EXE to the STARTUP.CMD.

Note When SMS Client Setup modifies system *.INI files, it comments out previous entries, by placing ;SMS in front of those entries. If the client is being removed, SMS Client Setup removes the comment to return the client to its previous state.

---

11. On computers running Windows NT, SMS Client Setup evaluates whether the client has the version of the operating system appropriate for the SMS services to be installed. Then it creates a *.CCR file on the SMS logon server for the Client Configuration Manager. For more information about how SMS services are installed on computers running Windows NT, see "How SMS Client Setup Installs SMS Client Services on Computers Running Windows NT" later in this chapter.

12. Writes INSTALLED in the **SetupPhase** entry of the [Local] section of the SMS.INI file, on all clients.

Removal Mode

When SMS Client Setup is started using the **/r** switch to remove a client (or if the DEINSTAL.BAT or DEINSTAL.CMD batch files are run), SMS Client Setup performs the following for each type of operating system.

For clients running only MS-DOS

1. Performs the checks listed in "SMS Client Setup General Actions" earlier in this chapter.

2. Removes the existing SMS component files. It also removes the SMS configurations from system files and restores the previous setting that existed before SMS was installed.

For clients running Windows version 3.1, Windows for Workgroups, Windows 95, and Windows NT:

1. Performs the checks listed in "SMS Client Setup General Actions" earlier in this chapter.
2. Writes DEINSTALL in the **SetupPhase** entry of the [LOCAL] section of SMS.INI and exits.
3. Depending on the operating system, the user must either restart Windows or log off and back on to the network.

   For computers running Windows version 3.1 and Windows for Workgroups, the user must start or restart Windows to complete the removal.

   For computers running **Windows 95** and Windows NT, at the computer, the user must log off and log on to the network.
4. The SMSRUN program starts and checks the **SetupPhase** entry.
5. SMSRUN starts the SMSSVR program with the **/c** switch, which tells SMSSVR to call SMS Client Setup to complete the removal, and then SMSRUN exits.
6. SMSSVR starts SMS Client Setup with the **/k** switch, which tells SMS Client Setup that it can remove SMS component files to complete the removal.
7. SMS Client Setup removes the existing SMS component files. It also removes the SMS configurations from system files and restores the previous setting that existed before SMS was installed.
8. On computers running Windows NT, SMS Client Setup creates a *.CCR file on the SMS logon server for the Client Configuration Manager so that the Client Configuration Manager can remove the SMS services from the client. For more information about how SMS services are removed from computers running Windows NT, see "How SMS Client Setup Installs SMS Client Services on Computers Running Windows NT" later in this chapter.

For clients running OS/2:

1. The user should close all Windows-based OS/2 sessions.

2. The user runs **CLI_OS2 /r** or **DEINSTAL.CMD** from an SMS logon server.

3. SMS Client Setup performs the checks listed in "SMS Client Setup General Actions" earlier in this chapter.

4. Writes DEINSTALL in the **SetupPhase** entry of the [LOCAL] section of SMS.INI, and then exits.

5. The user starts a new Windows-based OS/2 session.

6. The SMSRUN program starts and checks the **SetupPhase** entry.

7. SMSRUN starts the SMSSVR program with the **/c** switch, which tells SMSSVR to call SMS Client Setup to complete the removal, and then SMSRUN exits.

8. SMSSVR starts SMS Client Setup with the **/k** switch, which tells SMS Client Setup to remove SMS component files to complete the removal.

9. SMS Client Setup Removes the existing SMS component files. It also removes the SMS configurations from system files and restores the previous setting that existed before SMS was installed.

Upgrade Mode

When SMS Client Setup is started using the **/u** switch to upgrade a client (or if the UPGRADE.BAT or UPGRADE.CMD batch files are run), SMS Client Setup performs the following for each type of operating system.

For clients running only MS-DOS:

1. Performs the checks listed in "SMS Client Setup General Actions" earlier in this chapter.

2. Detects the computer's microprocessor type so that the files that are appropriate for the microprocessor type are installed.

3. Determines the network type using the **NetworkType** entry specified in the LOGON.SRV\DOMAIN.INI file on the SMS logon server.

   This entry specifies which network operating system is used by the SMS logon server.

4. Compares the **Components** and **AutoStart** entries in the [SMS] section of the DOMAIN.INI file on the SMS logon server with the **InstalledComponents** and **AutoStartComponents** entries in the [WorkstationStatus] section of the SMS.INI file on the client.

   By performing this comparison, SMS Client Setup determines which existing SMS client components need to be added, removed, or upgraded.

5. Removes the SMS configurations from system files and restores the previous setting that existed before SMS was installed.

6. Upgrades the SMS components on the client by removing unneeded components, installing new ones, or replacing existing ones.

7. Modifies the system configuration to configure the set of SMS components specified by the upgrade.

   For more information about how the system configuration is modified for the installation of SMS components, see step 10 in "Installation Mode" earlier in this chapter.

8. If SMS Client Setup cannot install a file, it will try again the next time SMS Client Setup runs.

For clients running Windows version 3.1, Windows for Workgroups, Windows 95, and Windows NT:

1. Performs the checks listed in "SMS Client Setup General Actions" earlier in this chapter.

2. Detects the computer's microprocessor type so that the files that are appropriate for the microprocessor type are installed.

3. Determines the network type using the **NetworkType** entry specified in the LOGON.SRV\DOMAIN.INI file on the SMS logon server.

   This entry specifies which network operating system is used by the SMS logon server.

4. Writes UPGRADE in the **SetupPhase** entry of the [LOCAL] section of SMS.INI, and then exits.

5. Depending on the operating system, the user must either restart Windows or log off and back on to the network.

   For computers running Windows version 3.1 and Windows for Workgroups, the user must start or restart Windows to complete the upgrade.

   For computers running **Windows 95** and Windows NT, at the computer, the user must log off and log on to the network.

6. The SMSRUN program starts and checks the **SetupPhase** entry.

7. SMSRUN starts the SMSSVR program with the **/c** switch, which tells SMSSVR to call SMS Client Setup to complete the upgrade, and then SMSRUN exits.

8. SMSSVR starts SMS Client Setup with the **/k** switch, which tells SMS Client Setup that it can remove SMS component files to complete the upgrade. SMSSVR waits for SMS Client Setup to complete the upgrade.

9. Compares the **Components** and **AutoStart** entries in the [SMS] section of the DOMAIN.INI file on the SMS logon server with the **InstalledComponents** and **AutoStartComponents** entries in the [WorkstationStatus] section of the SMS.INI file on the client.

   By performing this comparison, SMS Client Setup determines which existing SMS client components need to be added, removed, or upgraded.

10. Removes the SMS configurations from system files and restores the previous setting that existed before SMS was installed.

11. Upgrades the SMS components on the client by removing unneeded components, installing new ones, or replacing existing ones.

12. Modifies the system configuration to configure the set of SMS components specified by the upgrade.

   For more information about how the system configuration is modified for the installation of SMS components, see step 10 in "Installation Mode" earlier in this chapter.

13. If SMS Client Setup cannot install a file, it will try again the next time SMS Client Setup runs.

14. On computers running Windows NT, SMS Client Setup evaluates whether the client has the version of the operating system appropriate for the SMS services to be installed or upgraded. Then it creates a *.CCR file on the SMS logon server for the Client Configuration Manager. For more information about how SMS services are installed or upgraded on computers running Windows NT, see "How SMS Client Setup Installs SMS Client Services on Computers Running Windows NT" later in this chapter.

15. SMSSVR uses the SMSRUN16.INI/SMSRUN32.INI file to set up the SMS Client program group and start SMS components that are configured to start automatically, and then SMSSVR exits.

For clients running OS/2:

1. The user should close all Windows-based OS/2 sessions.

2. The user runs **CLI_OS2 /u** or **UPGRADE.CMD** from an SMS logon server.

3. SMS Client Setup performs the checks listed in "SMS Client Setup General Actions" earlier in this chapter.

4. Detects the computer's microprocessor type so that the files that are appropriate for the microprocessor type are installed.

5. Determines the network type using the **NetworkType** entry specified in the LOGON.SRV\DOMAIN.INI file on the SMS logon server.

   This entry specifies which network operating system is used by the SMS logon server.

6. Writes **UPGRADE** in the **SetupPhase** entry of the [LOCAL] section of SMS.INI, and then exits.

7. The user starts a new Windows-based OS/2 session.

8. The SMSRUN program starts and checks the **SetupPhase** entry.

9. SMSRUN starts the SMSSVR program with the **/c** switch, which tells SMSSVR to call SMS Client Setup to complete the upgrade, and then SMSRUN exits.

10. SMSSVR starts SMS Client Setup with the **/k** switch, which tells SMS Client Setup that it can remove SMS component files to complete the upgrade. SMSSVR waits for SMS Client Setup to complete the upgrade.

11. Compares the **Components** and **AutoStart** entries in the [SMS] section of the DOMAIN.INI file on the SMS logon server with the **InstalledComponents** and **AutoStartComponents** entries in the [WorkstationStatus] section of the SMS.INI file on the client.

    By performing this comparison, SMS Client Setup determines which existing SMS client components need to be added, removed, or upgraded.

12. Removes the SMS configurations from system files and restores the previous setting that existed before SMS was installed.

13. Upgrades the SMS components on the client by removing unneeded components, installing new ones, or replacing existing ones.

14. Modifies the system configuration to configure the set of SMS components specified by the upgrade.

    For more information about how the system configuration is modified for the installation of SMS components, see step 10 in "Installation Mode" earlier in this chapter.

15. If SMS Client Setup cannot install a file, it will try again the next time SMS Client Setup runs.

16. SMSSVR uses the SMSRUN16.INI file to set up the SMS Client program group and start SMS components that are configured to start automatically, and then SMSSVR exits.

How SMS Client Setup Installs SMS Client Services on Computers Running Windows NT

On a computer running Windows NT, SMS Client Setup runs via a logon script or batch file in the security context of the user logged on to that computer. For SMS 1.2, SMS services and device drivers must be installed and configured (as well as modifications to the registry) for the Client Inventory service, Remote Control Agent service, and SNMP Event to Trap Translator. However, service and device driver installation and configuration require Administrator privilege (in addition, some of the SMS services must also run in the context of a service account with Administrator privilege). In many cases, the user who logs on to a computer does not have this privilege. To enable users to log on to their computer with the appropriate level of access assigned to them *and* enable SMS to install and configure SMS services on clients running Windows NT, SMS 1.2 has enhancements to SMS Client Setup as well as two additional components (the Client Configuration Manager service and CLIMONNT.EXE).

This section describes how the following SMS client services and components are installed on computers running Windows NT:

- Remote Control Agent
- Client Inventory
- SNMP Event to Trap Translator

How SMS client services are installed, upgraded, and removed:

1. As described in "How SMS Client Setup Works" earlier in this chapter, SMS Client Setup determines which SMS client components need to be added, removed, or upgraded.

2. SMS Client Setup then evaluates whether the client has the version of the operating system appropriate for the SMS services to be installed or upgraded:

   - The Remote Control Agent service requires Windows NT version 3.51 or later. If the computer is running an earlier version of the Windows NT operating system, SMS Client Setup will not install this component.

   - The Client Inventory service is only installed if the SMS_INVENTORY _AGENT_NT service (the version of the Inventory Agent service that runs on SMS logon servers running Windows NT Server) is not already installed.

3. SMS Client Setup adds keys and values to the client's registry to specify configuration data required by the Client Configuration Manager to install, upgrade, or remove SMS client services.

   SMS Client Setup adds configuration data in the following key:

   HKEY_LOCAL_MACHINE\Software\Microsoft\SMS\Client Services

4. If any components needed to be installed, upgraded, or removed, SMS Client Setup creates a client configuration request file (*sms_id*.CCR where *sms_id* is the SMS ID for the computer requesting a configuration change) on the current SMS logon server in the LOGON.SRV\CCR.BOX directory.

   An *sms_id*.CCR file is an ASCII text file used to notify the Client Configuration Manager that a particular client needs a configuration change.

5. If the SMS logon server is a server running LAN Manager or LAN Server, the Maintenance Manager periodically collects the .CCR files from the LOGON.SRV\CCR.BOX directory of the SMS logon server and moves them to the LOGON.SRV\CCR.BOX directory of the site server.

   The Client Configuration Manager is available only on SMS logon servers and site servers running Windows NT Server. This means that the Maintenance Manager must move the .CCR files on servers running LAN Manager and LAN Server to the site server for processing.

6. At the SMS logon server (or the site server if the .CCR file was collected from an SMS logon server running LAN Manager or LAN Server), the Client Configuration Manager has a CCR processing thread that waits for .CCR files in the LOGON.SRV\CCR.BOX directory and processes the .CCR files.

   If the .CCR file was moved to the site server, the Client Configuration Manager service on the site server processes the .CCR file. In this case, connectivity between the site server and the client is required.

7. The CCR processing thread reads the .CCR file, connects to the target client registry, and checks whether it has access rights to the computer and its registry (that is, whether the SMS Service Account has access).

8. The CCR processing thread reads the client's registry to retrieve information needed to install, configure, or remove each SMS component (Remote Control Agent service, SNMP Event to Trap Translator, and Client Inventory service).

9. For each SMS component, the CCR processing thread performs the required configuration change by installing or removing services, changing service parameters, and so on.

10. For each SMS component, the CCR processing thread modifies the appropriate values within the Client Services key of the client's registry to reflect the new configuration.

11. If the CCR processing thread completes the configuration requested by a .CCR file, it deletes the .CCR file.

12. If the CCR processing thread cannot complete the configurations requested by a .CCR file, it performs one of the following actions:

   - If a .CCR file for the same target computer already exists in the LOGON.SRV\CCR.BOX\RETRY directory, the thread updates the CCR in the RETRY directory with the values for the .CCR file in the CCR.BOX directory. After updating the .CCR file in the RETRY directory, the thread deletes the .CCR file in the CCR.BOX directory.

   - If a .CCR file for the same target computer does not exist in the RETRY directory, the thread moves the .CCR file to that directory.

If the Error Reporting Delay time has passed and an event MIF file has not been created for this .CCR file, the Client Configuration Manager writes an event MIF file that reports the following:

- Last error (for example, access denied).

- Name of computer where Client Configuration Manager processed the .CCR file.

- Name of target computer.

- Date and time of the first and last attempt.

The Client Configuration Manager has a separate CCR retry thread to process .CCR files placed in the RETRY subdirectory. The CCR retry thread attempts to perform the incomplete configurations by periodically reprocessing the .CCR files in the RETRY directory. Note that the processing of the .CCR files by this thread is the same as the CCR processing thread. For each .CCR file, the CCR retry thread will continue retrying periodically until the retry duration expires for the .CCR file. If an event MIF file was reported for a .CCR file, the CCR retry thread creates an event MIF file for the .CCR file, reporting that the .CCR file has successfully been processed.

13. If a configuration change performed by Client Configuration Manager requires the client to be restarted, the Client Monitor program running on the client displays a message stating that a restart is required to finish the configuration of the SMS client components and prompts the user to restart or not.

Inventory

The following sections describe how inventory is collected and processed in SMS.

Collecting Inventory at Sites

The following sections describe how inventory is collected and reported at primary and secondary sites.

Collecting Inventory at a Primary Site

This section describes how SMS collects and uses inventory information at a primary site. The inventory collection process varies depending on your network operating system (Windows NT, LAN Manager, NetWare, or Macintosh). This process is summarized in the Figure 3.5, Collecting Inventory at a Primary Site.

At each SMS computer, the Inventory Agent scans and reports inventory.

At clients (such as computers running MS-DOS, Windows 3.1, Windows for Workgroups 3.11, OS/2, Macintosh, Windows 95, and Windows NT Workstation), the Inventory Agent runs in the following ways:

- If the Automatically Configure Workstation Logon Scripts feature has been set up for the SMS domain containing the client, the Inventory Agent program is started from the logon script when the user at the client logs on to the network.

- If the user connects to the SMS_SHR on an SMS logon server and runs the RUNSMS batch file, the Inventory Agent is started.

When the Inventory Agent runs on a client, the Inventory Agent scans the client for software (specified by the PACKAGE.RUL file) and hardware. Note that there are five versions of the Inventory Agent program for clients: INVDOS, INV32CLI, INVWIN32, INVOS2, and INVMac. The Inventory Agent checks its inventory scan interval (the inventory scan interval for hardware and software is set in the Inventory dialog box from the Site Properties dialog box). If the interval has elapsed, the Inventory Agent scans for inventory.

The Inventory Agent is installed as a service on all computers running Windows NT and on servers running LAN Manager. The Inventory Agent service wakes up every 24 hours to check the inventory scan interval, and takes inventory if the interval has elapsed.

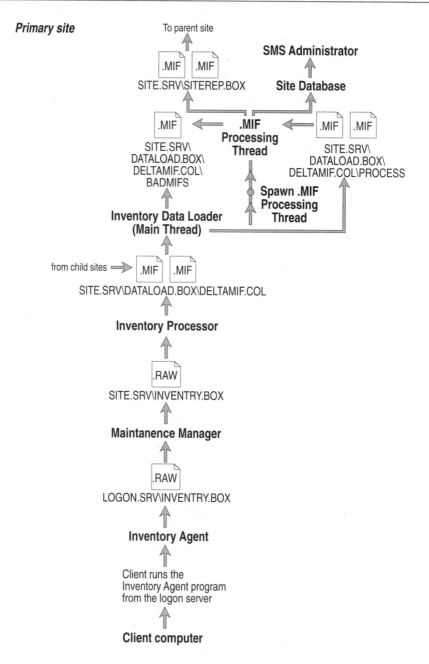

Figure 3.5   Collecting Inventory at a Primary Site

On SMS servers (site servers, SMS logon servers, or helper servers) running Windows NT Server and LAN Manager, the Inventory Agent (INVWIN32.EXE) is installed and run as a service. This service is run using the SMS Service Account, not the user's account. This service may run even when no user is logged on to the network. When this service takes inventory, it places the inventory file on an appropriate SMS logon server for processing.

On Windows NT-based computers that are not SMS servers, SMS installs a different version of the Inventory Agent service (INV32CLI.EXE). This service ensures that inventory is reported periodically, even if a user does not explicitly run SMS Client Setup. This service runs using the local system account, which means that it can take inventory even when no user is logged on to the computer, and that it can gather information that cannot be obtained when running in the user's context. The service stores the inventory file locally.

How SMS Modifies Logon Scripts

When you set up the Automatically Configure Workstation Logon Scripts feature, SMS modifies the logon scripts for each SMS domain in the site.

How SMS modifies logon scripts depends on the network operating system of the domain.

Windows NT and LAN Manager Domains

SMS uses the Directory Replicator service to place the SMSLS batch file and the SETLS utilities on the SMS logon server shares (NETLOGON) of the SMS logon servers in the site's domains. SMS modifies the logon scripts for users at the site's domains (for users who have existing logon scripts) or sets the users' logon scripts to the SMSLS batch file (for users who do not have existing logon scripts). When the SMSLS batch file is run in a logon script, the SMSLS batch file first runs the slow network detection program (NETSPEED.COM). The SMSLS batch file then runs the SMS Client Setup program to install SMS components on the client and the Inventory Agent to collect inventory for a client from an SMS domain's logon server.

NetWare Domains

SMS modifies the system login scripts for each SMS logon server in the site's NetWare domains. SMS adds lines to the script that run the SMSLS.SCR script, which runs the slow network detection program (NETSPEED.COM), SMS Client Setup, and Inventory Agent programs.

A companion program, the Client Monitor (CLIMONNT.EXE), copies the inventory files to an SMS logon server. This program runs in the user's context, and therefore can only copy inventory files to the SMS logon server when the user is logged on to the network.

For more information about how SMS collects inventory from computers running Windows NT, see "Collecting Inventory from Computers Running Windows NT" later in this chapter.

On servers running NetWare, the Maintenance Manager on the site server scans the NetWare server and reports the inventory as a text MIF file to the site server's SITE.SRV\DATALOAD.BOX\DELTAMIF.COL where the MIF file is processed by the Inventory Data Loader.

The Inventory Agent program reports the inventory for the client by creating a RAW Inventory Agent file (*.RAW) and placing this file in the INVENTRY.BOX directory of the SMS_SHR share on the client's SMS logon server.

For NetWare servers, the file is placed in the LOGON.SRV\INVENTRY.BOX directory under the SMS root directory on the volume where the SMS logon server components are installed. Note that OS/2 and Macintosh clients write *.MIF files instead of *.RAW files. *.MIF files are written to the LOGON.SRV\ISVMIF.BOX directory of an SMS logon server.

At the site server, the Maintenance Manager monitors the LOGON.SRV \INVENTRY.BOX directories of the SMS_SHR share on all SMS logon servers in the site. The Maintenance Manager collects the client inventory files (*.RAW files) from these directories on the SMS logon servers, and places them in the SITE.SRV\INVENTRY.BOX directory on the site server. Inventory history files are maintained in the SITE.SRV\INVENTRY.BOX\HISTORY directory. If NetWare servers are present, the Maintenance Manager polls the INVENTRY.BOX directory on these servers for inventory information.

The Inventory Processor processes the client inventory files (*.RAW and *.MIF) and places the processed binary MIF files (*.MIF) in the SITE.SRV \DATALOAD.BOX\DELTAMIF.COL directory on the site server. If the Inventory Processor cannot process a .RAW file, it places the file in the SITE.SRV\INVENTRY.BOX\BADRAWS directory. If the Inventory Processor cannot process a .MIF file, it places the file in the SITE.SRV\INVENTRY.BOX \BADMIFS directory. For more information about how the Inventory Processor processes the .RAW and .MIF files, see "How Inventory History Is Maintained" later in this chapter.

The Inventory Data Loader is a multi-threaded process (new for SMS 1.2). The main thread of the Inventory Data Loader takes the Binary MIF files in the SITE.SRV\DATALOAD.BOX\DELTAMIF.COL directory and places them into the PROCESS subdirectory. If the Inventory Data Loader does not have an active thread for processing .MIF inventory MIF files, it will spawn a .MIF processing thread. Note that the Inventory Data Loader can have a separate thread to process the five types of MIF files, which are distinguished by their file extensions. Also note that main thread limits the number of MIF files of each type to 1000 files of each type—when the count falls below 1000 for a type of MIF file, the main thread moves more MIF files of that type into the PROCESS subdirectory (if they exist). The thread terminates when there are no more .MIF files to process.

The .MIF processing thread renames the .MIF file before it attempts to process it; it adds an X to the beginning of the filename (for example, it would rename 12345678.MIF to X12345678.MIF). If the thread successfully processes the .MIF file, then it updates the database with the information in the file. If the MIF file is not valid, or if the thread cannot process the file for any reason, then the thread places the .MIF file in the SITE.SRV\DATALOAD.BOX\DELTAMIF.COL \BADMIFS directory. If the Inventory Data Loader terminates while processing the .MIF file, the X remains at the beginning of the filename. The thread will try to process the MIF file three times, each time adding another X to the beginning of the filename. If the thread cannot process the .MIF file successfully after three attempts, then it moves the file to the BADMIFs directory.

The .MIF processing thread updates the site database with inventory reported by the clients. After the thread has updated the site database, it moves the .MIF file to SITE.SRV\SITEREP.BOX directory to be forwarded to its parent site—if the current site has a parent site.

After the site database update, you can view the updates to the computer inventory using the SMS Administrator.

The SMS Administrator does not automatically refresh the Sites window with changes to the database (such as the addition of clients or changes to the inventories of existing clients). You may need to refresh the display for the Sites window to see new clients or changes to existing clients.

Collecting Inventory at a Secondary Site

At secondary sites, SMS collects inventory at SMS computers and collects all MIF files on the site server exactly as described in "Collecting Inventory at a Primary Site" earlier in this chapter. However, a secondary site stores all of its inventory in its parent site's database. There is no Inventory Data Loader at a secondary site to directly add the inventory information to a site database. Instead, a secondary site forwards its inventory MIF files to its parent so that the inventory information can be processed and added to the parent site's database by the Inventory Data Loader at the parent site. This process is summarized in Figure 3.6, Collecting Inventory at a Secondary Site.

Instead of writing Binary MIF files to the SITE.SRV\DATALOAD.BOX \DELTAMIF.COL directory, the Inventory Processor at a secondary site writes Binary MIF files to the SITE.SRV\SITEREP.BOX directory. The Site Reporter monitors the SITE.SRV\SITEREP.BOX directory for Binary MIF files. After it detects a queue of Binary MIF files, it creates a system job (*.JOB files in the SITE.SRV\SCHEDULE.BOX directory) to send the inventory information to the parent site. The system job file contains instructions for sending the Binary MIF files up to the parent site. The Site Reporter moves all inventory files to a subdirectory (SITECODE*) of the SITE.SRV\SITEREP.BOX directory.

The Scheduler starts the system job by compressing the Binary MIF files into a single file, *jobid*.P* (where *jobid* is the eight character job ID for the job). The *jobid*.P* file is placed in the SITE.SRV\SENDER.BOX\TOSEND directory in the SMS root directory.

The Scheduler also creates a despooler instruction file (*jobid*.I* where *jobid* is the eight character job ID for the job). The despooler instruction file contains instructions that the parent site uses to decompress the *jobid*.P* file and to process the Binary MIF files. The *jobid*.I* file is also placed in the SITE.SRV \SENDER.BOX\TOSEND directory.

The Scheduler then creates a send request file. A send request file (*.SRQ) contains instructions for sending the compressed package and the despooler instruction file to the parent site. Initially, the *.SRQ file is placed in the appropriate outbox directory (SITE.SRV\SENDER.BOX\REQUESTS*sender.000*, where *sender* is the specific sender's outbox directory name, such as LAN_DEFA.000, SNA_BATC.000, or RAS_ISDN.000) for the type of sender being used to send the Binary MIF files to the parent site. For example, if a package is sent to the parent site using the LAN Sender, the SRQ file would be placed in the LAN_DEFA.000 outbox directory. You can check these directories to verify that the Scheduler has processed the job properly.

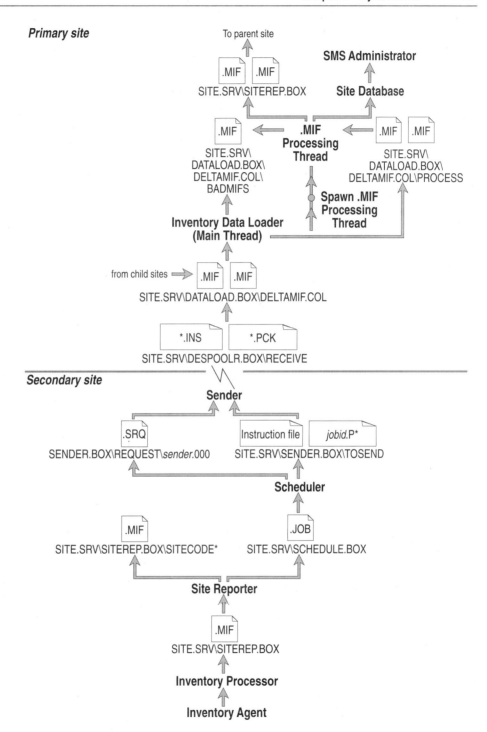

Figure 3.6   Collecting Inventory at a Secondary Site

The sender monitors its outbox for a valid send request. When it detects a send request, the sender renames it to *.SRS to indicate the send is in progress.

The sender connects to the target site and transfers the compressed package file and the despooler instruction file from the site server's TOSEND directory to the parent site's SITE.SRV\DESPOOLR.BOX\RECEIVE directory. The Despooler renames the compressed package to *.PCK. You can monitor this directory at the site server for the parent site to check the progress of the sender.

After the *.PCK file reaches its full size at the parent site, the sender transfers the instruction file as a .TMP file. When the instruction file transfer is complete, it is renamed as a valid instruction file (*.INS). This indicates that the sender has successfully processed the send request and sent the compressed file and its despooler instruction file.

At the target site server for the target site, the Despooler monitors the SITE.SRV\DESPOOLR.BOX\RECEIVE directory for despooler instruction files and processes them. The Despooler decompresses the inventory files and places them in the SITE.SRV\DATALOAD.BOX\DELTAMIF.COL directory. The Inventory Data Loader processes the Binary MIF files and updates the site database. For more detailed information about how the Inventory Data Loader processes Binary MIF files at a primary site, see "Collecting Inventory at a Primary Site" earlier in this chapter.

How Inventory Is Reported to a Parent Site

Any site that has a parent site above it in the site hierarchy reports its inventory to its parent site. If a primary site has a site above it in the site hierarchy, it updates its own database with the client inventory (reported as Binary MIF files) of its site and child sites. Then the site forwards the client inventory up to its parent site. The client inventory is processed and forwarded until it reaches the central site.

When a child site first attaches to a parent site, the Hierarchy Manager instructs the Inventory Data Loader to create a *.INV directory (usually, this is 00000000.INV but the eight character name is a unique name assigned by the Inventory Data Loader) in the SITE.SRV\SCHEDULE.BOX directory on the site server for the child site. The Inventory Data Loader stops processing inventory MIF files at the site (files with a *.MIF) and creates a snapshot image of the computer inventory in the site database. The inventory information is extracted as a series of files, which are placed in the *.INV directory. When all the computer inventory data is extracted, the Inventory Data Loader creates a system job to send the files in the *.INV directory to the parent site and resumes processing *.MIF files at the current site.

The Scheduler processes the system job and the files in the *.INV directory are sent up to the parent site by the sender. At the parent site, the Despooler creates a *.UPD directory (usually, this is 00000000.UPD but the eight character name is a unique name assigned by the Despooler) in the parent site's SITE.SRV \DATALOAD.BOX\DELTAMIF.COL directory. The parent site's Inventory Data Loader monitors the DELTAMIF.COL directory for a directory with the *.UPD name. When it detects a *.UPD directory, it stops processing *.MIF files at the site and begins processing the files in the *.UPD directory and adds the computers from the child site to the site database. When all the computer inventory data from the child site is added, the Inventory Data Loader renames the *.UPD directory to INV*.JOB and creates a system job to send the files in the INV*.JOB directory to the parent site and resumes processing *.MIF files at the current site. This process is repeated at this site's parent site, and so on up the site hierarchy—all the way up to the central site.

How SMS Collects Inventory from Computers

The following sections describe how SMS collects inventory from clients running Windows NT, Macintosh, and OS/2.

Collecting Inventory from Clients Running Windows NT

On SMS computers running Windows NT Workstation and Windows NT Server (with the role of standalone server within a domain), the Inventory Agent is installed as a service. This service is installed and works differently than the SMS_INVENTORY_AGENT_NT service that runs on SMS logon servers running Windows NT Server. These services run at the same interval and scan for information in the same way. However, the Inventory Agent service on computers running Windows NT Workstation runs in the context of the Local System account (not the SMS Service Account as with SMS logon servers), which provides the service full access to the client. This means that the Inventory Agent service does not have direct access to network resources because the Local System account does not have access to the network.

On computers running Windows NT Workstation, the Client Monitor program complements the Inventory Agent service by providing network access to the SMS logon server. The Inventory Agent service requires network access so that updates to the package rule files (as well as the hardware and software scan intervals) can be retrieved from the SMS logon server and RAW files containing inventory reports can be copied to the SMS logon server. After the Client Monitor has copied the files, the Inventory Agent service can then use the local files to get the inventory scanning information (instead of having to connect to the SMS logon server). The Inventory Agent service writes the .RAW file (which contains the inventory report for the client) to the MS\SMS\INVDATA directory on the client. The Client Monitor then moves the .RAW files from MS\SMS\INVDATA to the SMS logon server.

The Client Monitor has three threads. The main thread manages the Client Monitor program itself; the client service thread handles special requests for restarts by the Client Configuration Manager; and the inventory helper thread provides communication between the Inventory Agent and the SMS logon server.

From the SMS logon server, the Client Monitor inventory helper thread copies the following files to the MS\SMS\DATA directory on the client:

- DOMAIN.INI, which contains the scan intervals.
- PKG_16.CFG, which contains the list of package rules.
- *sms_id*.CFG (where *sms_id* is the SMS ID of the client), which is a file containing a **resync** command for the client.

To the SMS logon server, the Client Monitor inventory helper thread copies .RAW files from the MS\SMS\INVDATA directory on the client to the LOGON.SRV\INVENTRY.BOX directory.

When the Client Monitor starts, the inventory helper thread does the following:

- Checks the MS\SMS\INVDATA directory on the client for any .RAW files to be moved to the SMS logon server
- Checks the LOGON.SRV directory on the SMS logon server for any configuration files to be copied to the client. If there is a difference in date, time, or file size between the files (DOMAIN.INI, PKG_16.CFG, and *sms_id*.CFG) on the server and client, it copies the files from the server.

When the inventory helper thread copies .RAW files to the SMS logon server, it copies them as *.TMP to ensure that the Inventory Processor does not begin processing a file that is still being copied to the SMS logon server. After a .RAW file is copied as .TMP file, it renames *.TMP to a *.RAW file (with a unique file name) and deletes the *.RAW file on the client.

After this initial processing, the inventory helper thread sleeps and waits on the following events:

- Directory change notification on the MS\SMS\INVDATA directory. If a new *.RAW file is added to this directory, the inventory helper thread moves it to the SMS logon server.
- The time when the inventory configuration update interval has elapsed. The inventory helper thread checks the SMS logon server for any change in the three inventory configuration files at an interval that is one-third the Client Inventory service wake up interval. By default, the wake up interval is 24 hours; therefore, the update interval for Client Monitor is every 8 hours.

If the Inventory Agent service is not installed, the inventory helper thread spends most of its time sleeping, waiting for the client inventory installation state to change (this is set in the registry by SMS Client Setup). In this case, the inventory helper thread does not copy inventory configuration files from the SMS logon server. It will check once for any .RAW files and copy them to the SMS logon server. Thereafter, it will ignore changes to the MS\SMS\INVDATA directory—until the Inventory Agent service is installed.

Collecting Inventory from Macintosh Computers

To initiate inventory collection for the first time, a user at a Macintosh client must connect manually to an SMS logon server running Windows NT Server *and* Services for Macintosh, and run the Installer program. After that, inventory collection is automatic.

The user runs the Installer by selecting the Chooser to connect to the SMS logon server, and locating the MAC.BIN folder. When the user opens the Installer within the Macintosh folder, SMS files, including the INVMac program, are copied to the client. INVMac is copied to System Folder:Startup Items. When the Installer is completed, it requires that the Macintosh be restarted. At restart, INVMac runs automatically because it is a startup item.

When INVMac runs, it creates a local SMS.INI file as well as two files that store hardware and software inventory history: InvHWScanResult and InvSWScanResult. INVMac also launches the Package Command Manager (PCMMac).

INVMac puts inventory results in the LOGON.SRV\ISVMIF.BOX directory on the SMS logon server as a *.MIF file. The Maintenance Manager moves the MIF files from the Services for Macintosh logon server to the SITE.SRV \ISVMIF.BOX directory on the site server. The Inventory Processor processes these files and places them in the SITE.SRV\DATALOAD.BOX \DELTAMIF.COL directory.

At a primary site, the Inventory Processor processes these files into Binary MIF files and places them in the SITE.SRV\DATALOAD.BOX\DELTAMIF.COL directory. The Inventory Data Loader uses the Binary MIF files to update the computer inventory in the site database and places the MIF files in the SITE.SRV\SITEREP.BOX directory for the Site Reporter to forward the MIF files to the site's parent site. For more detailed information about how inventory is processed at a primary site, see "Collecting Inventory at a Primary Site" earlier in this chapter.

At a secondary site, the Inventory Processor processes these files into Binary MIF files and places them in the SITE.SRV\SITEREP.BOX directory for the Site Reporter to forward the MIF files to the site's parent site. For more detailed information about how inventory is processed at a secondary site, see "Collecting Inventory at a Secondary Site" earlier in this chapter.

Collected files are placed in the *.CFD directory on the Services for Macintosh logon server. If there are no collected files, this directory does not exist. Files in this directory include *.FIL which are collected from the Macintosh client and one cataloging file, COLLFILE.LST. The COLLFILE.LST file is an ASCII file relating the files 0000000x.FIL to the path on the Macintosh client.

Collecting Inventory from OS/2 Computers

When the Inventory Agent for OS/2 runs on servers running LAN Manager version 2.x and LAN Server and the Inventory Agent program runs on OS/2 clients, it scans for hardware and software inventory. However, the Inventory Agent for OS/2 does not report inventory as a RAW file in the LOGON.SRV \INVENTRY.BOX directory. Instead, it creates a text MIF file and places it in the LOGON.SRV\ISVMIF.BOX directory on the SMS logon server. The Maintenance Manager moves the MIF files from the SMS logon server to the SITE.SRV\ISVMIF.BOX directory on the site server.

At a primary site, the Inventory Processor converts these files into Binary MIF files and places them in the SITE.SRV\DATALOAD.BOX\DELTAMIF.COL directory. The Inventory Data Loader uses the Binary MIF files to update the computer inventory in the site database and places the MIF files in the SITE.SRV\SITEREP.BOX directory for the Site Reporter to forward the MIF files to the site's parent site. For more detailed information about how inventory is processed at a primary site, see "Collecting Inventory at a Primary Site" earlier in this chapter.

At a secondary site, the Inventory Processor converts these files into Binary MIF files and places them in the SITE.SRV\SITEREP.BOX directory for the Site Reporter to forward the MIF files to the site's parent site. For more detailed information about how inventory is processed at a secondary site, see "Collecting Inventory at a Secondary Site" earlier in this chapter.

How Custom Inventory Files Are Processed

SMS enables users to customize the SMS inventory by creating MIF files. MIF files are ASCII text files that contain information about a computer component, such as a hard drive or network card. You add the inventory information in a MIF file to the SMS inventory by placing it in one of the special directories dedicated for custom MIF files. SMS components periodically scan these directories and process the MIF files contained in them.

There are two types of MIF files for reporting customized client and server inventory: IDMIFs and NOIDMIFs.

IDMIFs are used for adding custom architectures and objects to the inventory. They contain Identification and Architecture groups.

NOIDMIFs are generally used for adding new groups to the inventory of a computer already existing in the database. These contain no Identification or Architecture groups.

For extensive information on customizing your inventory using MIF files, see the *Microsoft BackOffice Software Development Kit.*

Collecting IDMIFs

After you create an IDMIF, there are two locations that you can place the MIF file in order to add its inventory information to the SMS inventory:

- Place the IDMIF MIF file in the LOGON.SRV\ISVMIF.BOX directory on an SMS logon server.

- Place the IDMIF MIF file in the IDMIFs directory on an SMS client. The IDMIFs directory is specified by the **StandaloneISVMIFPath** entry in the [SMS] section of SMS.INI. Usually, this directory is MS\SMS\IDMIFS.

  If the Inventory Agent detects an IDMIF in the MS\SMS\IDMIFS directory on a computer running Windows NT or MS-DOS, it appends the *.MIF file to the *.RAW file it created as part of regular inventory collection. The Inventory Processor then extracts the *.MIF information from the *.RAW file and uses it to create Binary MIF files in the SITE.SRV\DATALOAD.BOX \DELTAMIF.COL directory.

  If the Inventory Agent detects an IDMIF on an OS/2 or Macintosh client (IDMIFs will be in the MS\SMS\IDMIFS on an OS/2 client, and in an SMS\IDMIF directory created by the user on a Macintosh client), it moves the file to the ISVMIF directory on the appropriate SMS logon server. The Maintenance Manager moves client (and server) *.MIF files found in this directory to the SITE.SRV\ISVMIF.BOX directory on the site server where they are processed by the Inventory Processor and written to the SITE.SRV \DATALOAD.BOX\DELTAMIF.COL directory as Binary MIF files. (Note that the Inventory Agent programs for OS/2 and Macintosh computers write *.MIF files to the LOGON.SRV\ISVMIF.BOX directory as part of the standard inventory process.)

For more detailed information about how inventory is processed at a primary site, see "Collecting Inventory at a Primary Site" earlier in this chapter. For more detailed information about how inventory is processed at a secondary site, see "Collecting Inventory at a Secondary Site" earlier in this chapter.

Collecting NOIDMIFs

After you create a NOIDMIF, you place the MIF file on an SMS client in order to add its inventory information to the SMS inventory.

NOIDMIFs are placed in the MS\SMS\NOIDMIFS directory on SMS clients. For example, when a user at a client enters a form by using the MIF Entry tool, a *.MIF file is put in the directory that is specified by the **MachineISVMIFPath** entry in the client's SMS.INI file. By default, **MachineISVMIFPath** is the MS\SMS\NOIDMIFS directory. The next time the Inventory Agent scans for software on client's running Windows NT, Windows 3.1, Windows for Workgroups, Windows 95, or MS-DOS, it appends the information to the inventory *.RAW file. If the client is an OS/2 or Macintosh client, the Inventory Agent copies the MIF file to the client's SMS logon server (in LOGON.SRV\ISVMIF.BOX). The groups defined by the MIF files are then added to the database.

NOIDMIFs can exist only on clients, except in one case: a user can place a NOIDMIF with a *.NIM extension in the ISVMIF.BOX directory on a NetWare logon server in order to extend inventory for that server. The Maintenance Manager processes the file, which includes appending the NetWare server's architecture and identification group to it, and writes it to the DELTAMIF.COL directory as a Binary MIF file.

The Inventory Processor creates inventory history files for IDMIFs and NOIDMIFs and places them in the SITE.SRV\INVENTRY.BOX\HISTORY directory. Note that history is not created if a user copies an IDMIF with an *.NHM extension to the LOGON.SRV\ISVMIF.BOX directory. Additionally, *.NIM files do not have history.

For more information about how inventory history is maintained, see the following section.

How Inventory History Is Maintained

For each SMS computer, the Inventory Processor maintains a history file that contains the current inventory for that computer. These history files are placed in the SITE.SRV\INVENTRY.BOX\HISTORY directory on the site server.

Note For computers running Windows NT, Windows 3.1, and MS-DOS, the Inventory Processor gives each history file a unique name—usually, a file name with the computer's SMS ID and the extension .HMS. For Novell NetWare servers, Macintosh, and OS/2 computers, the HISTORY.MAP file maps each computer to its history file—these history files usually have unique file names and the extension .SMH. The HISTORY.MAP file is divided into sections according to architecture; each computer is listed by NetcardID, SMSID, and SMSLocation.

When the Inventory Processor processes a subsequent RAW file (or MIF file) from a computer, it compares the inventory reported in the RAW file (groups are identified by their class and keyed attributes) to the inventory reported in the computer's history file. If there are changes, the Inventory Processor creates a Binary MIF file containing the groups whose inventories have changed (groups that have been added, updated, or deleted), and passes the file to the Inventory Data Loader. When the Inventory Data Loader detects a Binary MIF file, it then adds, updates, or deletes the groups specified in the Binary MIF file in the SMS database.

For example, the Operating System group has the class MICROSOFT|OPERATING_SYSTEM|1.0 and uses the Operating System Name attribute as a key. When the Inventory Processor reads a group of this class in the RAW file, it looks for a group with the same class and an identical value for the Operating System Name attribute. If it found a RAW file that contained a group with this class and an Operating System Name of MS-DOS, the Inventory Processor would search the history file for a group with the same class and an Operating System Name of MS-DOS. The Inventory Processor would then use the data for the group in the RAW file to update the computer's history file and add the update information to a Binary MIF file.

The Inventory Processor can add a PRAGMA statement to any group that it adds to the Binary MIF file. A PRAGMA statement tells the Inventory Data Loader what to do with a group:

Pragma	Meaning
SMS:Add	Adds the group to the computer's inventory in the database.
SMS:Update	Updates the group in the database with the information in the Binary MIF file.
SMS:Delete	Removes the group from the computer's inventory in the database.

For example, when the Inventory Processor detects that a group has been deleted, it reports the deletion by adding the group to the Binary MIF file, using a PRAGMA="SMS:Delete" statement. If no PRAGMA is specified, the Inventory Data Loader will determine the PRAGMA. If the group exists in the database, the Inventory Processor performs an SMS:Update; if the group doesn't exist in the database, it performs an SMS:Add.

If there is no change to the computer's inventory (that is, the inventory in the history file matches the RAW file), the Inventory Processor does not report a Binary MIF file. If a RAW file is processed later than four days after the last inventory report, and there is no change to the computer's inventory, the Inventory Processor will report a Binary MIF file to update the computer's Workstation Status group.

Resynchronizing Inventory Information

Whenever the Inventory Data Loader receives a Binary MIF file that does not correspond with information already existing in the site database, it issues a resynchronization (**resync**) command to update the site inventory.

Each Binary MIF file contains a series of group entries that describe some aspect of the computer they are associated with. MIF groups may contain an entry (called a *pragma*) that indicates the relationship of the group information to the information in the database. The PRAGMA can be ADD, UPDATE, or DELETE (if a PRAGMA statement is missing, it is assumed to be ADD). When a MIF file contains instructions to update or delete a group that is missing from the database, the Inventory Data Loader starts the resynchronization process. This process results in a full scan of the computer that generated the Binary MIF file.

For example, if you delete a computer from the inventory and do not change its reporting status, the Inventory Data Loader initiates a **resync** when it receives a MIF file for that computer. During the **resync**, it is likely that only the Identification group for that computer is available in the Personal Computer Properties - [*computername*] window. In this case, the event log contains an entry indicating that a **resync** is in progress.

Note that when a child site is attached to a parent site for the first time, a **resync** is not necessary. Instead, the Hierarchy Manager automatically sends up the inventory files when it detects attachment to the parent site.

The resynchronization process, also summarized in Figure 3.7, Resynchronizing Inventory Information, is as follows:

1. The Inventory Data Loader creates a system job that contains a command for the specific computer.
2. The job is passed to the Scheduler, which creates a resynchronization instruction and passes it to the sender to send to the target computer.
3. The target site Despooler runs the resynchronization instruction, which in turn creates a domain resynchronization instruction. (Because the Inventory Data Loader only sends a **resync** command for one computer at a time, only one domain is involved.)

When the Despooler runs the domain instruction, it writes a **resync** command to the master inventory command file (RESYNC.CFG) for the computer's domain. Any existing **resync** command for the computer is overwritten.

RESYNC.CFG is located in the SITE.SRV\MAINCFG.BOX\INVDOM.BOX
domain.000 directory on the site server. One copy of the file exists for each
SMS domain.

The Maintenance Manager replicates RESYNC.CFG to the LOGON.SRV
directory on all SMS logon servers. The Maintenance Manager also creates
separate resync files for use by computers that are running Windows NT, have the
Inventory Agent service installed, and do not have a role of SMS logon server.
For each computer running Windows NT, the Maintenance Manager creates a
resync file with only the **resync** command for that particular computer (in fact, the
Maintenance Manager creates a file for each **resync** command in the
RESYNC.CFG file but the individual files are only used by the specific type for
each computer running Windows NT, as mentioned earlier). The Maintenance
Manager places these resync files in the LOGON.SRV\INVENCFG.BOX. The
files are named *sms_id*.CFG where *sms_id* is the SMS ID for the computer for
which the **resync** command is intended.

At computers that are running Windows NT, have the Inventory Agent service
installed, and do not have a role of SMS logon server, the Client Monitor service
polls its current SMS logon server for the resync file for that particular computer
every 8 hours. The Client Monitor compares the date/time and size of the resync
file on the SMS logon server with the resync file on the local computer. If either
of these attributes have changed or a resync file does not exist, the Client Monitor
copies the resync file to the MS\SMS\INVDATA directory. If the user runs the
SMS Client Setup program (either manually or via a logon script), SMS Client
Setup will also compare the local and SMS logon server resync files and copies
over the resync file if necessary. The Inventory Agent service wakes up every 24
hours to check if the hardware and software scan intervals have changed or
elapsed. At this time, the Inventory Agent service also reads the resync file.
If the file contains a pending **resync** command, it performs a full software and
hardware scan.

At all other types of computers, RESYNC.CFG is read by the Inventory Agent
program the next time the program runs. On the SMS client computer, the
Inventory Agent runs manually via a RUNSMS batch file or automatically via a
logon script. On SMS logon servers, the Inventory Agent service wakes up every
24 hours to check if the hardware and software scan intervals have changed or
elapsed. The Inventory Agent reads the file and looks for the SMS ID of the local
computer. On that computer, it checks the history file (CMNDHIS.*) to see if a
resync command with a time later than the present **resync** command has already
run. If not, the Inventory Agent performs a complete hardware and software
inventory of the computer and sends the resulting *.RAW file (or *.MIF file for
Macintosh or OS/2 computers) to its current SMS logon server.

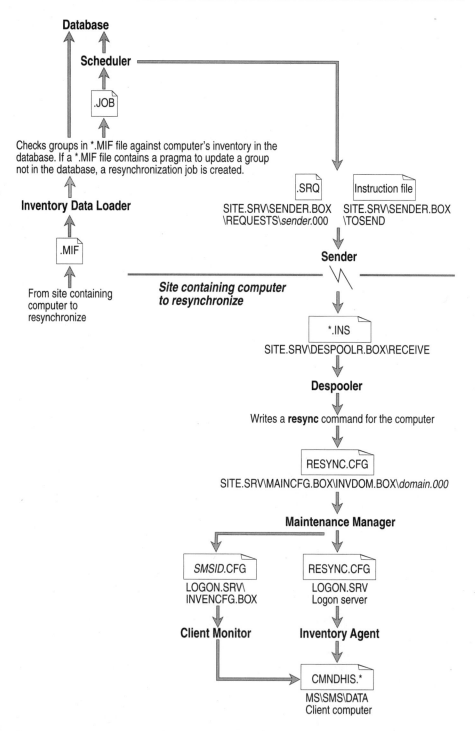

Database

Scheduler

.JOB

Checks groups in *.MIF file against computer's inventory in the
database. If a *.MIF file contains a pragma to update a group
not in the database, a resynchronization job is created.

Inventory Data Loader

.MIF

From site containing
computer to
resynchronize

.SRQ

SITE.SRV\SENDER.BOX
\REQUESTS\sender.000

Instruction file

SITE.SRV\SENDER.BOX
\TOSEND

Sender

*Site containing computer
to resynchronize*

*.INS

SITE.SRV\DESPOOLR.BOX\RECEIVE

Despooler

Writes a **resync** command for the computer

RESYNC.CFG

SITE.SRV\MAINCFG.BOX\INVDOM.BOX\domain.000

Maintenance Manager

SMSID.CFG

LOGON.SRV\
INVENCFG.BOX

Client Monitor

RESYNC.CFG

LOGON.SRV
Logon server

Inventory Agent

CMNDHIS.*

MS\SMS\DATA
Client computer

Figure 3.7   Resynchronizing Inventory Information

The Maintenance Manager collects the *.RAW file from the SMS logon servers and places them on the site server in the same way that it collects *.RAW files from a normal inventory report. For more information about how inventory is processed, see "Collecting Inventory at a Primary Site" earlier in this chapter.

The Inventory Processor creates a Binary MIF file from the RAW file and places a pragma:resync attribute in the Binary MIF to indicate that it represents a resynchronization. Then the Inventory Data Loader updates the database (and forwards the Binary MIF file to its parent site) and the computer's full inventory appears in the Sites window.

Note that the Inventory Processor deletes a computer's history file if the RAW file indicates that a resynchronization has taken place. The Inventory Processor then creates a new history file.

How SMS Collects Files

SMS collects files that have the Collect This File option enabled in the package Inventory properties. The inventory collection process varies depending on your network operating system (Windows NT, LAN Manager, NetWare, or Macintosh). When the Inventory Agent scans for software, it also collects files specified by the inventory rules set for packages.

On servers running Windows NT Server and clients running MS-DOS, Windows version 3.1, Windows for Workgroups, Windows 95, and Windows NT Workstation, the Inventory Agent appends collected files to the *.RAW file containing the inventory information being reported.

On servers running LAN Manager and clients running OS/2 and Macintosh, the Inventory Agent creates a *.CFD directory beneath LOGON.SRV \ISVMIF.BOX. If no files are collected, this directory does not exist. The *.CFD directory's name begins with eight characters, which are the same as the MIF file reporting the computer's inventory. For example, if the computer's MIF file is 00000000.MIF, its collected file directory is 00000000.CFD. The *.CFD directory contains all collected files (which are renamed *.FIL to ensure the file name is unique to that computer). The directory also contains a COLLFILE.LST file, which is an ASCII text file containing the package number, path, and name where the file is found, and the renamed file name (*.FIL) of each collected file.

On NetWare servers, Maintenance Manager handles collected files the same way as OS/2 and Macintosh clients, except that the MIF file and the *.CFD directory are placed in the SITE.SRV\INVENTRY.BOX directory on the site server.

At the site server, the Maintenance Manager monitors the LOGON.SRV \INVENTRY.BOX and LOGON.SRV\ISVMIF.BOX directories of the SMS_SHR share on all SMS logon servers in the site. The Maintenance Manager collects the client inventory files (*.RAW and *.MIF) and collected files from the directories previously mentioned on the SMS logon servers and places them in the SITE.SRV\INVENTRY.BOX directory on the site server. Inventory history files are maintained in the SITE.SRV\INVENTRY.BOX\HISTORY directory.

The Inventory Processor processes the client inventory files (*.RAW and *.MIF), extracts the collected files from the *.RAW files, places the processed files (*.MIF) in the SITE.SRV\DATALOAD.BOX\DELTAMIF.COL directory on the site server, compresses the collected files (files extracted from the *.RAW files and files collected as *.FIL files), and appends these compressed files to the *.MIF files. These processed files are called inventory Binary MIF files.

The Inventory Data Loader processes Binary MIF files and updates the site database with inventory reported by the clients. It also decompresses the collected files and places them in a subdirectory beneath SITE.SRV \DATALOAD.BOX \FILES.COL. The subdirectory structure reflects the hierarchy of sites, as follows: *site_code\range_of_smsids\smsid*. Note that *range_of_smsids* is the first ID in the range. All of the collected files for the computer are placed in that computer's SMSID subdirectory. If there is a conflict in the file name, a random four-digit sequence is appended to the extension. For example, if you collected two AUTOEXEC.BAT files from a computer with SMS ID RED12345, SMS will create a subdirectory RED\RED12300\RED12345 beneath the SITE.SRV \DATALOAD.BOX\FILES.COL directory. Both collected files are stored in that subdirectory; one as AUTOEXEC.BAT, the other as AUTOEXEC.BAT_4EBD (where the digits 4EBD appended to the file extension are four digits selected randomly for this example).

The Inventory Data Loader copies all Binary MIF files that cannot be processed to a BADMIFS subdirectory. For more detailed information about how the Inventory Data Loader processes Binary MIF files at a primary site, see "Collecting Inventory at a Primary Site" earlier in this chapter.

After the site database is updated, you can view the collected files using the SMS Administrator.

How SMS Maintains Package Inventory Rules and SMS Network Application Configurations

Package and program group properties defined in a site's database are used to define software for which the Inventory Agent should scan and to configure program group offerings within the site. If a site is part of site hierarchy, the package and program group configuration information is propagated from the parent site down to the current site. Each parent site propagates its own package and program group configurations as well as those of its parent site.

For example, if site A is a parent site of site B and site B is a parent site of site C, site A propagates all its package and program group configuration information to site B; site B propagates its own package and program group configuration as well as those received from site A down to site C. Site C contains package and program group configuration information for sites A and B as well as those defined at site C.

When you create, modify, or delete a package or program item, SMS modifies the site database. A site database contains properties for all packages and program groups created at the current site and the sites above it in the hierarchy. The Applications Manager monitors the site database but it does not make changes until the packages and program group windows go through a period of inactivity. Updating the PACKAGE.RUL file is dependent on the polling intervals of both the Applications Manager and Maintenance Manager.

If a user doesn't make changes to packages and program groups for 10 minutes, the Applications Manager processes the change. This gives users time to modify packages and program groups without causing unnecessary package and program group updates.

When the Applications Manager processes a change in package properties, it updates the inventory detection rules at the current site. For more information about how inventory detection rules are updated at the current site, see "Maintaining Package Inventory Rules Within a Site" later in this chapter.

When the Applications Manager processes the change in package properties or program group properties at the current site, the Applications Manager updates the configuration files that are used by Program Group Control at Windows-based clients to set up and run SMS network applications. For more information about how network applications are configured within a site, see "SMS Network Applications" later in this chapter.

After the Applications Manager updates the local site's configuration, it creates transaction files to be sent to all its direct child sites. This process is summarized in Figure 3.8,Transaction Files.

The Applications Manager creates the following types of transaction files:

- *.PAC (added or changed packages)
- *.DPK (deleted packages)
- *.GRP (added or changed program groups)
- *.DPG (deleted program groups)

The Applications Manager then creates a job that sends all package and program group information to the sites directly beneath it in the hierarchy.

The Scheduler compresses these files into a single *jobid*.P* file (where *jobid* is the eight character job ID for the job) and creates a despooler instruction file. For each target site specified, the Scheduler also creates a send request file. A send request file (*.SRQ) contains instructions for sending the compressed package and the despooler instruction file to the target site. The sender transfers the *jobid*.P* file and despooler instructions to the lower-level sites.

At each site, the Despooler decompresses the files in the package and places them in the SITE.SRV\SITECFG.BOX directory on the site server. The Applications Manager at the site updates the site's database with the package and program group information in the transaction files. After Applications Manager updates the database, it also updates that site's inventory and SMS network application configuration and creates a job to send all its database's package and program group properties to its subsites. When a package gets sent to a child site that is a secondary site, Applications Manager stores the *.PAC and *.GRP files in the SITE.SRV\APPMGR.BOX directory rather than in the site database.

Maintaining Package Inventory Rules Within a Site

A package's inventory rules resides at the site where the package was originally created and are propagated to all subsites. The SMS system scans for the package on all clients at the originating site and all of its subsites. For more information about how package inventory rules are propagated to subsites, see "How SMS Maintains Package Inventory Rules and SMS Network Application Configurations" earlier in this chapter.

When you define Inventory properties for a package, SMS adds the package's inventory rules to the site's database. A site's database contains properties for all packages created at the current site and the sites above it in the hierarchy. The Applications Manager monitors the site database but it does not make changes until the packages and program group windows go through a period of inactivity. Updating the PACKAGE.RUL file is dependent on the polling intervals of both the Applications Manager and Maintenance Manager.

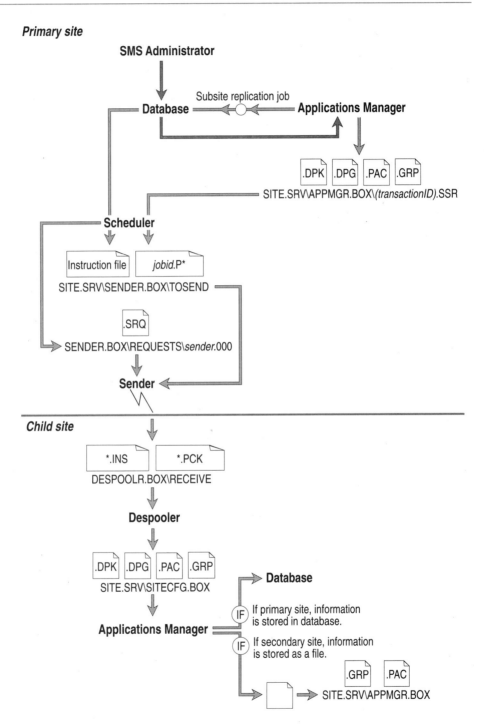

Figure 3.8   Transaction Files

If a user doesn't make changes to packages and program groups for 10 minutes, the Applications Manager processes the change. This gives users time to modify packages without causing unnecessary package property updates.

When the Applications Manager detects a change in a package's properties followed by a period of inactivity, it updates the site's PACKAGE.RUL file. The PACKAGE.RUL file contains rules for all packages inventoried at the site. Maintenance Manager uses the PACKAGE.RUL file to create the Inventory Agent program's configuration files, which contain rules for collecting inventory. Maintenance Manager replicates these configuration files (PKG_16.CFG) to all SMS logon servers for all SMS domains in the site. When the Inventory Agent program runs at a client in the site, it scans for packages defined in the site's database.

This process is summarized in Figure 3.9, Package Inventory Rules Update.

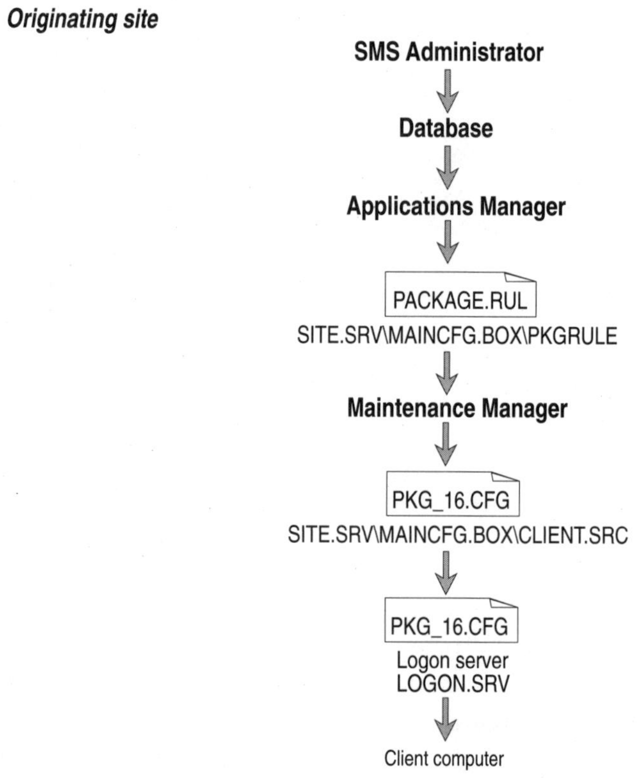

Originating site

SMS Administrator

↓

Database

↓

Applications Manager

↓

PACKAGE.RUL

SITE.SRV\MAINCFG.BOX\PKGRULE

↓

Maintenance Manager

↓

PKG_16.CFG

SITE.SRV\MAINCFG.BOX\CLIENT.SRC

↓

PKG_16.CFG

Logon server
LOGON.SRV

↓

Client computer

Figure 3.9   Package Inventory Rules Update

Software Distribution

The following sections describe how SMS processes Run Command On Workstation jobs, Share Package On Server jobs, Remove Package From Server jobs, and SMS network applications. It also describes how SMS selects default distribution servers for jobs.

Run Command On Workstation Jobs

This section describes how Run Command On Workstation jobs are transmitted from the site database to SMS logon servers and clients. This process is summarized in Figure 3.10, Run Command On Workstation Software Distribution.

A Run Command On Workstation job runs a command defined for a package at specified clients. You can use a Run Command On Workstation job to install a package or to run a command on individual clients.

To install a package on clients, you create a package with Workstations properties, and then create a Run Command On Workstation job for that package. After the job is created, it is added to the site database where the Scheduler monitors all jobs created at the site.

The Scheduler has a polling interval for checking jobs in the SMS database. This polling interval is based on the Response setting in the Services dialog box within Site Properties. This means that if the Scheduler is in the inactive state of a polling interval, it may not detect all new jobs or active jobs (or any changes to a job) at the moment that their Start After times elapse—the Scheduler will detect and process the new, active, or changed jobs when the current polling interval elapses, at which time it will check the jobs in the SMS database.

After the job's Start After time elapses, the Scheduler starts the job by creating a compressed package file (*packageid*.W* where *packageid* is the eight character package ID for the package used by the job) that contains all subdirectories and files within the package's source directory. The *packageid*.W* file is placed in the SITE.SRV\SENDER.BOX\TOSEND directory of the SMS root directory.

The Scheduler then creates a despooler instruction file for each target site. A despooler instruction file contains instructions for completing the job at each target site (*instructionid*.I* where *instructionid* is the five character unique ID in the job ID followed by the site code for the target site). The *instructionid*.I* file is placed in the SITE.SRV\SENDER.BOX\TOSEND directory.

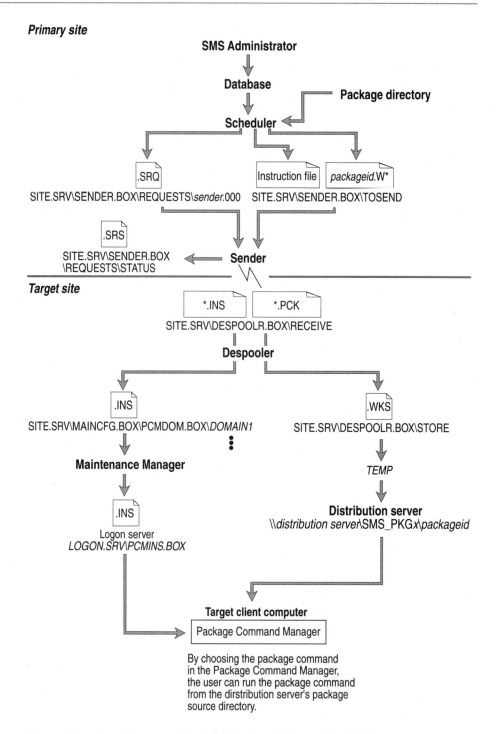

Figure 3.10   Run Command On Workstation Software Distribution

For each target site specified for the job, the Scheduler also creates a send request file. A send request file (*.SRQ) contains instructions for sending the compressed package and the despooler instruction file to the target site. Initially, the *.SRQ file is placed in the appropriate outbox directory (SITE.SRV\SENDER.BOX \REQUESTS\sender.000 where sender.000 is the specific sender's outbox directory name, such as LAN_DEFA.000, SNA_BATC.000, or RAS_ISDN.000) for the type of sender being used to send the job to the target site. For example, if a package is sent to the target site using the LAN Sender, the SRQ file would be placed in the LAN_DEFA.000 directory of the REQUESTS directory.

You can check these directories to verify that the Scheduler has processed the job properly.

Note If you have created a job with the current site as the target, SMS uses the same method for transmitting the package and instructions as a job targeted to child sites. When you install a primary site, a LAN Sender is automatically installed and a LAN Sender address is also automatically created for the site itself. This address is used for the sending process for jobs created at the current site *and* targeted at the site itself. You should never delete this address.

The sender monitors its outbox for a valid send request. When it detects a new send request, it renames it to *.SRS to indicate the send is in progress.

The sender connects to the target site and transfers the compressed package file and the despooler instruction file from the SITE.SRV\SENDER.BOX\TOSEND directory on the site server to the SITE.SRV\DESPOOLR.BOX\RECEIVE directory on the target site server. The Despooler renames the compressed package to *.PCK. This directory can be monitored at the site server to check the sender's progress.

After the *.PCK file reaches its full size at the parent site, the sender transfers the instruction file as a .TMP file. When the instruction file transfer is complete, it is renamed as a valid instruction file (*.INS). You can verify the compressed package and its instruction file were properly sent to the target site by checking the SITE.SRV\DESPOOLR.BOX\RECEIVE directory on the destination site server.

At the site server for the target site, the Despooler monitors the SITE.SRV \DESPOOLR.BOX\RECEIVE directory for instruction files and then processes the files. The Despooler moves the compressed package to the SITE.SRV \DESPOOLR.BOX\STORE directory. Packages for Run Command On Workstation jobs are saved as *packageID*.WKS.

Next, the Despooler at the target site decompresses the compressed package (.WKS file) into the package source directory's original files and directory structure. The Despooler decompresses the package directory into a temporary directory located at the root directory of the local drive with the most free space.

Note that if the package contains NTFS-format files (such as Macintosh files or files with a long file name or unique characters), the Despooler uses the local NTFS drive with the most free space for its temporary directory.

Note that a preferred drive can be set in the following registry key: HKEY_LOCAL_MACHINE\SOFTWARE\Microsoft\SMS\Components \SMS_DESPOOLER\Preferred Drive For Temp Directory.

The Despooler copies the decompressed package directory and files from the temporary directory to the target distribution servers specified by the job. Where the package directory is then placed on each target distribution server depends on the type of server:

- On SMS logon servers running Windows NT Server, LAN Manager, or LAN Server, the Despooler creates a subdirectory in the SMS_PKGx share where x specifies the drive where the directory is located. The package ID is used for the name of the new subdirectory, and the package is installed in this directory.

  If SMS_PKGx has not already been created, the Despooler determines the drive that contains the SMS_SHR share. If this share has at least 100 MB of free space, it is used. If there is less than 100 MB free, the Despooler uses the NTFS drive with the most available free space. If no NTFS drive has at least 100 MB free, it uses the non-NTFS drive with the most available free space. If no other drives have 100 MB free, the drive containing the SMS_SHR is used. Note that the minimum free space requirement is 100 MB by default; however, it can be set in the following registry key:

  HKEY_LOCAL_MACHINE\SOFTWARE\Microsoft\SMS\Components \SMS_DESPOOLER\SMS Drive Minimum Free Space in Mbytes

  The only exception to this is if the SMS root directory is on a drive formatted as FAT and the package requires NTFS (such as a Macintosh package or a package source directory that contains NTFS long names). In this case, the Despooler searches for a drive formatted as NTFS. If it finds an NTFS drive, the Despooler creates the SMS_PKGx directory at the root of that drive (where x is the drive letter), shares the directory as SMS_PKGx, creates a subdirectory (beneath that directory) with the same name as the package ID, and installs the package in this subdirectory. If no NTFS drive is found, the Despooler retries up to 100 times, waiting the amount of time specified by its set interval between each retry.

- On SMS logon servers running NetWare, the Despooler installs the package on the volume where the SMS logon server components are installed. The Despooler creates a subdirectory (beneath the *smsroot*\LOGON.SRV \PCMPKG.SRC directory) with a name that is the same as the package ID. The package is installed in this directory.

- On computers running Windows NT Workstation (or servers that are running Windows NT Server, LAN Manager, or LAN Server but are not SMS logon servers), the package is installed only if the SMS Service Account is a member of the computer's Administrators group. If the computer doesn't already have an SMS_PKGx share (where x is the drive letter), the Despooler creates an SMS_PKGx directory at the root of the drive with the most free disk space. It shares the directory as SMS_PKGx, creates a subdirectory with the same name as the package ID, and installs the package in this directory.

After the Despooler copies the decompressed package from the temporary directory to all the target distribution servers, the Despooler deletes the temporary directory and its contents. The Maintenance Manager creates a Package Location MIF file (*.PMF) that is reported back to the sending site. This information is written to the database. It indicates where the package has been installed. When you do Remove Package From Server jobs, the package can only be removed from servers reported in a Package Location MIF file.

For a Run Command On Workstation job, the Despooler uses the job's despooler instruction file to create a PCM instruction file for each target client in the target site's domains. PCM instruction files contain package installation instructions for individual clients. For each domain in the site, there is a domain master box where PCM instruction files for the domain are placed. The domain master box directory is SITE.SRV\MAINCFG.BOX\PCMDOM.BOX*domain_name*.000. For each target client, a PCM instruction file for the target client is placed on all SMS logon servers in the SMS domain containing that client.

You can verify the PCM instruction files (*workstation_unique_ID*.INS) were created by checking the SITE.SRV\MAINCFG.BOX\PCMDOM.BOX *domain_name*.000 directories on the site server.

Maintenance Manager replicates the PCM instruction files from the SITE.SRV\MAINCFG.BOX\PCMDOM.BOX*domain_name*.000 directories on the site server to the LOGON.SRV\PCMINS.BOX directory on all the SMS logon servers in the target domains. The PCM instruction file is named according to the client's SMS ID (for example, D9500002.INS).

At the SMS client, Package Command Manager monitors the LOGON.SRV \PCMINS.BOX directory of the client's SMS logon server for new PCM instruction files. A package appears in the Package Command Manager window when the client's time is later than the Offer After time set for the job. To run the package command, the user at the client selects the package and chooses the Run button. The Package Command Manager runs the package's command.

Note There are four possible extensions for an instruction file (*.INS, *.SNI, *.IST, and *.NIL). There are four possible file names for a package (*.PCK, *.PKG, *packageid*.SRV, and *packageid*.WKS).

SMS components only create instructions as *.SNI or *.INS. The *.INS files contain compressed instructions and the *.SNI files hold decompressed instructions. An *.INS or *.SNI instruction becomes *.IST or *.NIL when the Despooler starts processing the instruction. A *.IST file is for instructions which have an accompanying package file. A *.NIL file is for standalone instructions.

The *.PCK files become *.PKG files the moment their respective *.INS or *.SNI files become *.IST files. When the Despooler at the receiving site moves a compressed *.PKG file into the SITE.SRV\DESPOOLR.BOX\STORE directory, it renames it to *packageID*.WKS (for client packages) or *packageID*.SRV.

Status Reporting for Run Command On Workstation Jobs

After the Package Command Manager completes a package installation (that is, it has run the package command), it creates a despooler instruction file that reports status for the Run Command On Workstation job. The Package Command Manager places the file in the DESPOOLR.BOX directory specified by the **ResultsSharePoint** entry in the client's SMS.INI file. If the SMS logon server is a NetWare server, the file is placed on the volume containing the SMS installation directory on the server. If the package installation script calls the ISVMIF DLL to report status or writes a text status MIF file to the Windows directory, the Package Command Manager puts this file in the DESPOOLR.BOX as a *.MIF file.

After running a package, the Package Command Manager also modifies the PCMHIST.REG file to indicate the package was run. The PCMHIST.REG file is located in the MS\SMS\DATA directory on the client. All information about whether a command has been run, has been archived, or is pending is stored in this file.

The Maintenance Manager monitors the DESPOOLR.BOX on all SMS logon servers and moves files back to the SITE.SVR\DESPOOLR.BOX\RECEIVE directory on the site server. The Despooler reads the instruction file and processes the instruction. It also updates the master copy of the PCM instruction file in the DOMAINMASTERINBOX directory (SITE.SRV\MAINCFG.BOX \PCMDOM.BOX*domain.name*.000). The Maintenance Manager copies this file to the LOGON.SRV\PCMINS.BOX directory on all SMS logon servers in the SMS domain containing the client.

The Despooler then creates a job status MIF file which reports the package installation status from the client back to the site where the job was created. The job status MIF file has an extension of .JMF. This .JMF file is sent up the hierarchy just like an event MIF file, inventory MIF file, or other MIF file. Note that job status MIF files in SMS 1.0 had an extension of .MIF. For primary sites, the .JMF file is placed in the SITE.SRV\DATALOAD.BOX\DELTAMIF.COL directory. For secondary sites, the .JMF file is placed directly in the SITE.SRV \SITEREP.BOX directory. If the package command reports a failed status, the Despooler logs an event to the Windows NT event log on the site server and writes an error event MIF file (event MIF files have an extension of .EMF) to the SITE.SRV\DATALOAD.BOX\DELTAMIF.COL directory on the site server. If the package command created a text status MIF file, the description attribute is included in this event. For information about how events are reported, see "Event Processing" later in this chapter.

If the current site is the originating site for the job, the Inventory Data Loader reads the .JMF file and uses it to update the job's status in the site database. The Inventory Data Loader is a multi-threaded process (new for SMS 1.2). The main thread of the Inventory Data Loader takes the MIF files in the SITE.SRV \DATALOAD.BOX\DELTAMIF.COL directory and places them into the PROCESS subdirectory. If the Inventory Data Loader does not have an active thread for processing .JMF files, it will spawn a .JMF processing thread. Note that the Inventory Data Loader can have a separate thread to process the five types of MIF files, which are distinguished by their file extensions. Also note that the main thread limits the number of MIF files of each type to 1000 files—when the count falls below 1000 for a type of MIF file, the main thread moves more MIF files of that type to the PROCESS subdirectory. The .JMF processing thread updates the site database with job status reported by the clients. Note that the thread performs a syntax check on the .JMF file and places these files in the BADMIFS subdirectory if the MIF file cannot be processed. If there are no more MIF files to process, the thread terminates.

If the current site is a primary site that is *not* the originating site for the job, the Inventory Data Loader moves the .JMF file to the SITE.SRV\SITEREP.BOX directory. If the current site is a secondary site, the Despooler places the .JMF directly in the SITE.SRV\SITEREP.BOX directory (and never in the SITE.SRV \DATALOAD.BOX\DELTAMIF.COL directory).

When the Site Reporter detects a queue of MIF files, it creates a system job that sends the MIF files to the current site's parent site. The trigger queue length is determined by Service Response settings in the Site Properties dialog box.

The system job's instruction file is placed in the SITE.SRV\SCHEDULE.BOX directory. The Scheduler monitors this directory for system job instructions. For each system job, the Scheduler creates a despooler instruction file (*jobid*.I* where *jobid* is the eight character job ID for the job) and compresses the MIF files into a single file (*jobid*.P*). These files are placed in the SITE.SRV\SENDER.BOX \TOSEND directory.

The Scheduler then creates a send request file (*.SRQ) in the appropriate sender's outbox directory. The sender processes the request and transfers the data to the parent site. At the parent site, the Despooler reads the instruction file and carries out its instructions by decompressing the compressed file containing the MIF files in the SITE.SRV\DATALOAD.BOX\DELTAMIF.COL directory on the site server.

If the parent site is not the originating site for the job, the Inventory Data Loader moves the .JMF file to the SITE.SRV\SITEREP.BOX directory and forwards it to its parent site, and so on until it reaches the originating site.

If the parent site is the originating site for the job, the Inventory Data Loader reads the .JMF file, moves it to the SITE.SRV\DATALOAD.BOX\DELTAMIF.COL \PROCESS directory, and uses it to update the job's status in the site database.

To view job status reported by Package Command Manager, open the Job Properties dialog box for the job, choose the Status button, select the site for which you want to view status, and choose the Details button. The job's status at each client and distribution server is displayed in the list box.

How Package Command Status MIF Files Are Processed

A package command can write a MIF file to the Windows directory to provide more detailed status. This status MIF file is called a package command status MIF file. A program started by a package command can also call a function from the ISVMIF DLL to report status on the job that corresponds to the package command. For more information on reporting status with the ISVMIF DLL, see the *Microsoft BackOffice Development Kit.* For information about the package command status MIF file format, see Chapter 4, "File Formats."

If a program writes a MIF file to the Windows directory, Package Command Manager collects the file and places it (and the despooler instruction file) in the DESPOOLR.BOX directory specified by the **ResultsSharePoint** entry in the client's SMS.INI file. Note that the date and time on the MIF file must be later than the date and time specified for the job start time (or Package Command Manager will not collect the file).

The package command status MIF file has priority over the despooler instruction file. This means that the Despooler uses the status reported in the package command status MIF file to create a job status MIF file (*.JMF). The job status MIF file reports the job status up the hierarchy to the site where the job was created. If a failure occurs, the job status MIF file includes a text description of the failure reported by the package command status MIF file, and the Despooler logs an event in the Windows NT event log on the site server using this description.

A package command status MIF file includes one group (InstallStatus) that contains two attributes (Status and Description).

The Status attribute determines the status reported back to the originating site. This status is included in the job details status MIF file that the Despooler writes and that eventually makes its way back to the originating site's job details data for this job in the database.

The Description attribute is used only if the Status is FAILED—in which case, the Description is used as text in an SMS event and a Windows NT event. If the MIF file contains a FAILED status and includes a description string, the string is reported by the Despooler in a Windows NT event to the computer's site server Windows NT event log and is reported as an SMS event, which also eventually makes its way back up the site hierarchy to the originating site's database. If the MIF file contains a SUCCESS status, the description string is not reported back.

In the SMS Administrator, you can view the status in the Job Status Details dialog box for the job. If the package command reports a FAILED status, you can view the generated event in the Events window in the SMS Administrator.

Share Package On Server Jobs

This section describes how Share Package On Server jobs are transmitted from the originating site to the target site and distribution servers. This process is summarized in Figure 3.11, Share Package On Server Software Distribution.

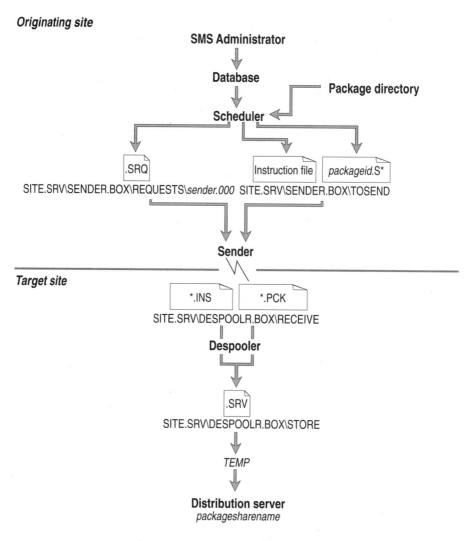

Figure 3.11   Share Package On Server Software Distribution

A Share Package On Server job installs a package on servers, shares the directory containing the package and all its files, and makes them available to users according to the access permissions specified by the job.

To share a package on servers, you create a package with Sharing properties, and then create a Share Package On Server job for that package. After the job is created, it is added to the site database where the Scheduler monitors all jobs created at the site.

The Scheduler and sender process is exactly the same as the process for Run Command On Workstation jobs—except that the Scheduler creates a compressed package with the name *packageid*.S* (whereas a Run Command On Workstation job uses the name *packageid*.W*). The process for Run Command On Workstations jobs is described in "Run Command On Workstation Jobs" earlier in this chapter.

At the site server for the target site, the Despooler monitors the SITE.SRV \DESPOOLR.BOX\RECEIVE directory for instruction files and then processes the files. The Despooler moves the compressed package to the SITE.SRV \DESPOOLR.BOX\STORE directory. Packages for Share Package On Server jobs are saved as *packageID*.SRV.

Next, the Despooler at the target site decompresses the compressed package (.SRV file) into the package source directory's original files and directory structure. The Despooler decompresses the package directory into a temporary directory located at the root directory of the local drive with the most free space. The selection and usage of the temporary directory is exactly the same as the process for Run Command On Workstation jobs.

The Despooler copies the decompressed package directory and files from the temporary directory to the target distribution servers specified by the job. Where the package directory is then placed on each target distribution server depends on the type of server:

- On SMS logon servers running LAN Manager or Windows NT Server, the Despooler creates a directory (with the same name as the share name specified for the package) at the root of the drive with the most free space. The Despooler shares that directory using the specified share name and installs the package in that directory. If the package share name already exists, the Despooler copies the package to the existing share.

- On SMS logon servers running NetWare, the Despooler tries to install the package to the volume specified for the package. Within the Sharing properties of the package, you should specify a volume name and a subdirectory for share name (for example, MYVOL\MYDIR).

  If you specify TEST\ONE as the share name, and TEST is an existing volume, the Despooler puts the package in *servername*\TEST\ONE. If TEST is not a volume name on the NetWare server, the Despooler puts the package in *servername**defaultvolume*\TEST\ONE.

  The default volume is the volume where SMS is installed; if SMS is not installed on the NetWare server, the Despooler creates the package share on the SYS volume.

  If you specify only TEST as the share name, and TEST is an existing volume on the NetWare server, the Despooler puts the package in *servername*\TEST *packageID*. If TEST is not a volume name on the NetWare server, the Despooler puts the package in *servername**defaultvolume*\TEST.

  Thus, if you specify TEST\ONE as your volume and share name, all NetWare distribution servers should have a volume called TEST with enough space to install the shared package directory. If you specify a share name that does not exist on NetWare servers, the default volume on each server must have enough room for the package. If adequate space is not available on the default volume, the shared package directory is not created and an event is written to the SMS event log.

- On computers running Windows NT Workstation, the package is installed only if the SMS Service Account is a member of the computer's Administrators group. The Despooler creates a directory (with the same name as the share name specified for the package) at the root of the drive with the most disk space. The Despooler shares this directory using the specified share name and installs the package in that directory.

Remove Package From Server Jobs

When a Remove Package From Server job is created, the Despooler removes all files from all or some target site distribution servers, depending on which job task is specified (Remove From All Distribution Servers or Remove From Selected Distribution Servers). SMS uses the Package Location data in the database to determine which servers have a copy of the package.

This process is summarized in Figure 3.12, Remove Package From Server Job Flow.

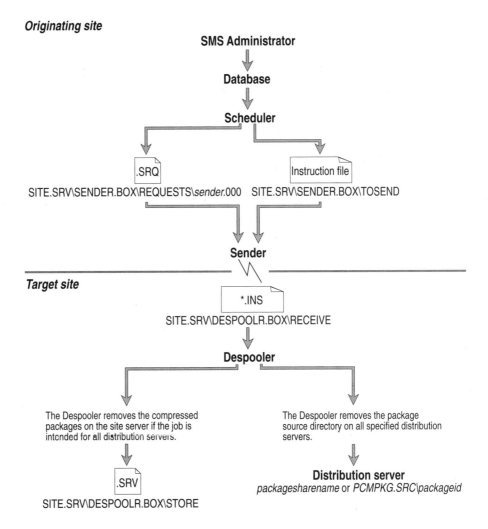

Figure 3.12   Remove Package From Server Job Flow

For the Remove From All Distribution Servers option, the Despooler:

- Removes the compressed version of the package from the target site servers.
- Removes the decompressed versions of the package from all distribution servers.
- Removes the commands from PCM instruction files for all target SMS computers for all jobs that use the removed package. Note that this is the only way to remove commands from PCM instruction files (except by using the SMS Administrator to cancel each job that uses the package).
- Leaves packages that have been installed on clients.
- Leaves the package source directory at the originating site.
- Leaves the compressed version of the package at the originating site. This is the compressed package created by the Scheduler in the SITE.SRV\SENDER.BOX\TOSEND directory on the originating site server. There are two ways to remove this compressed package: 1) Delete the package from the Packages window in the SMS Administrator. 2) Manually delete the compressed file (you can identify it by its file name: *packageid*.W* for a workstation package and *packageid*.S* for a server package).

For the Remove From Selected Distribution Servers option, the Despooler:

- Removes the decompressed versions of the package from all distribution servers in the specified machine group.
- Leaves packages that have been installed on clients.
- Leaves the package source directory at the originating site.
- Leaves the compressed version of the package at the originating site. This is the compressed package created by the Scheduler in the SITE.SRV\SENDER.BOX\TOSEND directory on the originating site server. There are two ways to remove this compressed package: 1) Delete the package from the Packages window in the SMS Administrator. 2) Manually delete the compressed file (you can identify it by its file name: *packageid*.W* for a workstation package and *packageid*.S* for a server package).

A Remove Package From Server job applies to both Run Command On Workstation and Share Package On Server jobs. After a Remove Package From Server job's Start After time elapses, SMS sends the job's instructions to designated sites. Using the job instructions, the Despooler removes the decompressed version of the package from the specified distribution servers. If you selected the Remove From All Distribution Servers option, the Despooler also removes the compressed version of the package from the site server's DESPOOLR.BOX\RECEIVE\STORE directory.

Note that if you limit package removal to sites A and B, and then specify a machine group containing a distribution server that is part of Site C, no files are removed from the server that is part of site C.

SMS Network Applications

This section discusses how configuration information for setting up and running SMS network applications is transmitted from the site database to SMS logon servers and clients. This process is summarized in Figure 3.13, SMS Network Application Software Distribution.

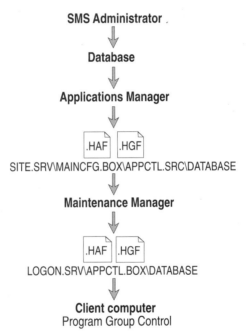

Figure 3.13   SMS Network Application Software Distribution

When you set up an SMS network application within SMS, you create program items within packages, create program groups that contain the program items you want to offer, and assign program groups to the user groups to which you want to offer program items. There are two SMS programs that configure and run the SMS network applications on clients: the Application Control program, and the Application Start program. Together, these programs are often referred to as the Program Group Control application. These programs are described later in this section.

Package and program group properties defined in a site's database are used to configure program group offerings within the site. If a site is part of site hierarchy, the package and program group configuration information is propagated from the parent site down to the current site. Each parent site propagates its own package and program group configurations as well as those of its parent site.

For example, if site A is a parent site of site B and site B is a parent site of site C, site A propagates all its package and program group configuration information to site B; site B propagates its own package and program group configuration as well as those received from site A down to site C. Site C contains package and program group configuration information for sites A and B as well as those defined at site C. For more information about how package configurations and program group configurations are propagated from the parent site to its child sites, see "How SMS Maintains Package Inventory Rules and SMS Network Application Configurations" earlier in this chapter.

As noted earlier, all configuration information needed to set up and run SMS network applications at the site is stored in the site database. From the configuration information in the site database, the Applications Manager creates configuration files that are used by Program Group Control at Windows-based clients to set up and run SMS network applications. The Applications Manager creates and maintains two sets of configuration files: one for program items (*.HAF) and one for program groups (*.HGF). These files are located in the SITE.SRV\MAINCFG.BOX\APPCTL.SRC\DATABASE directory. These files serve as a database that Program Group Control can query to find out which program groups are assigned to the current user at the client and to retrieve configuration information for the program groups and their program items.

The Maintenance Manager replicates the .HAF and .HGF files to the SMS logon servers for all SMS domains in the current site. On the SMS logon servers, .HAF and .HGF files are located in the LOGON.SRV\APPCTL.BOX\DATABASE directory.

The Application Control program reads the Program Group Control files and creates the program groups for the appropriate SMS network applications. The Application Control program runs only on Windows-based clients at the site. There are three versions of the Application Control program: APPCTL95 for Windows 95 clients, APPCTL32 for Windows NT clients, and APPCTL16 for 16-bit Windows clients.

When a user logs on to the network, the Application Control program retrieves the list of user groups of which the current user is a member. How this list is retrieved depends on the type of client:

- For clients running the Windows NT operating system, the Application Control program retrieves the list of user groups from the SMS domain containing the servers listed in the [Servers] section of SMS.INI.

- For clients running the LAN Manager network operating system, the Application Control program retrieves the list of user groups from the SMS domain containing the server specified by the **ValidatingServer** entry in the [SMSLSIni] section of SMS.INI. If no server is specified in this entry or if it is unavailable, the Application Control program searches for a network logon server in the domain where the client has been logged on and retrieves the list of user groups from that server.
- For clients running the NetWare network operating system, the Application Control program retrieves the list of user groups from all SMS logon servers listed in the [Servers] section of SMS.INI.

Next, the Application Control program connects to the server specified by **CurrentLogonServer** entry in the [Servers] section of the client's SMS.INI file. If this server is not available, it uses an algorithm to randomly select an SMS logon server from the other servers listed in the [Servers] section of SMS.INI.

Based on the user group memberships for the user, the Application Control program retrieves the list of assigned program groups and the configurations for the program items in those program groups. It then creates the assigned program groups in the client's Program Manager. It also creates entries in the client's registry to configure the program items for all assigned program groups.

Note that on clients running Windows 95 and Windows NT version 4, the Application Control program adds the groups as menu items under Programs in the Start menu.

When the Application Control program creates the program items for an SMS network application, it configures the program item command line to call the Application Start program. When the user selects the program item, the Application Start program actually installs, configures, and runs the SMS network application. There are three versions of the Application Start program: APPSTA95 for Windows 95 clients, APPSTA32 for Windows NT-based clients, and APPSTA16 for 16-bit Windows-based clients.

If either the Application Control program or the Application Start program encounters any errors, it logs the errors to a local log file called PGC.LOG. This log file is located in the MS\SMS\LOGS directory on the client. Some errors are reported to the SMS logon server as SMS event MIF files, which are eventually added to the site database so that you can view these errors in the SMS Events window in the SMS Administrator.

How Default Distribution Servers Are Selected

When the Scheduler activates either a Run Command On Workstation job or a Share Package On Server job, it builds the list of target distribution servers from the machine group you specified in the Put On Specified Distribution Servers box in the Job Details dialog box. The distribution server list is compiled at the time that the Scheduler activates the job, so if you added a computer to a machine group between the time the job was created and when it was activated, this new computer is included in the distribution server list. If you added a computer after the job is activated, the new computer is *not* included.

The Scheduler puts all the computers from this machine group into the distribution server list, regardless of what types of computer they are.

When the Despooler processes the job, it tries to install the package on the target servers.

If a target site for the job does not have a computer in the specified machine group, the Scheduler uses the servers listed in that target site's Default Servers group.

If you select the Default Servers machine group as the distribution target, the Scheduler creates the list of target distribution servers from the Default Servers set for each target site. When the Scheduler activates the job, the Scheduler uses the Default Servers currently stored in the site database for the target sites.

Note that the Default Servers group can contain computers that are not part of the SMS system. If you use a non-SMS computer, you must ensure that the SMS Service Account has administrative privilege for the computer. The Despooler treats a non-SMS computer like a computer running Windows NT Workstation.

Note that the Despooler retries failed instructions (including the instruction to place a package on a distribution server) 100 times at the retry interval before it stops processing the instruction and reports that the instruction could not be completed. The retry interval is set according to the site's service response rate.

Event Processing

SMS can have its system components installed on different computers in a site. For example, an SNA Sender can be installed on another server (that is, a server other than the site server).

When an SMS component reports an event to the SMS system, it first logs an event in the Windows NT event log of the computer where the component is running. The component then reports the event in two steps to the site server for the site:

1. At a primary site, the component writes an event MIF file (*.EMF) to the SITE.SRV\DATALOAD.BOX\DELTAMIF.COL directory of the SMS root directory on the site server. The Inventory Data Loader service updates the site database if the site is a primary site, and forwards the .EMF file to the site's parent site.

    At a secondary site, the component writes an .EMF file to the SITE.SRV\SITEREP.BOX directory on the site server. The Site Reporter creates a system job to send the .EMF file up to the site's parent site.

2. The component logs an event to the Windows NT event log on the site server.

This process is summarized in Figure 3.14, Figure 3.15, and Figure 3.16.

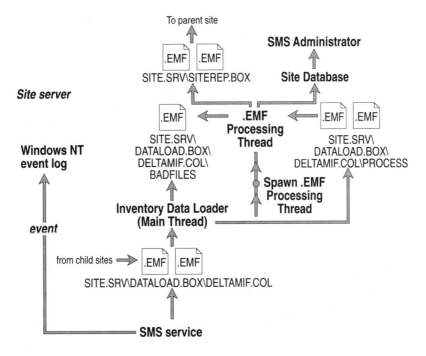

Figure 3.14   How events are reported in a site.

When the .EMF file is forwarded to the site's parent site, the Inventory Data Loader updates that site's database and forwards the event MIF file to its parent site. By processing and forwarding .EMF files, the system reports events up the site hierarchy—all the way up to the central site.

Using the Events window of the SMS Administrator, you can view events for the site where you are logged in and all sites beneath that site.

Note If a component cannot create or write the .EMF file (for example, if the site server is out of disk space), the event may not be reported to the site database. In this case, the Windows NT event log of the computer where the event occurred may contain the only record of the event.

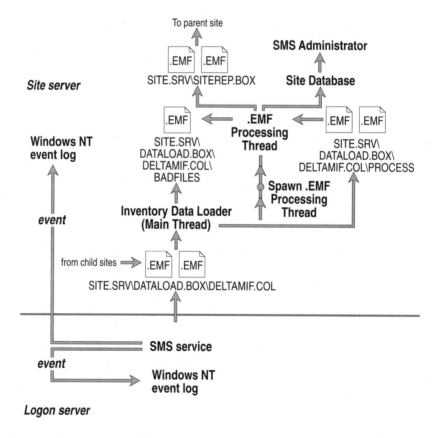

Figure 3.15   How events are reported by a service installed on another server (that is, a service not installed on the site server).

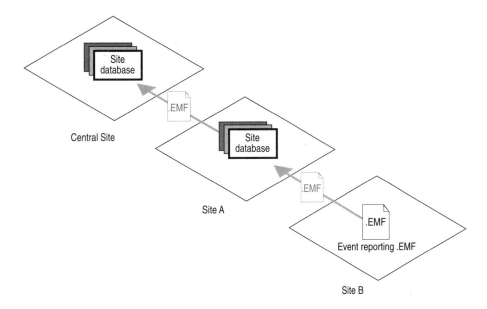

Figure 3.16   How events are forwarded up the site hierarchy.

The SMS Executive, Site Configuration Manager, and Hierarchy Manager services maintain event history on some of their events. When an event that uses event history occurs, the SMS service or component reads its event history file from the ERRORHIS subdirectory beneath the directory where the service or component is installed. The SMS Executive (SMS_EXEC.HIS), the Site Configuration Manager (SMS_SITE.HIS), and Hierarchy Manager (SMS_HIER.HIS) have their own history files. The component or service checks its event history file for a record of the condition that generated the event. If the condition is the same as the last recorded event, no event is reported. If the condition has changed, the event is reported with the updated status. If the status is a success or recovery report, the component clears the event record from its error history file.

How the Inventory Data Loader Processes .EMF Files

The Inventory Data Loader is a multi-threaded process (new for SMS 1.2). The main thread of the Inventory Data Loader takes the Binary MIF files in the SITE.SRV\DATALOAD.BOX\DELTAMIF.COL directory and places them into the PROCESS subdirectory. If the Inventory Data Loader does not have an active thread for processing .EMF event MIF files, it will spawn a .EMF processing thread. Note that the Inventory Data Loader can have a separate thread to process the five types of MIF files, which are distinguished by their file extensions. Also note that main thread limits the number of MIF files of each type to 1000 files   when the count falls below 1000 for a type of MIF file, the main thread moves more MIF files of that type into the PROCESS subdirectory.

The .EMF processing thread updates the site database with events reported by SMS components. After the thread has updated the site database, it moves the .EMF file to SITE.SRV\SITEREP.BOX directory to forward the .EMF to its parent site—if the current site has a parent site. Note that the thread performs a syntax check on the MIF file and does not copy to the SITE.SRV\SITEREP.BOX if the MIF file cannot be processed; these unprocessable MIF files are placed in theBADMIFS subdirectory. If there are no more .EMF files to process, the thread terminates.

Remote Troubleshooting

SMS supports remote troubleshooting for clients running MS-DOS, Windows, Windows for Workgroups, Windows 95, and Windows NT. This section contains information about the system flow of remote troubleshooting. For general information about remote troubleshooting, see the SMS version 1.2 *Administrator's Guide*.

The settings in the [Sight] section of the SMS.INI file on each client specify which remote troubleshooting utilities, if any, are enabled on the client. Users can modify these settings with the Help Desk Options program in the SMS Client program group. The remote troubleshooting agents and programs check the [Sight] section of the SMS.INI file for configuration settings. For more information about the SMS.INI file, see Chapter 4, "File Formats."

For all clients in the SMS inventory, the SMS Administrator uses the SIGHTNT.DLL program to obtain the computer address and the address type (a NetBIOS name or an IP or IPX address) from the database. When the Help Desk or Diagnostics icon is selected, SIGHTNT.DLL tries to connect to the client over a supported protocol (IP, IPX, or a NetBIOS protocol). Global defaults (such as time-out values for various NetBIOS Lana numbers and the IPX protocol) are stored in the Windows NT registry on the site server, under the following key:

HKEY_Local_Machine\Software\Microsoft\SMS\Components\SightNT

Remote Troubleshooting Across a RAS Connection

If the site address for a client is a RAS address, SMS uses GATEWAY.DLL to make an automatic RAS connection and gain access to the client. GATEWAY.DLL initiates the RAS connection to the remote LAN and authenticates the user by communicating with a RAS server that exists on the same LAN as the client. When a remote troubleshooting utility terminates, GATEWAY.DLL disconnects the target LAN, closes the RAS session, and frees up the port and modem.

The SMS remote troubleshooting utilities only support NetBIOS transports and IP across RAS. IPX transports are not supported. Also, GATEWAY.DLL does not support the SNA Sender and, for SNA links, will return the message Can't connect via SNA to SIGHTNT.DLL.

Remote Troubleshooting Across a WAN

You can remotely control clients across a bridged or routed WAN. In a bridged WAN environment, you can establish the remote control session over both NetBIOS-based and socket-based protocols. However, in a routed WAN environment, you cannot use NetBIOS-based protocols unless you also configure name management for the protocol.

For instance, Windows NT supports socket-based TCP/IP and NetBIOS-based TCP/IP. NetBIOS-based TCP/IP (NBT) can locate resources on a local IP network by name. However, resources located on remote subnets are not responsive to name query requests because routers do not pass IP-level broadcasts. For that reason, Windows NT uses a LMHOSTS file to map IP addresses to the NetBIOS names of computers outside the local subnet. LMHOSTS is a text file located in the *winntsystemroot*\SYSTEM32\DRIVERS\ETC directory. To remotely control an SMS client using NBT, a remote address must be matched with an entry in the TCP/IP LMHOSTS file on the SMS Administrator computer.

At start up, Windows NT reads LMHOSTS and stores entries in a system cache. NBT reads its internal cache. If no match is found, it sends a NetBIOS broadcast and retries the broadcast up to five times. If there is no response, NBT reads the LMHOSTS file directly. If it finds an entry for the computer name and corresponding remote IP address, NBT sends a datagram to that address. The query includes the address of the originating computer running Windows NT. When the target NetBIOS client receives the query, it sends a return packet to that address.

CHAPTER 4

File Formats

Microsoft Systems Management Server (SMS) uses files to identify and configure clients, servers, domains, sites, packages, and so on. The files are maintained by various SMS components. Some files are in binary format, and thus cannot be viewed or edited. Other files are in text format; it is possible to view and even edit these files, although in general you should not modify SMS system files.

Text-based files that can be viewed and potentially modified are described in this chapter. For a complete listing of the files used by SMS servers , see Chapter 1, "Server Reference." For a complete listing of the files used by SMS clients, see Chapter 2, "Client Reference."

Note Documentation of SMS system files is included for informational purposes only. You should not attempt to modify any of the system files that are maintained or used directly by SMS.

The file formats for the following text-based files are described in this chapter:

- SMS.INI
- Site control file
- SYSTEM.MAP
- Package and audit rule files
- Package definition files
- Management Information Format files
- SNMP export files
- Event to Trap Translator configuration tool format files
- Client configuration request files

SMS.INI

The SMS.INI file is installed on all computers when they are added to the SMS system. This file stores system information about the client and the SMS site in which it is contained. SMS Client Setup creates the SMS.INI file, however the file is maintained and used by all of the SMS client components. The SMS.INI file is located in the root of the first (alphabetical) local hard drive (usually drive C).

SMS.INI is created from a master template file named DOMAIN.INI, which is located in the LOGON.SRV directory (SMS_SHR) on all SMS logon servers. The DOMAIN.INI file contains a subset of SMS.INI entries that are valid in the domain. When SMS Client Setup creates the SMS.INI file on a client, some of the values in the SMS.INI file are derived from the DOMAIN.INI file; other values are based on the specific configuration of the client.

The following sections and entries are in the SMS.INI file:

- [Package Command Manager]
- [Servers]
- [Share]
- [Program Group Control]
- [AppCtlIniFiles]
- [AppCtlScripts]
- [MSTest16.20]
- [WorkstationStatus]
- [SMS]
- [SMSLSIni]
- [Local]
- [Sight]
- [LogonHistory]
- [UserName]
- [AppleServers]

These sections and entries are described in the following sections. In addition, a sample SMS.INI file is included in "Sample SMS.INI File" later in this chapter.

[Package Command Manager]

Information used by the Package Command Manager to locate its instruction files, results directory, and local status file.

InstructionSharePoint
> The location of the Package Command Manager instruction files on the SMS logon server. The location is a subdirectory of the SMS logon server share.

ResultSharePoint
> The location where the Inventory Agent places results of Package Command Manager actions.

LocalRegistryLocation
> The location of the registry file (PCMHIST.REG) used by the Package Command Manager to store package information.

PollingInterval
> Specifies how often (in minutes) the Package Command Manager checks for new packages. This value is the polling interval that is set in the Site Properties window of the SMS Administrator. If a value for PollingInterval is set in the [Local] section of SMS.INI, it overrides this value.

[Servers]

The servers available to the client components. These servers are SMS logon servers in the client domain. The client components use the entries in this section to determine where to read instructions or configuration information. In addition, these entries are used to determine where to send inventory and status information. Each server is listed as a separate entry in this section.

Domain
> The name of the domain that processed the current user's logon request.

CurrentLogonServer
> The name of the server that processed the current user's logon request.

Server*number*
> The name of a server that acts as a collection point for the current client. The *number* identifies each server entry (for example, Server1, Server2, and so on).

[Share]

The shares to be used by the SMS client components. Each entry corresponds to an entry in the [Servers] section.

CurrentLogonServer
> The share name on the current SMS logon server. On servers running Windows NT Server, LAN Manager, and LAN Server, this share is named SMS_SHR. On servers running NetWare, this entry specifies the volume name.

Server*number*
> The share name for the corresponding server listed in the [Servers] section.

[Program Group Control]

The location of the files that store the configuration information for SMS network applications. Program Group Control reads configuration information from the files and uses it to configure and run SMS network applications.

Directory
> The name of the directory containing the SMS network application files. The directory is relative to a server specified in the [Servers] section and the corresponding share name specified in the [Share] section.

[AppCtlIniFiles]

The location of the initialization files required by SMS network application configuration scripts. If an application requires a local copy of an initialization file, the configuration script can copy the file from this location to the local client.

Directory
> The name of the directory containing the initialization files. The directory is relative to a server specified in the [Servers] section and the corresponding share name specified in the [Share] section.

[AppCtlScripts]

The location of the SMS network application configuration scripts. If an application requires a configuration script, the Application Control program looks for its configuration script at this location and runs it.

Directory
> The name of the directory containing the configuration scripts. The directory is relative to a server specified in the [Servers] section and the corresponding share name specified in the [Share] section.

[MSTest16.20]

The location of the Package Command Manager installation scripts and SMS network application configuration scripts that are provided with SMS. This directory contains all default script processors.

Directory

> The name of the directory containing the default script processors. The directory is relative to a server specified in the [Servers] section and the corresponding share name specified in the [Share] section.

[WorkstationStatus]

Indicates the client status.

SysFilesNotModified

> Lists files, such as AUTOEXEC.BAT and WIN.INI, that SMS Client Setup could not modify. This indicates an error condition.

FilesNotDownloaded

> Lists files that SMS Client Setup could not download. This indicates an error condition.

InstalledComponents

> Indicates components installed on the client.

AutoStartComponents

> Indicates components that are automatically started on the client.

StandaloneWorkstation

> Reserved. Should be set to NO.

FailedHardwareChecks

> Lists any hardware failures encountered during the inventory process. These failures are also listed in the SMSSAFE.TMP file. For more information about SMSSAFE, see Chapter 2, "Client Reference."

[SMS]

The information that identifies the client and maintains its inventory.

BuildNo

> The SMS product build number. This number is compared to the build number in the DOMAIN.INI file on the SMS logon server. If the build numbers differ, the client software is automatically upgraded.

SPNumber

> The SMS Service Pack number.

INIFileVersion

The version reference of the INI file. The higher 16 bits are the actual INI file version; the lower 16 bits are the build number.

CopyListVersion

The version reference of the copy-list file.

SiteCode

The three-character code identifying the site that maintains the current client's inventory.

SMS Unique ID

The client's system identifier, which is included in RAW files sent to the SMS logon server. The ID consists of a three-character site code followed by a five-digit number, such as TTT00003.

SMSPath

The client directory that contains SMS files and directories. Package Command Manager, Program Group Control, Program Group Control Start, SMSRUN, and the Inventory Agent read this path from SMS.INI.

SMSBinPath

The client directory that contains the SMS binaries.

StandaloneISVMIFPath

The directory path containing standalone MIF files. Objects defined by standalone MIF files have a custom architecture and are not included in the client's inventory (displayed in the Inventory window and the Personal Computer Properties - [computername] window). Instead, these standalone MIF objects are added to the SMS system database using their own architecture. They are stored and handled separately from the computer inventory. The Inventory Agent uses this path to locate the MIF files.

MachineISVMIFPath

The path to the directory containing client MIF files. These MIF files add new types of objects (such as new types of hardware) to the client's inventory. The objects are appended to the client architecture as a new group. These objects are included in the client's inventory and can be viewed in the Personal Computer Properties - [computername] window for the client. The Inventory Agent uses this path to locate the MIF files.

LocalWindowsPath

The path to the directory that contains the WIN.INI and SYSTEM.INI files (if found).

SharedWindowsPath

The path to the directory that contains Windows operating system files.

SMSLogPath

The path to the directory that contains the SMS client log files.

SMSDataPath

The path to the directory that contains data files used by the SMS binaries.

SMSInvDataPath

The path to the directory that is used to store inventory data files (Windows NT-based clients only).

SMSTempPath

Reserved.

SMSLocalTempPath

Reserved.

SharedWindowsBinaries

Reserved.

SharedSMSBinaries

Reserved.

ModifyAutoexecBat

Reserved.

LogonRoot

The path on a NetWare server between the volume name and the LOGON.SRV directory (including LOGON.SRV).

LastLogonServerPath

Indicates the relative path (*servername**sharename*) of the SMS logon server that last ran SMS Client Setup.

UniqueIdPath

The path to the unique ID file. This file is used to generate unique IDs.

LastSoftwareScan

The actual date and time that the software inventory was scanned.

LastHardwareScan

The actual date and time that the hardware inventory was scanned.

SoftwareScanInterval

By default, this setting is equivalent to the Software Inventory Frequency setting in the Inventory dialog box of Site Properties. A zero (0) indicates the software is scanned each time the Inventory Agent runs.

HardwareScanInterval

By default, this setting is equivalent to the Hardware Inventory Frequency setting in the Inventory dialog box of Site Properties. A zero (0) indicates the hardware is scanned each time the Inventory Agent runs.

InvAgtFalseLogonCount

The number of times it takes to log on to another site/domain before inventory is taken.

InventoryCollectionPoint (client only)

The path to the directory on the logon server where the Inventory Agent places inventory files.

SlowNetFlag

Determines when a slow network link, such as a RAS link, exists between the SMS logon server and the client. If a slow link is present, the Package Command Manager prompts the user to make selective decisions regarding software installation.

OS

The operating system that the client uses. If SMS Client Setup finds that this key is different from the operating system currently running, it prints a message and exits. The following values are possible:

Number	Meaning
1	MS-DOS
2	Windows 3.x
3	OS/2
4	Windows NT
5	Windows 95

InventoryConfigurationPath

Path (relative to the LOGON.SRV directory) to the resync files on a Windows NT-based computer.

ConfigurationRequestPath

Path (relative to the LOGON.SRV directory) to the client configuration request files on a Windows NT-based computer.

ISVMIFCollectionPoint

For OS/2 and Macintosh clients, the directory where the Inventory Agent places inventory MIF files. By default, the directory is ISVMIF.BOX.

InvAgtServiceWakeupInterval

Specifies how often the Inventory Agent services for Windows NT and OS/2 wake up and check to see if the inventory frequency interval has elapsed. By default, the InvAgtServiceWakeupInterval value is 24 hours (1440 minutes).

CompanyName

The company name entered when SMS was installed at the local site.

NetworkType

Refers to the type of network software used by the SMS logon server. The following values are possible:

Number	Meaning
1	Unknown
2	Windows NT
3	LAN Manager version 1.x
4	LAN Manager version 2.x (includes WFWNET)
5	NetWare 2.x
6	NetWare 3.x
7	NetWare 4.x

[SMSLSlni]

Added by SETLS when domain mapping of clients is enabled.

ValidatingServer

The name of the current SMS logon server.

FileName

The name of the file that contains the domain mappings. By default, this file is named SMSLS.INI.

FileTime

The time stamp of the domain mapping file. This time stamp is used to determine if any domain mapping changes have been made.

SectionMatch

The section in the mapping file that was used to map the client.

KeyMatch

The value of the section in the mapping file that was used to map the client.

Domain

The SMS domain that the client was mapped to as a result of the mapping file.

[Local]

Specifies the local Package Command Manager configuration. These settings are modified in the Package Command Manager Options dialog box.

SetupPhase

Indicates the present state of SMS (INSTALLED, UPGRADE, VERIFY_FILES, COMPONENT_DEINSTALL, DEINSTALL) on the client. SMS Client Setup writes this entry and checks it the next time it runs. SMSRUN uses this entry to maintain clients.

LanguageCode

Identifies the language version of the SMS client. This entry is written by SMS Client Setup.

NetCardID

The network card ID number as obtained by the Inventory Agent.

MachineName

The network computer name as obtained by the Inventory Agent.

SystemRole

The SMS system role. For example, server.

SystemType

The SMS system type. For example, x86-based personal computer.

LastPCMFileTime

Shows the most recent instruction file date used by Package Command Manager. The Package Command Manager checks this date to see if a new instruction file has arrived.

ShowPCMIntroDialog

Indicates whether the introductory message box should be displayed when Package Command Manager starts.

PollingInterval

A value set by the user to specify the Package Command Manager polling interval. If set, this value overrides the PollingInterval value specified in the [Package Command Manager] section.

UserName

Allows the user to enter a default name to be used by the Package Command Manager installation scripts.

CompanyName

Allows the user to override the default company name through which Package Command Manager installation scripts specify a company name when installing software.

NextAvailableSiteSMSUniqueID

This entry resides on the site server only. It is only written when a site is removed. This entry indicates the next available SMS unique ID that can safely be used. If the site is installed again with the same site code, this number is used as the starting point for all future SMS unique IDs.

[Sight]

Contains settings for remote control options. Some of these settings can be modified in the Help Desk Options dialog box.

Allow Takeover

Allows the computer running the SMS Administrator to take remote control of the client.

Allow Reboot

Allows the computer running the SMS Administrator to remotely restart the client.

Allow File Transfer

Allows file transfer to and from the client.

Allow Chat

Allows the Remote Chat utility to run.

Allow Remote Execute

Allows the computer running the SMS Administrator to remotely run programs on the client.

Visible Signal

Provides a visible signal to the user to indicate that the client is being controlled remotely.

Audible Signal

Provides an audible signal to the user to indicate that the client is being controlled remotely.

Allow Ping Test

Allows the computer running the SMS Administrator to remotely ping the client.

Allow DOS Diagnostics

Allows the computer running the SMS Administrator to remotely run the MS-DOS diagnostics utilities on the client.

Allow Windows Diagnostics

Allows the computer running the SMS Administrator to remotely run the Windows-based diagnostics utilities on the client.

Permission Required

Specifies whether the administrator running the SMS Administrator needs permission to remotely control the client.

Force Name

When set to yes, the computer name used between SMS and the client can be different from the LAN Manager computer name. If Force Name is set to yes, a MachineName entry must also be listed in the [Local] section.

Default Protocol

Default network protocol to be used for remote control. Valid protocols are NetBIOS, IP, and IPX.

LANANUM

Default Lana number to be used for remote control. Only valid for remote control over a NetBIOS protocol.

InstallWin16RCTSR

Indicates whether the remote control TSR (USERTSR / USERIPX) should be installed. Applies only to clients running Windows 3.1 (any network) or Windows for Workgroups (NetWare).

[LogonHistory]

Keeps track of logon attempts to another site or SMS domain. This information is used to determine if and when a computer's inventory should be reported to a new site or domain.

LastLoggedUser

The user name of the last user to log on to the network at the client.

Entry

When a user attempts to log on to a different site or SMS domain, this entry is used to store the last site or SMS domain where the client logged on. When the number of logon attempts reaches the number specified for InvAgtFalseLogonCount (in the [SMS] section), this entry is cleared.

Counter

Keeps track of the number of logon attempts to a different site or SMS domain. When the counter reaches the number specified for InvAgtFalseLogonCount, inventory is taken, and the computer is added to the new site/domain.

InventoryEntity

Specifies whether the Inventory Agent runs as a service or as an executable. Applies only to computers running Windows NT.

[UserName]

This user logon information is used for two purposes:

- SMS Client Setup uses this information to create unique, friendly names for NetWare clients. Since NetWare clients don't have friendly computer names, the name is created by combining the user name and IPX address. If another user logs on at the computer, inventory is skipped until the third logon attempt. At that time, the computer name is changed to reflect the new user name. When the computer name is changed, SMS creates a new inventory record for the computer.

- This information is also used to determine if and when a computer's inventory should be reported to a new site or domain.

The following keys are possible:

Current
   The name of the user currently logged on at the client.

LastLoggedUser
   The name of the previous user that logged on at the client.

Counter
   The number of times that the current user has logged on at the client.

[AppleServers]

The servers available for Macintosh clients.

CurrentLogonServer
   The name of the zone and server that processed the current user's logon request.

Server*number*
   The name of the zone and server that acts as a collection point for the current client. The *number* identifies each server entry (for example, Server1, Server2, and so on).

Sample SMS.INI File

```
[Package Command Manager]
InstructionSharePoint=pcmins.box
ResultSharePoint=despoolr.box
LocalRegistryLocation=C:\MS\SMS\DATA\pcmhist.reg
PollingInterval=60

[Servers]
Domain=S1DOMAIN
CurrentLogonServer=STEVEBDC
Server1=STEVEBDC
Server2=STEVEPDC

[Share]
CurrentLogonServer=SMS_SHR
Server1=SMS_SHR
Server2=SMS_SHR

[Program Group Control]
directory=appctl.box\database

[AppCtlIniFiles]
directory=appctl.box\inifiles

[AppCtlScripts]
directory=appctl.box\scripts

[MSTest16.20]
directory=mstest

[WorkstationStatus]
SysFilesNotModified=
FilesNotDownloaded=
InstalledComponents=PCM, MIFENTRY, APPCONTROL, REMOTE_CONTROL
AutoStartComponents=PCM, MIFENTRY, APPCONTROL
StandaloneWorkstation=No

[SMS]
BuildNo=786
SPNumber=0
INIFileVersion=66302
CopyListVersion=835643765
SiteCode=SKZ
SMS Unique ID=SKZ01000
SMSPath=C:\MS\SMS
SMSBinPath=C:\MS\SMS\BIN
```

```
StandaloneISVMIFPath=C:\MS\SMS\idmifs
MachineISVMIFPath=C:\MS\SMS\noidmifs
LocalWindowsPath=C:\NT351
SharedWindowsPath=C:\NT351
SMSLogPath=C:\MS\SMS\LOGS
SMSDataPath=C:\MS\SMS\DATA
SMSInvDataPath=C:\MS\SMS\INVDATA
SMSTempPath=C:\MS\SMS\TEMP
SMSLocalTempPath=C:\MS\SMS\TEMP
SharedWindowsBinaries=No
SharedSMSBinaries=No
ModifyAutoexecBat=Yes
LogonRoot=
LastLogonServerPath=\\STEVEPDC\SMS_SHR
UniqueIdPath=\\STEVEPDC\SMS_SHR\SMSID\
LastSoftwareScan=19960715135536.000000+000
LastHardwareScan=19960715135536.000000+000
SoftwareScanInterval=0
HardwareScanInterval=0
InvAgtFalseLogonCount=3
InventoryCollectionPoint=inventry.box
SlowNetFlag=no
OS=4
InventoryConfigurationPath=invencfg.box
ConfigurationRequestPath=ccr.box
ISVMIFCollectionPoint=isvmif.box
InvAgtServiceWakeupInterval=1440
CompanyName=MS
NetworkType=2

[Local]
SetupPhase=installed
LanguageCode=00000409
NetCardID=52:41:53:48:00:01
MachineName=STEVEK1
SystemRole=Workstation
SystemType=X86-based PC
ShowPCMIntroDialog=FALSE
LastPCMFileTime=837217035

 [Sight]
Allow Takeover=Yes
Allow Reboot=Yes
Allow File Transfer=Yes
Allow Chat=Yes
Allow Remote Execute=Yes
Visible Signal=Yes
```

```
Audible Signal=Yes
Allow Ping Test=No
Allow DOS Diagnostics=No
Allow Windows Diagnostics=No
Permission Required=Yes

[SMSLSIni]
ValidatingServer=\\stevepdc
FileName=\\RED1\NETLOGON\smsls.ini
FileTime=300cafc8
SectionMatch=WIN.INI
KeyMatch=S1DOMAIN
Domain=S1DOMAIN

[LogonHistory]
LastLoggedUser=stevek
Entry=
Counter=0
InventoryEntity=EXE
```

Site Control File

The site control file provides a record of site configuration parameters. Each primary and secondary site has a unique master site control file (SITECTRL.CT0) located in the SMS\SITE.SRV\SITECFG.BOX directory. This file defines the site properties, including information such as the type of site, SMS service and SQL Server accounts, SMS domains and logon servers, SMS services and components, and specific site configuration options, such as inventory scanning intervals and SMS Client Setup options.

When site properties are modified, the Hierarchy Manager creates a temporary site control file (*.CT1), which is read by the Site Configuration Manager. The Site Configuration Manager overwrites SITECTRL.CT0 with the information in *.CT1 and creates another file named *.CT2, which is used to update the database.

The site control file begins with a line indicating the SMS build number and the syntax version number. For example:

```
SITE CONTROL FILE [786][1.08]
```

Additional sections then are used to define specific site properties. Section names in the site control file are typically grouped with a BEGIN and an END statement. For example, the following section defines the File Definition:

```
BEGIN_FILE_DEFINITION
  <2>
  <Setup-based site creation>
  <SKZ>
  <SKZ>
  <837492602>
  <1>
END_FILE_DEFINITION
```

The following sections and entries are in the site control file:

- FILE_DEFINITION
- TRANSACTION
- SITE_ACCOUNT
- PROPERTY
- PROPERTY_LIST
- DOMAIN
- ADDRESS
- OUTBOX
- SERVER
- COMPONENT
- SENDER

These sections and entries are described in the following sections. In addition, a sample site control file is included in "Sample Site Control File" later in this chapter.

FILE_DEFINITION

Provides information about the site control file.

File Type

The file type for site control can be one of the following:

File type	Description
Actual (1)	Refers to a version of the site control file that contains the actual status of the site after completing the most recent changes. Such a file usually has a .CT2 extension.
Proposed (2)	Refers to site control files that contain proposed changes for the site. These files have a .CT1 extension and are used by the Site Configuration Manager as a basis for reconfiguring the site.
New site (3)	Used by SMS Setup to instruct Site Configuration Manager to begin creating a new site, either locally or remotely.
Transactions (4)	Contains specific one-time instructions for the Site Configuration Manager. These files initiate changes to the site hierarchy.
Local transactions (5)	Used by the Site Configuration Manager, Hierarchy Manager, and SMS Setup to pass along site upgrade or removal instructions within a site.

Comment

The description of the operation that generated the file. For example:

```
Setup-based site creation
```

Target site

The site code for the site being modified.

Originating Site

The site code for the site that originated the site modifications.

GMT time stamp

The file creation time (using Greenwich Mean Time).

Posted/Not Posted

A value of 1 (posted) indicates that the file is used internally by the Hierarchy Manager. A 0 indicates no handling by the Hierarchy Manager.

TRANSACTION

A list of one-time transactions, usually a set of instructions to the Hierarchy Manager or Site Configuration Manager. If the file type is transactions only, this section will be the only other entry in the file. If there are no transactions to be done, this section is not present.

Transactions have the following format:

```
TRANSACTION<TransactionType><PersistentFlag><DWORDValue><String1><String2>
```

The TransactionType field is described in the following sections. The PersistentFlag field is used to indicate whether the transaction applies to all transactions or only to this transaction. The remaining 3 fields are data fields for the transactions.

The following transaction types are possible:

Change@
Transaction sent to change the SMS Service Account and password.

SqlChange@
Transaction sent to change the SQL Server account and password.

InactiveDomains, InactiveServers, InactiveComponents, InactiveSenders
These transactions are used by the Site Configuration Manager to report inactive items. A count of inactive items is displayed in the SMS Administrator; Windows NT and SMS events are also generated for each inactive item.

The first string in these transactions is a comma-separated list of up to 20 items. The second string is blank. The DWORD parameter gives a total count of inactive items of this type. For example:

```
TRANSACTION InactiveDomains<0><2><DomainX,DomainY><>
```

DeinstallSite
Transaction sent to the Site Configuration Manager to remove the site from the site hierarchy.

InitiateDeinstall
Transaction sent to the Hierarchy Manager to initiate the removal of a site from the site hierarchy.

InitiateUpgrade

Transaction sent to the Hierarchy Manager to initiate a site upgrade.

DeinstallSiteAck

Transaction sent by the Site Configuration Manager to indicate that it has successfully removed a site from the site hierarchy.

Shutdown

Transaction sent to the Site Configuration Manager to shut down (stop and remove) all SMS services in the site.

ShutdownAck

Transaction sent by the Site Configuration Manager when shutdown is completed.

Upgrade

Transaction sent to the Site Configuration Manager to upgrade files for SMS services at the site.

DeleteSite

Transaction sent whenever a site needs to be deleted from the site hierarchy in all parent site databases. Each Hierarchy Manager forwards this to its parent site until the top of the tree is reached. The site is deleted only if the parent site code matches.

SyncParentDetach

Transaction used by the Hierarchy Manager to synchronize a detachment from a parent site.

ParentDetach

Transaction forwarded up the site hierarchy to detach from a parent site.

Heartbeat

Transaction sent in a site control file every 24 hours.

RequestNewSCFile

Transaction sent when the Site Configuration Manager detects no master site control file (SITECTRL.CT0).

TriggerWatchdog

Transaction that causes the Site Configuration Manager to do a watchdog cycle.

TriggerWatchdogHeartbeat

Transaction that causes the Site Configuration Manager to do a watchdog cycle and write a CT2 status file with a heartbeat transaction.

TriggerUserGroupMIF

Transaction that causes the Site Configuration Manager to do a watchdog cycle and write a user group MIF file.

TriggerLogonScriptConfig

Transaction that causes the Site Configuration Manager to do a watchdog cycle and modify logon scripts as specified by the Automatically Configure Logon Scripts setting.

LogEventForBootstrap

This transaction causes the Hierarchy Manager to log an event on behalf of the Bootstrap service.

SMSBaseID

Transaction sent by the Site Configuration Manager to log the last used SMS ID range from a previous SMS installation (if applicable).

NoEnumeration

Transaction sent to the Site Configuration Manager to suppress the enumeration of user groups.

SITE_ACCOUNT

Describes SMS account and configuration information.

SiteType

Defined by the following values:

Site Type	Value
9	Secondary site
6	Primary site

Site code

A three-character code that the SMS system uses to identify the site. The site code for any site must be unique across the SMS system. It is not case sensitive.

Parent site code

A three-character code that the SMS system uses to identify the parent site. This field is blank if the site does not have a parent site.

Site server

The name of the site server.

Site server domain

The Windows NT domain to which the site server belongs.

Site name

The name of the site.

Installation directory at the site

The path and directory name containing SMS files.

Service account domain name

The name of the domain that contains the SMS service account.

Service account name

The encrypted name for the SMS Service Account.

Password

The encrypted password for the SMS Service Account.

Public encryption key

The security mechanism used by SMS.

SQLServer name

The location of the SQL Server database that services the site.

SQL Login account

The encrypted login account for the SQL Server.

SQL Login password

The encrypted password for the SQL login account.

SQL database name

The name of the SQL Server database specified during SMS Setup.

SQL public encryption key

The security mechanism for SQL Server operations.

User name

The name the user entered during SMS Setup.

Organization

The name of the organization that the user entered during SMS Setup.

PROPERTY

Properties are various configurations used by different components. Property definitions include the property name followed two optional strings and a mandatory DWORD integer. (The DWORD value is 0 if there is no flag.) The following example uses two strings but no flag:

```
PROPERTY <User And Organization><AlexanderSeth><Siblings Inc><0>
```

Site Server Platform

The hardware platform (Intel, MIPs, RISC, and so on) of the site server. For example:

```
<Site Server Platform><INTEL X86><><0>
```

Site Server Language

The language platform of the site server (English, French, and so on).
For example:

```
<Site Server Language><english><><0>
```

Last Valid @

The most recently known valid service password. The encrypted user name
and password are defined by the first and second strings, respectively. The
DWORD parameter contains the time stamp when the user name and password
were created.

Last Valid SQL @

The last valid password for the SQL Server. The encrypted user name and
password are defined by the first and second strings, respectively. The
DWORD parameter contains the time stamp when the user name and password
were created.

Hardware Scan/Software Scan

Two separate properties that define the frequency at which hardware and
software scans occur. The frequency is defined using one of the following
values:

Value	Scan frequency
1 (always)	A scan occurs each time a log on occurs.
2 (daily)	A scan occurs at most once a day.
3 (interval)	The property HardwareScanInterval (or SoftwareScanInterval) is also defined, and a scan occurs at most once during that interval.

Hardware Scan Interval/Software Scan Interval

Two separate properties that define the scan interval (in days).

User and Organization

The user name and company name specified during the site installation.
For example:

```
<User And Organization><SaraElizabeth><Siblings Inc><0>
```

SNA Local Address

Defines the local LU alias for the SNA Sender. For example:

```
<SNA Local Address><MYLU1234><><0>
```

Note When creating an LU alias for use with the SNA Sender, do not use
numerals in the first position; numerals are allowed in positions 2 through 8 only.

Service Response

Indicates the monitoring mode for the SMS services. The faster the response rate, the heavier the system load. The following values are possible:

Value	Monitoring mode
1	Test (1 minute)
2	Fast (5 minutes)
3	Medium (15 minutes)
4	Slow (30 minutes)

Slow Net Strategy

Specifies how SMS clients at the site report their inventory when they have a slow communications link to their SMS logon server. This setting applies to all clients in the site. The following values are possible:

Value	Meaning
1	Clients always report their inventory to the SMS logon server, even if the Inventory Agent detects a slow network.
2	The Inventory Agent prompts the user if it detects a slow network. A message box requests permission for Inventory Agent to scan the client and report any inventory changes to the SMS logon server.
3	The Inventory Agent does not scan when it detects a slow network.

Client Config Manager On Servers

Specifies where the Client Configuration Manager service is running. The following values are possible:

Flag	Meaning
0x00000001	The Client Configuration Manager is automatically installed on the site server.
0x00000002	The Client Configuration Manager is automatically installed on all SMS logon servers (if there is an agent for that type of server).
0x00000004	The Client Configuration Manager is automatically installed on all helper servers.

Package Command Manager on Servers

Specifies where the Package Command Manager service is running. The following values are possible:

Flag	Meaning
0x00000001	The Package Command Manager is automatically installed on the site server.
0x00000002	The Package Command Manager is automatically installed on all SMS logon servers (if there is an agent for that type of server).
0x00000004	The Package Command Manager is automatically installed on all helper servers.

Inventory Agent On Servers

Specifies where the Inventory Agent service is running. The following values are possible:

Flag	Meaning
0x00000001	The Inventory Agent is automatically installed on the site server.
0x00000002	The Inventory Agent is automatically installed on all SMS logon servers (if there is an agent for that type of server).
0x00000004	The Inventory Agent is automatically installed on all helper servers.

PCM Polling

Specifies, in minutes, how frequently the Package Command Manager checks for new packages. This DWORD value applies to all clients but it can be overridden at an individual client through the Package Command Manager user interface.

LogonScripts

Indicates whether SMS is configured to alter logon scripts automatically. The following values are possible:

Flag	Meaning
0x00000000	Do not automatically configure workstation logon scripts.
0x00000001	The Automatically Configure Workstation Logon Scripts option is enabled.
0x00000002	When existing logon scripts are automatically configured, SMS adds them at the bottom of the script.

Client Installation

Indicates whether SMS modifies the AUTOEXEC.BAT file on clients. The following values are possible:

Flag	Meaning
0x00000001	Install Package Command Manager.
0x00000002	Automatically start Package Command Manager.
0x00000008	Install Program Group Control.
0x00000010	Automatically start Program Group Control.
0x00000020	Install Help Desk.
0x00000040	Automatically start Help Desk.
0x00000100	Install MIF Entry.
0x00000200	Automatically start MIF Entry.

Version

The version of SMS software specified by SMS Setup. For example:

```
<version><549><><0>
```

Default Package Server

Always set to Default Package Server.

Account Checking

Indicates whether SMS should attempt to validate the SMS Service Account before using it to install the SMS services. This property is currently used by SMS Setup only. The following values are possible:

Value	Meaning
1	Account checking is enabled for the site.
0	Account checking is disabled.

Remote Control Install Video Driver

Indicates whether or not to install support for the IDIS_NT.DLL remote control video driver.

Value	Meaning
0	Do not install support for the remote control video driver.
1	Install support for the remote control video driver.

Remote Control Command Line

Indicates the remote control command line to run on Windows NT clients. This command line lets you specify the default protocol and Lana number to be used on the clients.

GlobalUserGroupEnum

Indicates whether user group enumeration will be performed. The following values are possible:

Flag	Meaning
0x00000000	Enumerate the user groups.
0x00000001	Do not enumerate the user groups.

PROPERTY_LIST

Contains miscellaneous information about the site.

DOMAINTYPE

Supported domain types.

ADRSTRFMT

Supported sender address string types.

SoftwareUnits

Currently installed software units.

Remote Control Permitted Viewers

List of users and user groups that can remotely control Windows NT computers in the site.

Remote Control Supported Video Drivers

List of video adapters supported for accelerated screen transfer mode (valid only for computer running Windows NT).

NET_PROVIDERS

List of network provider types in the site. May include sub-lists.

Desktop Services

List of services installed on SMS logon servers.

Logon Script Files

A list of files used by the SMS logon script.

TrapFilter *number*

A description of each SNMP trap filter that has been defined in the site.

DOMAIN

Describes each SMS domain that participates in the site hierarchy.

Domain name

The name of the SMS domain.

Domain type

Specifies either Windows NT, LAN Manager, or NetWare.

Autoenumerate SMS logon servers

A 1 indicates that SMS is configured to autoenumerate SMS logon servers. A 2 indicates a user-defined list of servers and is followed by the SMS logon server list.

Logon server

SMS logon servers in the domain.

ADDRESS

Contains information about the site addresses. The format of the address string is:

```
ADDRESS <Originating Site Code><Destination Site Code><Sender
Type><Address string format><Address String>
```

The sender type can be LAN Sender, SNA Sender, or RAS Sender. The address string format also refers to a sender type.

The address string begins with a number that indicates how many address characters are to be read in the rest of the string that follows. Most of the address string is encrypted because it contains passwords.

OUTBOX

An Outbox entry exists for each defined sender. The format of the outbox string is:

```
OUTBOX <Outboxname><Drive><Address string format><Schedule string>
<CreateFlag><Server name>
```

SERVER

Various types of auxiliary servers are specified in this section. The format for the server string is:

```
SERVER <Server name><Server type><Flags><Install drive letter>
```

COMPONENT

Describes each of the Windows NT services (or their subcomponents) required by SMS.

Installation flags

The following table lists and describes the service installation flags.

Service	Flag	Description
INSTALL	0x00000001	Install this component.
LOCALSYSACCT	0x00000002	If this is a service, install it on the SMS logon server as a system account (instead of the SMS Service Account).
STARTSERVICE	0x00000004	Start this component if it is stopped.
SETREGISTRY	0x00000008	Configure the initial SMS registry values for this component.
EXE	0x00000010	Not currently used.

(continued)

Service	Flag	Description
LITERALPATH	0x00000020	The file ID for this component is a full path to the executable file instead of an ID in the system map file.
PRIMARYSITE	0x00000040	Install this component if the site is a primary site.
SECONDARYSITE	0x00000080	Install this component if the site is a secondary site.
AUTOSTART	0x00000100	If this is a service, install it to start automatically during system startup.
SENDER	0x00000200	This component is a sender.
OPTIONALSVC	0x00000400	This component is optional at this site.
AS_THREAD	0x00000800	This component runs under the control of SMS Executive.
DONTSTOPSVC	0x00001000	This service is not stopped or removed during a site shutdown or site removal.

Service or thread name
The name of the service or component, such as SMS_EXECUTIVE or SMS_DESPOOLER.

File ID of the service or subcomponent
This ID is used to look up the list of file names in the system map file to determine the executable files (EXEs and DLLs) for this component.

Server on which to install the component
The name of the site server or a helper server where this component should be installed.

Drive on which to install the service
The drive letter to which the executable files are copied when the component is installed on the server named in the preceding entry.

SENDER

Describes the senders in use at the site. Senders are similar to components but have special characteristics, such as the type of address format they support and the outboxes they monitor.

Installation flags
See the Installation flags entry in "COMPONENT," earlier in this chapter.

Address string format type
The type of address format that this sender understands and, therefore, the type of outbox it uses. For example, MS_LAN_SENDER.

File ID of the sender

This ID is used to look up the list of file names in the system map file to determine the executable files (EXEs and DLLs) for the sender.

Drive on which to install

The drive letter where the executable files are copied to when the sender is installed on the server named in the next entry.

Server on which to install

The name of the site server or helper server where this sender should be installed.

Sender name

The name of the sender. For example, SMS_LAN_SENDER.

Outbox

The outbox the sender is monitoring.

Sample Site Control File

```
SITE CONTROL FILE [786][1.08]

BEGIN_FILE_DEFINITION
  <2>
  <Setup-based site creation>
  <SKZ>
  <SKZ>
  <837492602>
  <1>
END_FILE_DEFINITION

BEGIN_SITE_ACCOUNT
  <6>
  <SKZ>
  <>
  <STEVEPDC>
  <S1DOMAIN>
  <STEVE'S SITE>
  <D:\SMS>
  <S1DOMAIN>

  <348CF4B23D7AAA97E1A7B3AA0A6AC6928635E7D2D73153B170AD60DBD6399B3EC737DF5
  52980A8>

  <98355E11DFCE1EAC93E29AAFD2D9D5A98512BD5D69B4C0295B38A1076A18FE00DF2B453
  CD0E6E9>
  <CEEBEA96831AABAB878E184E207C5C906D9E210404>
  <stevebdc>
```

```
<448FF9F6711B80A74B8DD27549A3216CD120D2C726A390C639DE59CC3B4ED7868E7E3A8
62DB95F>

<E411C8506516A50C6AFB7CBD2E7B1805A72ECB29ED5937882AD7539F71806BBACA70572
5EB8F10>
  <SMS>
  <9FD1B8FFE4FA969BAC0B6854349E7036E5C48E6CCE>
  <>
  <>
END_SITE_ACCOUNT

PROPERTY <Site Server Platform><INTEL X86><><0>
PROPERTY <Site Server Language><ENGLISH><><0>
PROPERTY <Last Valid @><><><831190761>
PROPERTY <Last Valid Sql @><><><831190761>
PROPERTY <Hardware Scan><><><1>
PROPERTY <Software Scan><><><1>
PROPERTY <Hardware Scan Interval><><><0>
PROPERTY <Software Scan Interval><><><0>
PROPERTY <User And Organization><Steve Kaye><MS><1>
PROPERTY <SNA Local Address><><><0>
PROPERTY <Service Response><><><1>
PROPERTY <Slow Net Strategy><><><1>
PROPERTY <CLIENT CONFIG MANAGER ON SERVERS><><><3>
PROPERTY <PACKAGE COMMAND MANAGER ON SERVERS><><><7>
PROPERTY <INVENTORY AGENT ON SERVERS><><><7>
PROPERTY <PCM Polling><><><60>
PROPERTY <Logon Scripts><><><0>
PROPERTY <Client Installation><><><891>
PROPERTY <Version><786><><0>
PROPERTY <Default Package Server><Default Package Server><><0>
PROPERTY <Account Checking><><><1>
PROPERTY <Remote Control Install Video Driver><><><1>
PROPERTY <Remote Control Command Line><-L0><><0>

BEGIN_PROPERTY_LIST
   <ADRSTRFMT>
   <MS_LAN_SENDER>
   <MS_BATCH_SNA_SENDER>
   <MS_INTER_SNA_SENDER>
   <MS_ASYNC_RAS_SENDER>
   <MS_ISDN_RAS_SENDER>
   <MS_X25_RAS_SENDER>
END_PROPERTY_LIST
```

```
BEGIN_PROPERTY_LIST
   <Remote Control Permitted Viewers>
   <Administrators>
END_PROPERTY_LIST

BEGIN_PROPERTY_LIST
   <Remote Control Supported Video Drivers>
   <ART>
   <FRAMEBUF>
   <MGA>
   <QV>
   <S3>
   <TGA>
   <VGA>
   <VGA256>
   <VGA64K>
   <WEITEKP9>
   <W32>
   <XGA>
END_PROPERTY_LIST

BEGIN_PROPERTY_LIST
   <NET_PROVIDERS>
   <Microsoft Windows NT or LAN Manager, Dri&ve:,  15, 15, 2, 0x10000109
,NETMSLM.DLL>
   <Novell NetWare,   &Volume:, 15, 48, 16, 0x20000204 ,NETNVNW.DLL>
END_PROPERTY_LIST

BEGIN_PROPERTY_LIST
   <Novell NetWare>
   <>
END_PROPERTY_LIST

BEGIN_PROPERTY_LIST
   <Microsoft Windows NT or LAN Manager>
   <PACKAGE COMMAND MANAGER ON SERVERS|WINDOWS NT
3.X=SMS_PACKAGE_COMMAND_MANAGER_NT>
   <INVENTORY AGENT ON SERVERS|WINDOWS NT 3.X=SMS_INVENTORY_AGENT_NT>
   <INVENTORY AGENT ON SERVERS|LAN MANAGER 2.X (OS/2)=SMS_INV_OS2LM>
   <CLIENT CONFIG MANAGER ON SERVERS|WINDOWS NT
3.X=SMS_CLIENT_CONFIG_MANAGER>
END_PROPERTY_LIST

BEGIN_PROPERTY_LIST
   <DOMAINTYPE>
   <Novell NetWare>
   <Microsoft Windows NT or LAN Manager>
END_PROPERTY_LIST
```

```
BEGIN_PROPERTY_LIST
   <Desktop Services>
   <INVENTORY AGENT ON SERVERS|0X00000007>
   <PACKAGE COMMAND MANAGER ON SERVERS|0X00000007>
   <CLIENT CONFIG MANAGER ON SERVERS|0X00000003>
END_PROPERTY_LIST

BEGIN_PROPERTY_LIST
   <SoftwareUnits>
   <INTEL CLIENT>
   <SCRIPTS>
   <INTEL SERVER>
   <INTEL NETWORK MONITOR>
   <INTEL SMS ADMINISTRATOR>
   <ALPHA CLIENT>
   <ALPHA SERVER>
   <MIPS CLIENT>
   <MIPS SERVER>
END_PROPERTY_LIST

BEGIN_PROPERTY_LIST
   <TrapFilter 0>
   <Valid 1>
   <Active 1>
   <IPAddress >
   <EnterpriseOID *>
   <GenericTrapID 16>
   <SpecificTrapID >
   <TrapAction 1>
   <Description Save Authentication Failure traps>
END_PROPERTY_LIST

BEGIN_PROPERTY_LIST
   <TrapFilter 1>
   <Valid 1>
   <Active 1>
   <IPAddress >
   <NTEventSourceOID *>
   <GenericTrapID 127>
   <SpecificTrapID *>
   <TrapAction 1>
   <Description Save Windows NT Events>
END_PROPERTY_LIST
```

```
BEGIN_PROPERTY_LIST
  <TrapFilter 2>
  <Valid 1>
  <Active 1>
  <IPAddress 123.123.123.123>
  <EnterpriseOID *>
  <GenericTrapID 127>
  <SpecificTrapID *>
  <TrapAction 1>
  <Description Save traps from Server TrafficCop>
END_PROPERTY_LIST

BEGIN_PROPERTY_LIST
  <TrapFilter 3>
  <Valid 1>
  <Active 1>
  <IPAddress >
  <EnterpriseOID *>
  <GenericTrapID 127>
  <SpecificTrapID *>
  <TrapAction 0>
  <Description Discard everything else>
END_PROPERTY_LIST

BEGIN_DOMAIN
  <S1DOMAIN>
  <Microsoft Windows NT or LAN Manager>
  <1>
  LOGONSERVER <STEVEBDC><><0><D:>
  LOGONSERVER <STEVEPDC><><0><D:>
END_DOMAIN

ADDRESS <SKZ><SKZ><MS_LAN_SENDER><LAN_DEFAULT>
  #182({}{\\STEVEPDC\SMS_SITE
348CF4B23D7AAA97E188E0407752F221FAE8ECD62E76BF6355E1F8CE113DFC85DCE587F1
5F7CB3
98355E11DFCE1E33390B0992F20A40BB44F7D58EB3E3381D0E800B3C06AC203576DA4D1B
CDA1AA})
ADDRESS <SKZ><DF1><MS_LAN_SENDER><>
  #185({}{\\ASSIMILATOR1\SMS_SITE
359BFFA27F67A180F408A57531D7596CA854DAC021D993C74AD920B34B33D0F18E064EFE
2DC02B
9A355E11DF6FDA7C17FC0BBD560F6005DE5AC32EEA23348959D02AE001FD6CCDCA08235D
EBF664})
OUTBOX <LAN_DEFAULT><><MS_LAN_SENDER>

<FFFFFFFFFFFFFFFFFFFFFFFFFFFFFFFFFFFFFFFFFFFFFFFFFFFFFFFFFFFFFFFFFFFFFFFF
FFFFFFFFFFFFFFFFFFFFFFFFFFFFFFFFFFFFFFFFFFFFFFFFFFFFFFFFFFFFFFFFFFFFFFFFFF
FFFFFFFFFFFFFFFFFFFFFFFFFFF><1><D><STEVEPDC>
OUTBOX <SNA_BATCH_DEFAULT><><MS_BATCH_SNA_SENDER>
```

```
<FFFFFFFFFFFFFFFFFFFFFFFFFFFFFFFFFFFFFFFFFFFFFFFFFFFFFFFFFFFFFFFF
FFFFFFFFFFFFFFFFFFFFFFFFFFFFFFFFFFFFFFFFFFFFFFFFFFFFFFFFFFFFFFFFF
FFFFFFFFFFFFFFFFFFFFFFFFF><1><D><STEVEPDC>
OUTBOX <SNA_INTER_DEFAULT><><MS_INTER_SNA_SENDER>

<FFFFFFFFFFFFFFFFFFFFFFFFFFFFFFFFFFFFFFFFFFFFFFFFFFFFFFFFFFFFFFFF
FFFFFFFFFFFFFFFFFFFFFFFFFFFFFFFFFFFFFFFFFFFFFFFFFFFFFFFFFFFFFFFFF
FFFFFFFFFFFFFFFFFFFFFFFFF><1><D><STEVEPDC>
OUTBOX <RAS_ASYNC_DEFAULT><><MS_ASYNC_RAS_SENDER>

<FFFFFFFFFFFFFFFFFFFFFFFFFFFFFFFFFFFFFFFFFFFFFFFFFFFFFFFFFFFFFFFF
FFFFFFFFFFFFFFFFFFFFFFFFFFFFFFFFFFFFFFFFFFFFFFFFFFFFFFFFFFFFFFFFF
FFFFFFFFFFFFFFFFFFFFFFFFF><1><D><STEVEPDC>
OUTBOX <RAS_ISDN_DEFAULT><><MS_ISDN_RAS SENDER>

<FFFFFFFFFFFFFFFFFFFFFFFFFFFFFFFFFFFFFFFFFFFFFFFFFFFFFFFFFFFFFFFF
FFFFFFFFFFFFFFFFFFFFFFFFFFFFFFFFFFFFFFFFFFFFFFFFFFFFFFFFFFFFFFFFF
FFFFFFFFFFFFFFFFFFFFFFFFF><1><D><STEVEPDC>
OUTBOX <RAS_X25_DEFAULT><><MS_X25_RAS_SENDER>
<FFFFFFFFFFFFFFFFFFFFFFFFFFFFFFFFFFFFFFFFFFFFFFFFFFFFFFFFFFFFFFFF
FFFFFFFFFFFFFFFFFFFFFFFFFFFFFFFFFFFFFFFFFFFFFFFFFFFFFFFFFFFFFFFFF
FFFFFFFFFFFFFFFFFFFFFFFFF><1><D><STEVEPDC>
SERVER <STEVEPDC><Default Package Server><0><>

BEGIN_COMPONENT
  <2125>
  <SMS_ALERTER>
  <ALERTER.DLL>
  <STEVEPDC>
  <D>
END_COMPONENT

BEGIN_COMPONENT
  <2125>
  <SMS_TRAP_FILTER>
  <TRAPFLTR.DLL>
  <STEVEPDC>
  <D>
END_COMPONENT

BEGIN_COMPONENT
  <77>
  <SMS_HIERARCHY_MANAGER>
  <PREINST.EXE>
  <STEVEPDC>
  <D>
END_COMPONENT
```

```
BEGIN_COMPONENT
  <2253>
  <SMS_APPLICATIONS_MANAGER>
  <APPMGR.DLL>
  <STEVEPDC>
  <D>
END_COMPONENT

BEGIN_COMPONENT
  <457>
  <SMS_SITE_CONFIG_MANAGER>
  <SITEINS.FXF>
  <STEVEPDC>
  <D>
END_COMPONENT

BEGIN_COMPONENT
  <205>
  <SMS_EXECUTIVE>
  <SMSEXEC.EXE>
  <STEVEPDC>
  <D>
END_COMPONENT

BEGIN_COMPONENT
  <2253>
  <SMS_MAINTENANCE_MANAGER>
  <MAINTAIN.DLL>
  <STEVEPDC>
  <D>
END_COMPONENT

BEGIN_COMPONENT
  <2253>
  <SMS_SITE_REPORTER>
  <SITEREP.DLL>
  <STEVEPDC>
  <D>
END_COMPONENT

BEGIN_COMPONENT
  <2253>
  <SMS_SCHEDULER>
  <SCHED.DLL>
  <STEVEPDC>
  <D>
END_COMPONENT
```

```
BEGIN_COMPONENT
  <2125>
  <SMS_INVENTORY_DATA_LOADER>
  <DATALDR.DLL>
  <STEVEPDC>
  <D>
END_COMPONENT

BEGIN_COMPONENT
  <2253>
  <SMS_INVENTORY_PROCESSOR>
  <INVPROC.DLL>
  <STEVEPDC>
  <D>
END_COMPONENT

BEGIN_COMPONENT
  <2253>
  <SMS_DESPOOLER>
  <DESPOOL.DLL>
  <STEVEPDC>
  <D>
END_COMPONENT

BEGIN_SENDER
  <2765>
  <MS_LAN_SENDER>
  <SENDER.DLL>
  <D>
  <STEVEPDC>
  <SMS_LAN_SENDER>
  OUTBOX <LAN_DEFAULT>
END_SENDER
```

SYSTEM.MAP

The SYSTEM.MAP file lists the platforms, languages, directories, and files that SMS can use. It tells SMS Setup which directories to create for specific language IDs and platforms. SMS Setup uses the SYSTEM.MAP file to copy files and directories from the Microsoft Systems Management Server version 1.2 compact disc to the site server disk. The Maintenance Manager uses the SYSTEM.MAP file to create copy-list files; these files are used to specify the files that should be copied to clients. Copy-list files are copied to each type of client that SMS supports.

The SYSTEM.MAP file is located in the SMSSETUP directory on the Microsoft Systems Management Server version 1.2 compact disc. For an installed site, it is located in the SMS root directory on the site server. Because the SYSTEM.MAP file is used by SMS to control site configuration, this file should not be modified.

The SYSTEM.MAP file contains the following sections:

- Platforms
- Copylists
- Languages
- Units
- IDList
- Service
- Package
- Directories

These sections provide mappings from one or more items to a single keyword; for instance, the following IDList maps the substrings that can be used to indicate the Intel x86 platform:

```
IDLIST "INTEL X86" = "386", "486", "PENTIUM", "X86"
```

The sections in the SYSTEM.MAP file are described next.

Platforms

List of supported platforms (CPU architectures). SMS 1.2 supports Intel, DEC Alpha, MIPS, and Macintosh platforms. This is indicated in the following line which appears in the SYSTEM.MAP file for the U.S. English version of SMS 1.2:

```
PLATFORMS = "INTEL X86", "DEC ALPHA", "MIPS R4000", "MAC 68000"
```

Copylists

Each entry indicates a client group for which files must be copied. For instance, in the following COPYLISTS section, the WIN95:PCM entry indicates the copy-list to be used to copy files to a Windows 95 client if the Package Command Manager is to be installed.

The COPYLISTS entry from the SMS version 1.2 SYSTEM.MAP file follows:

```
COPYLISTS = "DOS:STANDARD", "DOS:PCM", "DOS:REMOTE_CONTROL",
"DOS:REMOTE_CONTROL_386", "DOS:REMOTE_CONTROL_NETWARE",
"DOS:REMOTE_CONTROL_LANMAN", "DOS:MIFENTRY", "WIN16:STANDARD",
"WIN16:PCM", "WIN16:APPCONTROL", "WIN16:REMOTE_CONTROL",
"WIN16:REMOTE_CONTROL_386", "WIN16:REMOTE_CONTROL_NETWARE",
"WIN16:REMOTE_CONTROL_LANMAN", "WIN16:MIFENTRY", "WIN95:APPCONTROL",
"WIN95:STANDARD", "WIN95:PCM", "WIN95:REMOTE_CONTROL",
"WIN95:REMOTE_CONTROL_386", "WIN95:REMOTE_CONTROL_NETWARE",
"WIN95:REMOTE_CONTROL_LANMAN", "WIN95:MIFENTRY", "WIN95:LANMAN",
"WIN95:NETWARE", "OS2:STANDARD", "OS2:PCM", "OS2:MIFENTRY",
"WINNT:REMOTE_CONTROL", "WINNT:STANDARD", "WINNT:PCM",
"WINNT:APPCONTROL", "WINNT:MIFENTRY", "WIN16:LANMAN",
"WIN16:NETWARE", "DOS:LANMAN", "DOS:NETWARE", "WINNT:LANMAN"
```

Languages

List of languages supported by this version of SMS. For example, the following line is included in the SYSTEM.MAP file for the U.S. English version of SMS 1.2:

```
LANGUAGES = "ENGLISH"
```

Units

List of the valid installable software units for this version of SMS. This information is used by SMS Setup to properly configure the site. The UNITS entry from the SMS version 1.2 SYSTEM.MAP file follows:

```
UNITS = "ALPHA SERVER", "MIPS SERVER", "INTEL SERVER", "INTEL
CLIENT", "ALPHA CLIENT", "MIPS CLIENT", "MACINTOSH CLIENT",
"SCRIPTS", "INTEL SMS ADMINISTRATOR", "ALPHA SMS ADMINISTRATOR",
"MIPS SMS ADMINISTRATOR", "INTEL NETWORK MONITOR", "ALPHA NETWORK
MONITOR", "MIPS NETWORK MONITOR"
```

IDList

Define new associations to be used by the SMS system. For instance, IDLists define the default platforms, languages, CPU identifiers, directories, allowable installation or upgrade options, and so on. A sampling of the IDLists that appear in the SMS version 1.2 SYSTEM.MAP file follows:

```
IDLIST "BUILDNUMBER" = "786"
IDLIST "SPNUMBER" = ""
IDLIST "SYSMAPVERSION" = "786", "FINAL", "SMS V1.2", "FULL"
IDLIST "SMSVERSIONINFO" = "V1.2", "712"
IDLIST "LANGUAGE_DEFAULT" = "ENGLISH"
IDLIST "PLATFORM_DEFAULT" = "INTEL X86"
IDLIST "PERMITTED_UPGRADES" = "479:479", "521:531", "531:786"
IDLIST "INTEL X86" = "386", "486", "PENTIUM", "X86"
IDLIST "DEC ALPHA" = "ALPHA", "DEC", "DIGITAL"
IDLIST "MIPS R4000" = "R4000", "R4400", "MIPS", "RPC 44", "ARCSBIOS"
IDLIST "MAC 68000" = "MAC", "APPLE", "68000"
IDLIST "PLATFORM_DIRECTORY" = "INTEL X86=X86.BIN", "DEC
ALPHA=ALPHA.BIN", "MIPS R4000=MIPS.BIN", "MAC 68000=MAC.BIN"
```

Service

Defines how to install the SMS services. The Service sections use the BEGIN and END keywords. They also use the FLAGS, MAIN, and SUBCOMPONENT keywords, as follows:

- The FLAGS keyword is used to indicate how the service should be installed and configured. See the following table to interpret the Flag bits.

- The MAIN keyword is used to indicate the primary executable file associated with the service or component.

- The SUBCOMPONENT keyword is used to indicate the secondary executable files associated with the service or component.

The following is an example of the Service entry for the SMS service, SMS_ASYNC_RAS_SENDER.

```
SERVICE "SMS_ASYNC_RAS_SENDER"
BEGIN
    FLAGS = 3789
    MAIN "SENDER.DLL"
    SUBCOMPONENT "CONNRAS.DLL"
END
```

The following table lists the service flag bits.

Service	Flag	Description
INSTALL	0x00000001	Installs this component.
LOCALSYSACCT	0x00000002	If this is a service, installs it on the SMS logon server as a system account instead of the SMS Service Account.
STARTSERVICE	0x00000004	Starts this component if it is stopped.
SETREGISTRY	0x00000008	Configures the initial SMS registry values for this component.
EXE	0x00000010	Not currently used.
LITERALPATH	0x00000020	The file ID for this component is a full path to the executable file instead of an ID in the system map file.
PRIMARYSITE	0x00000040	Installs this component if the site is a primary site.
SECONDARYSITE	0x00000080	Installs this component if the site is a secondary site.
AUTOSTART	0x00000100	If this is a service, installs it to start during system startup.
SENDER	0x00000200	This component is a sender.
OPTIONALSVC	0x00000400	This component is optional at this site.
AS_THREAD	0x00000800	This component runs under the control of the SMS Executive.
DONTSTOPSVC	0x00001000	This service is not stopped or removed during a site shutdown or site removal.

Package

Defines how to install the SMS services on SMS logon servers and Windows NT-based clients. The Package section uses the BEGIN and END keywords. It also uses the FLAGS, MAIN, and SUBCOMPONENT keywords (see the preceding section for a description of how these keywords are used).

An example follows:

```
PACKAGE "SMS INVENTORY_AGENT_NT"
BEGIN
   FLAGS = 0
   MAIN "INVWIN32.EXE"
END
```

Directories

The remainder of the SYSTEM.MAP file consists of directories and files that must be created or installed on the site server. The directories and files are installed based on the microprocessor architecture platform, language, and software installable units specified in the section. For instance, the following section creates the PRIMSITE.SRV\AUDIT directory, and installs the files AUDIT.RUL and RUL2CFG.BAT in the directory:

```
DIRECTORY "PRIMSITE.SRV\AUDIT"
PLATFORM "" LANGUAGE "" SOURCE "COMMON\INTNL" FLAGS = 42
UNIT = "SCRIPTS"
BEGIN
   "AUDIT.RUL", SIZE(1, 1033292, 1033292), "AUDIT.RUL", "AUDIT.RU_",
   REMOTE=NO, COPYLISTS(), COMPRESS=NO, FLAGS = 1
   "RUL2CFG.BAT", SIZE(1, 991, 991), "RUL2CFG.BAT", "RUL2CFG.BA_",
   REMOTE=NO, COPYLISTS(), COMPRESS=NO, FLAGS = 1
END
```

Package and Audit Rule Files

Package rule files and audit rule files are both used by SMS to determine information about the software installed on clients. Package rule files are used when SMS performs software inventory on clients. Audit rule files are used when SMS runs a special Run Command On Workstations job on clients (the job runs the Audit program and uses the audit rules in the audit rule file). For more information about software inventory and audit, see the SMS version 1.2 *Concepts and Planning*.

Although the software inventory process differs from the auditing process, the package rule file and the audit rule file have the same format. To simplify terminology in this chapter, the term *package rule file* will generally be used to refer to both software inventory rule files and to audit package rule files.

A package rule file is a text file that contains rules for identifying software installed on SMS clients. A package rule file must be converted into a binary (*.CFG) file before SMS can use the package rule file. When packages are enabled for software inventory, the Maintenance Manager automatically converts the package rule file into CFG format. When you want to perform an audit, you must manually convert the package rule file to CFG format using the RUL2CFG program.

The package rule file is a list of software items called packages. For each package, there is a set of rules that are used to identify it. Each rule is the name of a file and, optionally, a set of attributes for that file.

The definition of a package begins with the package keyword, a package ID, and a package name:

package *packageID* "*packagename*"

packageID
> An integer that uniquely identifies the package within the package rule file. The *packageID* must be unique within the package rule file.

packagename
> A string (enclosed in quotation marks) that serves as a text label for the package. This string is used for the Package Name attribute when the package is reported to the SMS inventory.

This package identification is followed by a list of files that identifies the package. Each file must have a file name. Optionally, you can specify additional attributes (such as file size, file date, checksum, and so on) for each file.

The file keyword is followed by the file name and the optional file attributes:

file "*filename*" [*fileattributes*]

filename
> A string (enclosed in quotes) that specifies the name of the file. This can be an 8.3 file name or a long file name.

fileattributes
> Can be one or more attributes of the file. Each type of attribute begins with a keyword followed by the specific value (or values) for the attribute. Numerical values and offset values (such as BYTE, CHECKSUM, and so on) must be specified in decimal rather than hexadecimal. These values can be determined in the SMS Administrator when you set up the package for inventory.

> The following file attributes are possible:

BYTE
> An 8-bit value stored at a specific location in the file.

> **BYTE** *offset* *value*

> where *offset* is the data offset from the start of file (in bytes); and *value* is the value (in decimal notation) stored at the location specified by *offset*.

CHECKSUM

The sum of all values stored at a specific set of bytes.

CHECKSUM *offset length value*

where *offset* is the data offset at the beginning of the summed values (in bytes); *length* is the total number of bytes that are summed; and *value* is the summed value (in decimal notation) of all values stored in the specific range of bytes.

COLLECT (for use with Inventory Agent only)

A keyword that tells the Inventory Agent to collect the file and send it with the computer's inventory. This keyword has no affect on the Software Audit program.

CRC

The sum (and sequence) of all values stored at a specific set of bytes. Unlike CHECKSUM, CRC takes into account the sequence of the summed bytes. This makes it a more reliable identification of a file.

CRC *offset length value*

where *offset* is the data offset at the beginning of the summed values (in bytes); *length* is the total number of bytes that are summed; and *value* is the summed value (calculated with the CCITT-CRC algorithm and specified in decimal notation) of all the values stored in the specified range of bytes. SMS uses the CCITT-CRC standard to evaluate the CRC value. You must specify a CRC value computed with the CCITT-CRC algorithm.

DATE

The date of the file.

DATE *mm/dd/yy*

where *mm* is the decimal value for the month; *dd* is the decimal value for the day; and *yy* is the decimal value for the year. Single digit months and days must have a leading zero (for example, 01/03/95).

LONG

A 4-byte (32-bit) value stored at a specific location in the file.

LONG *offset value*

where *offset* is the data offset (in bytes); and *value* is the 32-bit value (in decimal notation) stored at the offset.

SIZE

The size of the file (in bytes).

SIZE *filesize*

where *filesize* is the size of the file in bytes.

STRING (TOKEN)

A string value stored at a specific location in the file. It appears as STRING in the user interface and as TOKEN in PACKAGE.RUL.

STRING *offset "string"*

where *offset* is the data offset in bytes; and *string* is the string value stored at the location starting at *offset*. The string value must be enclosed in quotation marks.

TIME

The time associated with the file.

TIME *hh:mm*

where *hh* is the decimal value (using the 24-hour clock) for hours; and *mm* is the decimal value for minutes. Single digit hours and minutes must have a leading zero (for example, 01:05). Midnight is written as 00:00.

WORD

A 2 byte (16-bit) value stored at a specific location in the file.

WORD *offset value*

where *offset* is the data offset from the start of file (in bytes); and *value* is the 16-bit value (in decimal notation) stored at the location specified by *offset*.

You can specify up to four STRING/TOKEN values per file. You can only specify one value for all other attributes.

Combining File Rules

The list of files for a package can be combined together using the AND and the OR operators. If no operator is specified between adjacent files, the AND operator is used. AND has precedence over OR.

An AND clause is true when both expressions connected by the AND are true. An OR clause is true when either (or both) of the expressions connected by the OR are true.

The Inventory Agent and Software Audit program search for the files connected in an AND clause in a single directory. Therefore, in order for an AND clause to evaluate to true, all files specified in the AND clause must be found in the same directory. For example, the following package rule specifies two files connected by an AND operator:

```
PACKAGE 1 "Configuration Files"
  FILE "CONFIG.SYS"
  AND
  FILE "SYSTEM.INI"
```

When SMS evaluates this rule, if the two files are not found, or they are found but they exist in different directories, then the rule is evaluated to false, and the package is not detected. The example package would be found if CONFIG.SYS and SYSTEM.INI existed in the same directory (for example, in C:\BACKUP).

For files connected by an OR operator, one or both must exist in a directory for the package to be detected. For example, if a package is defined as two files connected by an OR operator and the two files exist in the same directory, one instance of the package is detected:

```
PACKAGE 1 "Configuration Files"
  FILE "CONFIG.SYS"
  OR
  FILE "SYSTEM.INI"
```

In the preceding example, if CONFIG.SYS is detected in C:\BACKUP and SYSTEM.INI is detected in C:\WINDOWS, two instances of the example package are detected, because the file rule evaluates to true in both directories.

As another example, consider the following package rule:

```
PACKAGE 1 "Corporate Accounting Application"
  FILE "CORAPP.EXE"
  OR
  FILE "CORAPP.DLL"
  FILE "COR3D.DLL"
```

Because there is no operator specified between the files CORAPP.DLL and COR3D.DLL, SMS uses the AND operator between these files. The package rule is evaluated as follows:

1. First, SMS processes the AND clause. It looks for the files COR3D.DLL and CORAPP.DLL. If found in the same directory, this clause evaluates as true. If the files are not found, or they are found in different directories, then this clause is false.

2. Next, SMS processes the OR clause. If the AND clause was true, then the OR clause is also true. If the AND clause was false, then SMS looks for the file CORAPP.EXE. If it finds this file in any directory, the OR clause is true. If the AND clause was false and the file CORAPP.EXE is not found, then the OR clause is false.

Using Parentheses to Group File Rules

You can use parentheses to group files together as a single entity. Groups have higher precedence than the AND and OR operators. You can use parentheses to clarify how a package rule with a mix of AND and OR operators will be evaluated.

For example, consider the following package rule:

```
PACKAGE 1 "Good MS-DOS and Windows Configuration"
  FILE "CONFIG.SYS"
  AND
  FILE "SYSTEM.INI"
  OR
  FILE "VER.DLL"
```

This rule contains no groups, and so SMS evaluates the AND clause (CONFIG.SYS AND SYSTEM.INI) and then the OR clause (OR VER.DLL). The package is detected if CONFIG.SYS and SYSTEM.INI are found in the same directory or if VER.DLL is found in any directory.

However, if you add parentheses to the rule as follows:

```
PACKAGE 1 "Good MS-DOS and Windows Configuration"
  FILE "CONFIG.SYS"
  AND
  (
    FILE "SYSTEM.INI"
    OR
    FILE "VER.DLL"
  )
```

SMS evaluates the OR clause in parentheses before it evaluates the AND clause. The package is detected if CONFIG.SYS is found in a directory and either SYSTEM.INI or VER.DLL is found in that same directory.

Using File Attributes to Create Complex Rules

In the preceding examples, the rules used only the filename to identify packages. In order to identify files more certainly, you can specify additional file attributes in the package rule. These attributes were described earlier in this chapter. The allowable file attributes are:

- **BYTE** *offset value*
- **CHECKSUM** *offset length value*
- **CRC** *offset length value*
- **DATE** *mm/dd/yy*
- **LONG** *offset value*
- **SIZE** *filesize*
- **STRING** *offset "string"*
- **TIME** *hh:mm*
- **WORD** *offset value*

The following example uses the AND operator to detect a package if all three files (WINWOOD.EXE, WINWOOD.INI, and DIALOG.FON) are found on the client. It also requires that the WINWOOD.EXE file must have a *filesize* of 3483136 bytes, that the value of **BYTE** 10000 is 114, and that the **CHECKSUM** of the file (from byte 5000 to byte 5100) is 6851.

```
FILE winwood.exe  SIZE 3483136 BYTE 10000 114 CHECKSUM 5000 100 6851
AND
FILE winwood.ini
AND
FILE dialog.fon
```

Although this example includes only three files, and specifies file attributes for only one of the files, you can create rules which include many more files, and you can specify file attributes for all files in the package rule. For more package rule examples, look at some of the PDFs supplied with SMS version 1.2 (you can import the PDFs in the Packages window of the SMS Administrator). For more information about PDFs, see the following section.

Package Definition Files

A package definition file (PDF) is a text file that contains predefined Workstations, Sharing, and Inventory property settings for a package. When you create a new package, you can use the Import command from the Package Properties dialog box to define the properties for the package, using a PDF.

A PDF follows the standard *.INI file format. It is an ASCII text file containing keys (the key names are enclosed within brackets). Key names can be separated by spaces. Each key contains one or more entries, where each entry follows the format:

name = value1, value2, ...

Values are separated by a comma and at least one space.

A PDF has specific keys and entries that are used by the system to set the properties of a package. The following keys are allowed in a PDF file:

- [PDF] (required)
- [Package Definition] (required)
- [*SetupVariation* Setup]
- [Setup Package for Sharing]
- [Program Item Properties *Index*] (required for shared applications)
- [Setup Package for Inventory]
- [File *Index*] (required for inventory)

These keys are described in the following sections. A sample PDF file is included at the end of this section.

[PDF] (required)

Identifies the file as a PDF. This section contains a single entry:

Version (required)

The version of the PDF format used by the file.

Example:

```
Version = 1.0
```

[Package Definition] (required)

Defines the overall properties of the package.

Product (required)

The name of the product.

Example:

```
Product = Microsoft Excel
```

Version (required)

The version of the product.

Example:

```
Version = 4.0a
```

Comment

The comment used for the package's Comment setting. When the PDF is imported into SMS, this string is used as the Comment in the Package Properties dialog box.

Example:

```
Comment = version 4.0a for Windows
```

SetupVariations (required for setting up workstation packages)

A list of the setup variations supported by the package. Each setup variation name corresponds to the [*SetupVariation* Setup] key, described in the following section.

Example:

```
SetupVariations = Typical, Complete, Laptop, Automated
```

WorkstationAccess

The access permissions to the packages created with this PDF. You can assign either read or write permissions to the Users and the Guests groups. Thus, there are four permissions that you can assign:

UserRead

Permits users in the Users group to read and copy files, run programs, change directories within the shared directory, and read extended attributes of files.

GuestRead

Permits users in the Guests group to read and copy files, run programs, change directories within the shared directory, and read extended attributes of files.

UserWrite

Permits users in the Users group to write the contents and extended attributes of files.

GuestWrite

Permits users in the Guests group to write the contents and extended attributes of files.

To run a program file (that is, one with a .COM, .EXE, or .BAT extension), the user must have Read permission. The default is for both Users and Guests to have both Read and Write permissions.

Example:

```
WorkstationAccess = UserRead, UserWrite, GuestRead
```

Note The values for WorkstationAccess are case-sensitive; they must be specified exactly as shown in the preceding section.

[*SetupVariation* Setup]

For the setup variations specified in the SetupVariations entry in the [Package Definition] key (described in the preceding section), the PDF must have a key that defines each variation. For SMS, the setup variations specify the package commands that will be defined for the package's Workstations property. Typical setup variations for Microsoft applications include Typical, Complete, Laptop, and Automated setups.

CommandName (required)

The name used for this package command. When the PDF is imported into SMS, this string is used as the Command Name for this package command.

Example:

```
CommandName = Automated Minimum Installation
```

CommandLine (required)

The command line used for this package command. When the PDF is imported into SMS, this string is used as the Command Line for this package command. The command should be relative to the package directory.

Example:

```
CommandLine = setup.exe
```

SystemTask (required)

Specifies whether this package command can run in background mode on unattended computers running Windows NT. Specify TRUE if the command can be run as a system background task; FALSE if the command cannot be run as a system background task.

Example:

```
SystemTask=TRUE
```

Note If you wish to set SystemTask to TRUE, you must also set UserInputRequired (described in the following section) to FALSE. For both keys, the TRUE and FALSE values are case-sensitive and must be specified as all uppercase.

UserInputRequired (required)

Specifies whether this package command requires interaction with the user to complete the command. You can specify TRUE or FALSE.

Example:

```
UserInputRequired = TRUE
```

SynchronousSystemExitRequired

The meaning of this key depends upon the client platform on which the package command is running.

On Windows-based clients, this key is used to automate package commands that require a system restart (typically these package commands set up applications). When this key is set to TRUE, Package Command Manager allows the application launched by the package command to restart the computer. When set to FALSE, Package Command Manager will not permit the launched application to restart the computer. If this key is not specified, it defaults to FALSE.

On MS-DOS clients, this key is used to provide additional memory for the application launched by the package command. When this key is set to TRUE, Package Command Manager launches the application specified by the package command and then ends. This allows more memory for the package command, but it also means that Package Command Manager does not regain control after the package command application ends. When this key is set to FALSE (or not specified), Package Command Manager remains loaded in memory and regains control after the package command application ends.

Example:

```
SynchronousSystemExitRequired = FALSE
```

SupportedPlatforms (required)

Specifies the operating systems where the package can be installed and run. Each operating system name must be separated by a comma and a space. Supported platforms are MS-DOS, Windows 3.1, Windows95, Windows NT (x86), Windows NT (MIPS), Windows NT (Alpha), and Macintosh.

Note In previous versions of SMS, this key required a platform version for MS-DOS (for instance, MS-DOS 6.0) and for Windows NT (for instance, Windows NT 4.0 (x86)). In SMS version 1.2, the platform version is no longer required. PDFs that specify a version for these platforms will be accepted by SMS version 1.2, however the platform version will be discarded.

Example:

```
SupportedPlatforms = Windows 3.1, Windows95, Windows NT (Alpha),
Windows NT (MIPS), Windows NT (x86)
```

[Setup Package for Sharing]

Defines the Sharing properties of the package. Sharing properties are used for installing the package on servers and sharing it from those servers (Share Package On Server jobs).

ShareName (required)

The share name that you want to assign to the shared package when it is installed on a server.

Example:

```
ShareName = exc40ash
```

ShareAccess (required)

The access permissions to the package's share when the shared package is installed on a server. You can assign either read or write permissions to the Users and the Guests groups. Thus, there are four permissions that you can assign:

UserRead

Permits users in the Users group to read and copy files, run programs, change directories within the shared directory, and read extended attributes of files.

GuestRead

Permits users in the Guests group to read and copy files, run programs, change directories within the shared directory, and read extended attributes of files.

UserWrite

Permits users in the Users group to write the contents and extended attributes of files.

GuestWrite

Permits users in the Guests group to write the contents and extended attributes of files.

Example:

```
ShareAccess = UserRead, UserWrite, GuestRead, GuestWrite
```

Note The values for ShareAccess are case-sensitive; they must be specified exactly as shown in the preceding section.

[Program Item Properties *index*] (required for shared applications)

Contains keys that are used to specify the program item properties for SMS network applications contained in the package. Each program item will be defined in the package's Sharing property. The value for *index* is a unique integer that identifies the program item within the PDF. The *index* should start at 1 and increase by 1 for each additional program item.

Description (required)

The program item description displayed to the user when they run the SMS network application. When the PDF is imported into SMS, this entry is used as the description for the program item.

Example:

```
Description = Microsoft Excel
```

CommandLine (required)

The command used to start the SMS network application.

Example:

```
CommandLine = EXCEL.EXE
```

ConfigurationScript (required)

The configuration script file used to configure the SMS network application at clients. This value can be NULL. If an explicit path is not specified, the package source directory is the default path to the configuration script.

Example:

```
ConfigurationScript = exc40a0n.PCD
```

RegistryName (required)

The name of the key where the SMS network application's configuration information is stored in the Windows registry.

Example:

```
RegistryName = EXCEL4
```

DefaultINIFile (required)

The file that the SMS network application uses as a default initialization file. Specify the filename only, not a path to the file. The specified INI file must be in the same directory as the PDF file.

Example:

```
DefaultINIFile= EXCEL4.ini
```

RunMinimized (required)

Specifies whether the SMS network application should be minimized to an icon each time the user starts it by using the program item. You can specify TRUE or FALSE.

Example:

```
RunMinimized = TRUE
```

RunLocalCopyIfPresent (required)

Specifies whether the SMS APPSTART program should search for the file specified by CommandLine locally in the client's path. If APPSTART finds the file, it starts the local version; otherwise, it starts the network version. You can specify TRUE or FALSE.

Example:

```
RunLocalCopyIfPresent = TRUE
```

DriveMode (required)

Specifies how the SMS APPSTART program should connect to the server and shared directory where the SMS network application is located. You can specify one of three values:

UNC

APPSTART runs the SMS network application by using a UNC name. No drive letter is connected to the application's shared directory.

ANY_DRIVE_LETTER

APPSTART must connect to the application's shared directory by using a drive letter—but APPSTART can use any available drive letter on the client.

SPECIFIC_DRIVE_LETTER *DriveLetter*:

APPSTART must connect to the application's shared directory by using a specific drive letter. *DriveLetter* specifies the drive letter that APPSTART must use. The drive letter must be followed by a colon (:).

Note All DriveMode values are case-sensitive and must be specified as all uppercase.

Example:

```
DriveMode = SPECIFIC_DRIVE_LETTER W:
```

SupportedPlatforms (required)

Specifies the supported operating systems platforms on which the program item is to be made available. Separate the operating system names with commas. Supported platforms are MS-DOS, Windows 3.1, Windows95, Windows NT (x86), Windows NT (MIPS), Windows NT (Alpha), and Macintosh.

Note In previous versions of SMS, this key required a platform version for MS-DOS (for instance, MS-DOS 6.0) and for Windows NT (for instance, Windows NT 4.0 (x86)). In SMS version 1.2, the platform version is no longer required. PDFs that specify a version for these platforms will be accepted by SMS version 1.2, however the platform version will be discarded.

Example:

```
SupportedPlatforms = Windows 3.1, Windows95, MS-DOS, Macintosh
```

DisplayIconInProgGroup

Specifies whether an application icon is placed in a program group. This entry should be FALSE for utility applications, such as MSAPPS, that are to be distributed along with other SMS network applications.

Example:

```
DisplayIconInProgGroup=FALSE
```

SetupIcon

Specifies the file containing the icon that you want to use for the SMS network application. This must be a *.ICO file.

Example:

```
SetupIcon = exc40a01.ico
```

[Setup Package for Inventory]

Defines the Inventory properties for the package. The Inventory properties are used by the SMS system to maintain inventory on the package.

The SMS system identifies a package by searching for a set of files that you specify in the package's Inventory properties. For each file, you specify the attributes used to detect the file (such as file date, file size, CRC, and so on). If the Inventory Agent program detects files that satisfy the conditions set by the package's Inventory properties, the Inventory Agent reports that the package has been detected on the client.

Within the Inventory properties, you can also set an option that enables SMS to collect specified files from clients and store them on the site server.

InventoryThisPackage (required)

Specifies whether the package should be included in the SMS inventory. You can specify TRUE or FALSE.

Example:

```
InventoryThisPackage = TRUE
```

Detection Rule Part *index* (required)

Specifies the inventory rule used to identify the package. A package's inventory rule is the set of files used to identify the package. Using the AND and OR operators, you can specify the set of files required to detect the package. The Part *index* indicates the order in which the rules are evaluated. The *index* should start at 1 and increase by 1 for each part of the rule.

For the files specified in the rule (except Boolean operators and grouping operators), the PDF must have a [File *index*] key. (This key is described in the next section).

You combine the file specifications by using the following rules:

- Files are combined using AND and OR operators. AND has precedence over OR.

- Files can be grouped and ungrouped with parentheses. Files within a group are treated as a single entity. For example, the rule File1 AND (File2 OR File3) specifies that SMS detects the package when File1 is found and either File2 or File3 is found—that is, File1 = TRUE and (File2 OR File3) = TRUE. Groups have precedence over AND and OR.

Example:

```
Detection Rule Part 1 = File1
Detection Rule Part 2 = AND
Detection Rule Part 3 = File2
Detection Rule Part 4 = OR
Detection Rule Part 5 = (
Detection Rule Part 6 = File3
Detection Rule Part 7 = AND
Detection Rule Part 8 = File4
Detection Rule Part 9 = )
```

[File *Index*] (required for inventory)

For the files specified in the Detection Rule Part *index* entry in the [Setup Package for Inventory] key, the PDF must have a key that defines each file. Each file corresponds to a key that defines the attributes of the file. The value for *index* is a unique integer that identifies the file within the PDF and the inventory rule. The *index* should start at 1 and increase by 1 for each additional file.

The Filename is required. All other attributes are optional.

Filename (required)

The name of the file.

Example:

```
Filename = EXCEL.EXE
```

Collect

Specifies whether the SMS system should collect a copy of this file and store it on the site server. You can specify TRUE or FALSE.

Example:

```
Collect = FALSE
```

BYTE

Specifies a value stored at a specific location in the file. This attribute requires two entries (separated by a comma and a space):

- *Location* is the data offset in bytes.

- *Value* is the value stored at the offset.

By default, the entries are decimal. To specify a hexadecimal number, start the hexadecimal number with 0x.

Example:

```
BYTE = 20000, 216
```

Checksum

Detects the sum of all values stored at a specific set of bytes and compares the sum to a specified value. This attribute requires three entries (separated by a comma and a space):

- *Start location* is the data offset where the summed values begin (in bytes).

- *Length* is the total number of bytes that are summed.

- *Checksum value* is the value checked against the summed values.

By default, the entries are decimal. To specify a hexadecimal number, start the hexadecimal number with 0x.

Example:

```
Checksum = 10000, 300, 32444
```

CRC

Detects the sum of all values stored at a specific set of bytes and compares the sum to a specified value. Unlike Checksum, CRC takes into account the sequence of the summed bytes. This makes it a more reliable identification of a file.

This attribute requires three entries (separated by a comma and a space):

- *Start location* is the data offset where the summed values begin (in bytes).
- *Length* is the total number of bytes that are summed.
- *Checksum value* is the value checked against the summed values.

SMS uses the CCITT-CRC standard to evaluate CRC. You must specify a CRC value computed with the CCITT-CRC algorithm.

By default, the entries are decimal. To specify a hexadecimal number, start the hexadecimal number with 0x.

Example:

```
CRC = 5000, 300, 38707
```

Date

The date of the file in decimal format: *mm, dd, yy*. The entries must be separated by a comma and a space.

Example:

```
Date = 9, 2, 93
```

Size

The size of the file (in bytes).

Example:

```
Size = 2766592
```

Time

The time of the file (using the 24-hour clock) in hours and minutes (*hh, mm*). The entries must be separated by a comma and a space.

Example:

```
Time = 14, 18
```

LONG

An unsigned LONG value. This attribute requires two entries (separated by a comma and a space):

- *Location* is the data offset in bytes.
- *Value* is the value stored at the offset.

Example:

```
LONG = 30000, 1346373702
```

WORD

A WORD value. This attribute requires two entries (separated by a comma and a space):

- *Location* is the data offset in bytes.
- *Value* is the value stored at the offset.

Example:

```
WORD = 40001, 15488
```

Token # (1–4)

A string value. This attribute requires two entries (separated by a comma and a space):

- *Location* is the data offset in bytes.
- *Value* is the string value stored at the offset. The string value must be enclosed by quotation marks. You can define up to four separate token entries.

Example:

```
Token 1 = 710, "WIN"
Token 2 = 714, "EXCEL"
```

For information about using PDFs to distribute software, see Chapter 5, "Working with Systems Management Server."

Sample Package Definition File

The following text is from the PDF file for Microsoft Excel for Windows 95 (EXC95.PDF file):

```
[PDF]
Version=1.0

[Package Definition]
Product=Microsoft Excel 95
Version=7.0
Comment=Microsoft Excel 95
SetupVariations=Compact, Typical, Complete, Custom, Uninstall
WorkstationAccess = UserRead, UserWrite, GuestRead

[Compact Setup]
CommandLine=setup.exe /Q1 /B2
CommandName=Compact
UserInputRequired=FALSE
SupportedPlatforms=Windows95, Windows NT (x86)
SystemTask=FALSE

[Typical Setup]
CommandLine=setup.exe /Q1 /B1
CommandName=Typical
UserInputRequired=FALSE
SupportedPlatforms=Windows95, Windows NT (x86)
SystemTask=FALSE

[Complete Setup]
CommandLine=setup.exe /Q1 /B3
CommandName=Complete
UserInputRequired=FALSE
SupportedPlatforms=Windows95, Windows NT (x86)
SystemTask=FALSE

[Custom Setup]
CommandLine=setup.exe
CommandName=Custom
UserInputRequired=TRUE
SupportedPlatforms=Windows95, Windows NT (x86)
SystemTask=FALSE
```

```
[Uninstall Setup]
CommandLine=setup.exe /Q1 /U
CommandName=Uninstall
UserInputRequired=TRUE
SupportedPlatforms=Windows95, Windows NT (x86)
SystemTask=FALSE

[Setup Package for Sharing]
ShareName=exc95sh
ShareAccess=UserRead, GuestRead

[Program Item Properties 1]
CommandLine=excel.exe
Description=Microsoft Excel 95 Install
ConfigurationScript=smsacm32.exe exc95+install setup.stf "SETUP.EXE /B4
/Q1" "SETUP.EXE /U /Q1"
RegistryName=exc95+install
DefaultINIFile=
RunMinimized=FALSE
RunLocalCopyIfPresent=FALSE
DriveMode=UNC
SupportedPlatforms=Windows95
SetupIcon=EXC9501.ICO
DisplayIconInProgGroup=TRUE

[Setup Package for Inventory]
InventoryThisPackage=TRUE
Detection Rule Part 1=File 1
; These lines are comments
; Detection Rule Part 2=AND
; Detection Rule Part 3=File 2

[File 1]
FILE=EXCEL.EXE
COLLECT=FALSE
Checksum=
DATE=7,20,95
SIZE=4828160
TIME=00, 00
```

Management Information Format Files

The management information format (MIF) is a standard format for describing desktop computer components (hardware and software). The MIF was defined by the Desktop Management Task Force (DMTF). For more information about the MIF, see the Desktop Management Interface Specification version 4.5 (DMI45.DOC) provided on the *Microsoft BackOffice Resource Kit* compact disc.

A MIF file is a text file that uses the MIF format to describe computer components. SMS uses six types of MIF files to provide information to the SMS database:

- Personal Computer MIF files (*.MIF)
- SMSEvent MIF files (*.EMF)
- UserGroup MIF files (*.UMF)
- JobDetails MIF files (*.JMF)
- PackageLocation MIF files (*.PMF)
- Custom architecture MIF files (*.MIF)

Note In previous versions of SMS, all MIF files were named with the .MIF file extension. If you have any computers running a previous version of SMS, those computers will continue to report all MIF files with the .MIF file extension.

Using MIF files, you can add objects with custom architectures to the inventory (such as printers and routers), add a new object to an existing architecture, and add groups (such as device driver information, hardware peripherals, and monitors) to computers already existing in the SMS database.

Basic MIF File Keywords

In an SMS site database, the inventory has a hierarchical structure. An architecture is the highest level in the SMS hierarchy, defining the structure for a set of objects. Each object is composed of one or more groups. Each group contains one or more attributes.

This hierarchy is reflected in the MIF file format. The following keywords are used in MIF files to describe computer components:

Architecture

A standard structure for describing a set of related objects in SMS. An architecture is defined by the Architecture group, which specifies a unique architecture name. For example, the Personal Computer architecture has a structure for describing Intel x86, Alpha, MIPS, and Macintosh-based computers.

Object

A specific item within a specific architecture. For example, a specific Macintosh computer (for example, Mac1) can be an object in the Personal Computer architecture. In a MIF file, an object is equivalent to a component block.

For a specific object, the attributes of its Identification group combine to form a unique identifier for the object. The Identification group for Personal Computer objects contains six attributes that are used to uniquely identify a computer.

Group

A structure for defining the distinct parts of an object. A group combines a set of attributes into a single, identifiable entity. For example, Processor, Network, and Operating System are some of the groups that exist on a computer with the Personal Computer architecture.

A group is identified by its class and keyed attributes. For a group class, each attribute's data type and size is set when that attribute is first reported to the SMS database.

In the Personal Computer architecture, groups can be used to store the properties of a hardware device (such a COM port or mouse), a piece of software (such as the operating system or a defined software package), or any logical entity (such as asset or employee information through custom MIF files).

Attribute

A property of a group. For example, a Disk group on a computer has attributes such as Drive Index, Storage Type, Free Storage, and so on. Each attribute is assigned a value. For example, a Disk Index attribute is assigned a value such as A, B, C, and so on.

Object Syntax

An SMS object is a specific item that uses a specific architecture. For example, the SMS system uses the Personal Computer architecture to inventory computers as objects. An object contains groups. For SMS, an object must have an Identification group and an Architecture group.

An object definition within a MIF file starts with the line Start Component and ends with the line End Component. Within an object definition, you should have the following entry:

Name

A string (enclosed by quotation marks) that labels the object.

Example of an object definition:

```
Start Component
    Name = "EMPLOYEE"
    Start Group
        Name = "Architecture"
        ID = 1
        Class = "MICROSOFT|ARCHITECTURE|1.0"
        Start Attribute
            Name = "ArchitectureName"
            ID = 1
            Access = READ-ONLY
            Storage = SPECIFIC
            Type = String(10)
            Value = "Employee"
        End Attribute
    End Group
    Start Group
        Name = "Identification"
        ID = 2
        Class = "MICROSOFT|IDENTIFICATION|1.0"
        Start Attribute
            Name = "Employee Name"
            ID = 1
            Access = READ-ONLY
            Storage = SPECIFIC
            Type = String(32)
            Value = "Steven Andrew"
        End Attribute
    End Group
End Component
```

Group Syntax

A group is a set of one or more attributes. When the inventory for an object is displayed in the object's Properties window, all the groups for the object are displayed in the left pane. The attributes for the selected group are displayed in the right pane.

Objects (called Components in the DMTF structure) for every architecture must have an Identification group and an Architecture group.

A group starts with the line Start Group and ends with the line End Group. Within the group, specify the following entries:

Name
> A string (enclosed by quotation marks) that labels the group. When the group is displayed in the Properties window, this string is used to label the group in the left pane.

ID
> A number that identifies the group. The ID must be unique for each group within the object. The ID is an integer value. Group IDs must be 1 or greater.

Key
> Applies only to multiple-instance groups. For example, an object such as a disk drive can have multiple instances on a computer. One or more keys are used to differentiate the instances. For example, the Disk Drive group has a key defined for the Drive Index attribute. The Key entry specifies one or more IDs for the attributes used to uniquely identify an instance of a group. If you have multiple keys, you must separate them with commas. If a group can have only a single instance, then no key should be defined.

Class
> A required string describing the source of the group definition.

A group also contains one or more attributes.

Example of a group:

```
Start Group
    Name = "Employee Name"
    ID = 1
    Class = MICROSOFT|EMPLOYEE NAME|1.0
    Start Attribute
        Name = "Last Name"
        ID = 1
        Access = READ-ONLY
        Storage = SPECIFIC
        Type = String(32)
        Value = "Smith"
    End Attribute
```

```
    Start Attribute
        Name = "First Name"
        ID = 2
        Access = READ-ONLY
        Storage = SPECIFIC
        Type = String(32)
        Value = "John"
    End Attribute
End Group
```

Identification Group Syntax

Objects for every architecture must have an Identification group. The Identification group can have any number of attributes. However, you should ensure that all attributes are included in all objects that are part of a single custom architecture.

```
Start Group
    Name = "Identification"
    ID = 1
    Class = "MICROSOFT|IDENTIFICATION|1.0"
    Start Attribute
        Name = "Employee Name"
        ID = 1
        Access = READ-ONLY
        Storage = SPECIFIC
        Type = String(32)
        Value = "Mitch Duncan"
    End Attribute
End Group
```

Architecture Group Syntax

Objects for every architecture must also have an Architecture group. The Architecture group contains one attribute. The value of the ArchitectureName attribute should be the label you want to display for the architecture in the SMS Administrator. For example, when you view an object with a custom architecture named EMPLOYEE, the ArchitectureName attribute value EMPLOYEE is displayed in the Properties window title bar.

```
Start Group
    Name = "Architecture"
    ID = 1
    Class = "MICROSOFT|ARCHITECTURE|1.0"
```

```
        Start Attribute
            Name = "ArchitectureName"
            ID = 0
            Access = READ-ONLY
            Storage = SPECIFIC
            Type = String(10)
            Value = "Employee"
        End Attribute
End Group
```

Attribute Syntax

When the inventory for an object is displayed in the object's Properties window, all the groups for the object are displayed in the left pane. The attributes for the selected group are displayed in the right pane.

An attribute starts with the line Start Attribute and ends with the line End Attribute. Within the attribute, you should have the following entries:

Name

A string (enclosed by quotation marks) that labels the attribute. When the attribute is displayed in the Properties window, this string is used to label the attribute in the right pane.

ID

A number that identifies the attribute. The ID must be unique for each attribute within the group. The ID is an integer value.

Access

Determines the access type of the table where the attribute will be stored. Values can be READ-ONLY, READ-WRITE and WRITE-ONLY. The Access statement is optional and defaults to READ-ONLY.

Storage

Assists management applications to optimize storage requirements. Values can be common or specific. Common attributes are for properties that are likely to be common among many on most computers (for example, the processor name should be a common attribute). Specific attributes are for properties that are likely to have unique values on most computers (for example, the amount of free disk space should be a specific attribute). The Storage statement is optional.

Type

The data type used to store the value of the attribute. There are two data types. Counter is an integer. String is a character string. For strings you must specify the maximum length for the string.

The SQL Server database has a limit of 255 characters for any attribute value. Any string longer than 255 characters will be truncated. In addition, any values longer than the originally defined length will be silently truncated. For example, if attribute Employee Name is defined as string(40), SMS will add only the first 40 characters for an Employee Name value that is longer than 40 characters.

The SMS system uses the first definition of type. For example, if you first defined Employee Name as string(40), the SMS system will always use that type. You cannot change the Type after you have first defined it.

Value

The value assigned to the attribute. The value must be in the form specified by Type. Strings must be enclosed within quotation marks. Counters must be decimal integers. The Value statement is optional.

Example of an attribute definition:

```
Start Attribute
    Name = "Hours Worked"
    ID = 1
    Access = READ-ONLY
    Storage = SPECIFIC
    Type = Counter
    Value = 500
End Attribute
```

Differences Between SMS and the DMI 4.5 MIF Specification

In general, the SMS system can use any MIF file that complies with version 4.5 of the Desktop Management Interface (DMI) specification. However, SMS treats some aspects of the MIF syntax in a way that is unique to SMS. In addition, although the full DMI 4.5 syntax is accepted by the SMS MIF parser, some fields are not used. The following sections outline the differences between SMS and DMI MIF files:

ComponentID group is supported but not enforced.

DMI 4.5 requires this group; however, the SMS MIF parser does not enforce this requirement. The ComponentID group is checked for correct syntax only. If the group does not exist in the MIF file, the parser will not report an error.

Some data types are simplified or merged.

DMI 4.5 has numerous data types: five types of integers, three types of strings, and one date type. SMS handles these data types in the following manner:

- All integer types (int, integer, int64, integer64, gauge, counter, and counter64) are treated as signed 32-bit values. Therefore, values exceeding 32 bits will not be correctly evaluated. Likewise, 32-bit unsigned values above 0x7FFFFFFF will be variously interpreted as unsigned 32-bit values or signed 32-bit values, depending on the context. However, the MIF parser will forward these values to other components as signed 32-bit integers.

- All string types (displaystring, string, octetstring) are treated as the same type for database purposes. Because SQL Server places a limit of 255 characters on strings, any strings longer than 255 characters in the MIF file will be truncated. However, there is no string length limitation in the syntax itself for attribute values. Strings should not exceed 255 characters in length, and they should not contain embedded NULL characters via an escape sequence.

- Enumeration types are evaluated as the symbolic string and not as the integral value represented by the enumeration string. The enumeration string is preserved as a database item. Enumeration types take on the string type when the MIF file has been parsed and evaluated. Enumeration types may be specified by using either the integer symbol or the enumeration string itself in all contexts where an attribute value is required.

Unicode MIF files are detected but not supported.

DMI 4.5 allows Unicode MIF files. The SMS Inventory Processor will not process a Unicode MIF file, and will report an error. The MIFCHECK utility will report that Unicode MIF files are not supported.

The Language statement is parsed but not used.

DMI 4.5 allows a Language statement that describes the language of the MIF file. SMS parses the Language statement but does not use it for any purpose.

PRAGMA is a keyword for SMS.

DMI 4.5 does not specify PRAGMA as a keyword. SMS uses the PRAGMA keyword to send commands between components. The PRAGMA statement can be used in a MIF group definition. The PRAGMA statement specifies a string that contains a command. The PRAGMA string is case-insensitive. If no PRAGMA is specified, the command is **Add** by default.

SMS supports three pragma types:

- Pragma **SMS:Add** adds the group to the computer's inventory in the database.

- Pragma **SMS:Update** updates the group in the database with the information in the Delta-MIF file.

- Pragma **SMS:Delete** removes the group from the computer's inventory in the database. Deleting the Identification group removes all records for the computer from the database.

Description statements are not used in SMS.

With DMI 4.5, you can use a Description statement to describe a component, group, or attribute. SMS parses Description statements but does not use them for any purpose.

The class string is converted to uppercase but not checked for internal format.

The class string is converted to uppercase, but not checked for internal format, because this is not a strict requirement in the specification. The conversion to uppercase is done to force all subsequent users of the CLASS string to treat it in a case-insensitive manner. Rather than relying on other components to do this, the parser converts the string to uppercase.

Path definitions are parsed but not used.

With DMI 4.5, you can use a Path statement to locate component instrumentation files. SMS parses Path statements but does not use them for any purpose.

Attributes that use Instrumentation Symbolic Names are parsed but not used.

With DMI 4.5, you can use a Path statement to specify Instrumentation Symbolic Names to specify paths to libraries that contain the actual value of an attribute. SMS parses attributes that use Instrumentation Symbolic Names but does not use them for any purpose.

The Unsupported keyword forces an attribute to be ignored in the SMS system.

With DMI 4.5, you can specify the keyword Unsupported to tell the DMI service layer that an attribute is not supported by a component.

For SMS, an Unsupported keyword applied to an attribute value causes that attribute to be specially marked. The MIF parser will retain the Unsupported tag; however, the Inventory Processor will ignore such attributes, treating them as though they were not present in the MIF file.

The Access statement is parsed but not used.

DMI 4.5 lets you use an Access statement to specify the access to an attribute. SMS parses Access statements but does not use them for any purpose. The Access statements have meaning only to the DMI service layer. However, the restrictions in the DMI specification on the correct or incorrect placement of these values with regard to enumerated types or key values are still enforced.

There are several restrictions on the Date data type.

The Date data type has the following restrictions:

- The value for an attribute with the Date data type must be represented using the full 25 octets required for the Date data type. You should pad values with zeroes if necessary (for example, the month of May should be represented as 05, not 5). If a date field has no value, you should place zeroes in that field.

- The microsecond field is ignored. SMS will store dates only to the resolution of one second. However, you must still specify zeros in the microsecond field.

- The UTC offset is parsed and available for use by SMS components, but currently no SMS components use the UTC offset information.

- An attribute cannot contain a date before 1980 or after 2030. Date attributes outside of this range will be considered errors by the SMS MIF parser.

- The asterisk character (*) in a date field is replaced with the value for the current date in the corresponding field on the computer where the MIF parser is running.

  With DMI 4.5, you can use asterisks to avoid specifying a part of a date. SMS requires that a date value be a complete date value because SQL Server cannot store partial date values. An attribute that contains all asterisks will be considered a NULL or blank date in the SMS database.

  For example, if the current date is November 11, 1995, the value 1995**01130000.000000+000 would be processed as 1:00 P.M., November 1, 1995 (** is replaced by 11, the current month).

- For non-English versions of SMS, the MIF syntax and keywords must be in English, but the string data can be in the localized language of the client.

For the String data type, you should use escape characters for characters outside the standard ANSI range (32 through 127).

Literal (non-escape) characters embedded in quoted strings outside of the range 32 to 127 will be parsed and passed on to the rest of the system. These values may have different appearances, depending upon the active display font. Strictly speaking, for string types, you should restrict the characters to the ISO 8859-1 character set. However, the parser does not currently enforce this particular character set.

All escape characters are fully interpreted as the correct 8-bit value. You should be careful when using escape characters. For example, a NULL in the middle of a string "abc\0abc" causes SMS to interpret the string as having a length of only three characters. Although the parser supports a stream of bytes by this mechanism, SMS truncates the string when it detects an escape NULL.

Also note that how the escape character is stored in the SMS database depends on the character set used by the SQL Server containing the database. How the escape character is displayed depends on the code page used by the computer running the SMS Administrator.

For the String data type, you should explicitly declare the string length, which must be 255 characters or less.

DMI 4.5 does not require you to specify the string length of an attribute with a String data type, and it does not impose limits on the string length. However, for SMS you should explicitly declare the length of all String data types, and you should limit the string length to 255 characters or less.

Because of the 255-character limit for SQL Server, the Inventory Processor does not support string lengths longer than 255 characters. Any string that is longer than 255 characters will be truncated to the first 255 characters. The SMS MIF parser will not report an error if the declared string length exceeds 255 characters.

If an attribute with a String data type does not have a declared string length, SMS will use the string length of the value that is specified for the first occurrence of the attribute. This string length will be used as the declared string length of the attribute. Any attributes of the same type will use the declared string length as the string length of the attribute.

For Groups and Tables, the SMS MIF parser does not enforce the uniqueness of key attributes.

DMI 4.5 requires that the key attributes be unique. You should follow the DMI recommendations. If a key attribute is not unique, SMS will store only the last instance of the duplicated key attribute.

Checking MIF Files

You can check the syntax of a MIF file using the MIFCHECK utility. The MIFCHECK utility runs the same MIF parser used by the SMS components. Therefore, any MIF file accepted by MIFCHECK will also be accepted by the SMS system. MIFCHECK verifies that the specified MIF files adhere to the syntax of the DMI Specification version 4.5 with the exceptions noted in the preceding section.

The MIFCHECK utility is provided on the *Microsoft BackOffice Resource Kit* compact disc. See the SMSTOOLS.HLP file on the compact disc for more information.

Predefined Architecture MIF Files

There are six architectures predefined in the SMS database. These architectures are:

- Personal Computer
- SMSEvent
- UserGroups
- JobDetails
- PackageLocation
- SNMP Traps

You can use MIF files to add information about five of these six architectures to the SMS database (you cannot use MIF files to add information about SNMP traps). These MIF files can vary in size, but in general they are too large to include examples for all types in this manual. You can view samples of each of these MIF files on an SMS site server in the SITE.SRV\DELTAMIF.COL\PROCESS directory.

Package Command Status MIF File

When Package Command Manager runs a package command on an SMS client, the package command can write a detailed status MIF file to the Windows directory. This status MIF file is called a package command status MIF file. This file is processed by the Despooler and is used to create a job status MIF file (*.JMF). For more information about how these files are processed, see "How Package Command Status MIF Files Are Processed" in Chapter 3.

This is a template for a package command status MIF file. Items in italics are variables that must be replaced.

```
START COMPONENT
  NAME = "WORKSTATION"
  START GROUP
    NAME = "ComponentID"
    ID = 1
    CLASS = "DMTF|ComponentID|1.0"
    START ATTRIBUTE
      NAME = "Manufacturer"
      ID = 1
      ACCESS = READ-ONLY
      STORAGE = SPECIFIC
      TYPE = STRING (string length up to 255)
      VALUE = "Manufacturer"
```

```
            END ATTRIBUTE
            START ATTRIBUTE
              NAME = "Product"
              ID = 2
              ACCESS = READ-ONLY
              STORAGE = SPECIFIC
              TYPE = STRING(string length up to 255)
              VALUE = "Product"
            END ATTRIBUTE
            START ATTRIBUTE
              NAME = "Version"
              ID = 3
              ACCESS = READ-ONLY
              STORAGE = SPECIFIC
              TYPE = STRING(string length up to 255)
              VALUE = "Version"
            END ATTRIBUTE
            START ATTRIBUTE
              NAME = "Serial Number"
              ID = 4
              ACCESS = READ-ONLY
              STORAGE = SPECIFIC
              TYPE = STRING(string length up to 255)
              VALUE = "Serial Number"
            END ATTRIBUTE
            START ATTRIBUTE
              NAME = "Installation"
              ID = 5
              ACCESS = READ-ONLY
              STORAGE = SPECIFIC
              TYPE = STRING(string length up to 255)
              VALUE = "Date Time"
            END ATTRIBUTE
          END GROUP
          START GROUP
            NAME = "InstallStatus"
            ID = 2
            CLASS = "MICROSOFT|JOBSTATUS|1.0"
            START ATTRIBUTE
              NAME = "Status"
              ID = 1
              ACCESS = READ-ONLY
              STORAGE = SPECIFIC
              TYPE = STRING(string length up to 255)
              VALUE = "Success" or "Failed"
            END ATTRIBUTE
```

```
      START ATTRIBUTE
        NAME = "Description"
        ID = 2
        ACCESS = READ-ONLY
        STORAGE = SPECIFIC
        TYPE = STRING(string length up to 255)
        VALUE = "Error Message"
      END ATTRIBUTE
    END GROUP
END COMPONENT
```

Custom Architecture MIF Files

When you add a new type of object to the SMS database, the MIF file containing the object's inventory must have an Architecture group and an Identification group. This type of MIF file is called an IDMIF.

When you add a new group to an existing object, the MIF file containing the group(s) must not have an Architecture group or an Identification group. This type of MIF file is called a NOIDMIF.

When creating a MIF file to add or update an object with a custom architecture, observe the following rules:

- The full definition for the object starts with the keyword Start Component and ends with End Component. You should define only one object (component) per MIF file.

- The object definition begins with the Name entry for the object.

- The Identification and Architecture groups must be included in the MIF file, using the structure you defined for the architecture.

- The Class value for the Identification group should be:

  `MICROSOFT|IDENTIFICATION|1.0.`

- The Class value for the Architecture group should be:

  `MICROSOFT|ARCHITECTURE|1.0.`

- If you want the object to appear in the Sites window of the SMS Administrator, you must include the Name, Site, Domain, SystemRole, and SystemType attributes in the Identification group; and the values for the Site and Domain attributes must be those of sites and SMS domains existing in the SMS database. If a custom architecture does not have these attributes defined, its objects are not displayed in the Sites window; you must display these objects by using a query.

- The group and attribute ID values must be 1 or greater.
- The attributes for an object must be specified in groups that adhere to the structure you defined for the architecture.

Important When updating inventory information for an object already existing in the SMS database, make sure to specify values for all of the attributes defined in the previous MIF file for that object; otherwise the values for those attributes will be set to NULL.

Sample Custom Architecture MIF File

The following MIF file adds an object with a custom architecture called "Employee" to the SMS database. The group types are Identification, Architecture, Employee Status, Location, and Position.

```
Start Component
    Name = "EMPLOYEE"
    Start Group
        Name = "Identification"
        ID = 1
        Class = "MICROSOFT|IDENTIFICATION|1.0"
        Start Attribute
            Name = "Site"
            ID = 1
            Access = READ-ONLY
            Storage = COMMON
            Type = String(3)
            Value = "PIT"
        End Attribute
        Start Attribute
            Name = "Domain"
            ID = 2
            Access = READ-ONLY
            Storage = COMMON
            Type = String(15)
            Value = "SHUPPDOM"
        End Attribute
        Start Attribute
            Name = "SystemType"
            ID = 3
            Access = READ-ONLY
            Storage = COMMON
            Type = String(50)
            Value = "Person"
        End Attribute
```

```
          Start Attribute
              Name = "SystemRole"
              ID = 4
              Access = READ-ONLY
              Storage = COMMON
              Type = String(50)
              Value = "Writer"
          End Attribute
          Start Attribute
              Name = "Name"
              ID = 5
              Access = READ-ONLY
              Storage = SPECIFIC
              Type = String(64)
              Value = "Ben Cole"
          End Attribute
          Start Attribute
              Name = "Project"
              ID = 6
              Access = READ-ONLY
              Storage = COMMON
              Type = String(32)
              Value = "SMS"
          End Attribute
          Start Attribute
              Name = "Company"
              ID = 7
              Access = READ-ONLY
              Storage = COMMON
              Type = String(32)
              Value = "Siblings Inc"
          End Attribute
      End Group
      Start Group
          Name = "Architecture"
          ID = 2
          Class = "MICROSOFT|ARCHITECTURE|1.0"
```

```
            Start Attribute
                Name = "ArchitectureName"
                ID = 1
                Access = READ-ONLY
                Storage = SPECIFIC
                Type = String(10)
                Value = "Employee"
            End Attribute
    End Group
    Start Group
        Name = "Employee Status"
        ID = 3
        Class = "MICROSOFT|EMPLOYEE STATUS|1.0"
        Start Attribute
            Name = "Hours Worked"
            ID = 1
            Access = READ-ONLY
            Storage = SPECIFIC
            Type = Counter
            Value = 500
        End Attribute
        Start Attribute
            Name = "Done?"
            ID = 2
            Access = READ-ONLY
            Storage = COMMON
            Type = String(40)
            Value = "No"
        End Attribute
    End Group
    Start Group
        Name = "Location"
        ID = 4
        Class = "MICROSOFT|LOCATION|1.0"
        Start Attribute
            Name = "Building"
            ID = 1
            Access = READ-ONLY
            Storage = COMMON
            Type = String(40)
            Value = "1"
        End Attribute
```

```
                    Start Attribute
                        Name = "Office Number"
                        ID = 2
                        Access = READ-ONLY
                        Storage = SPECIFIC
                        Type = String(40)
                        Value = "222"
                    End Attribute
                    Start Attribute
                        Name = "Phone"
                        ID = 3
                        Access = READ-ONLY
                        Storage = SPECIFIC
                        Type = String(40)
                        Value = "M"
                    End Attribute
                End Group
                Start Group
                    Name = "Position"
                    ID = 5
                    Class = "MICROSOFT|POSITION|1.0"
                    Start Attribute
                        Name = "Title"
                        ID = 1
                        Access = READ-ONLY
                        Storage = COMMON
                        Type = String(40)
                        Value = "Technical Writer"
                    End Attribute
                    Start Attribute
                        Name = "Level"
                        ID = 2
                        Access = READ-ONLY
                        Storage = COMMON
                        Type = Integer
                        Value = 2
                    End Attribute
                End Group
            End Group
        End Component
```

SNMP Export Files

The SMS Event to Trap Translator allows you to export trap configurations that you have defined in the SMS Administrator. You can export definitions in two formats: the configuration tool (CNF) format, and the trap text (TXT) format. The CNF format is used to export configurations that can be used with the Event Configuration tool to configure the Event to Trap Translator on computers running Windows NT. The TXT format is used to export configurations that can then be imported into other SNMP systems.

These file formats are described in the following sections.

SNMP Configuration Tool Format Files

The configuration tool included with SMS is used to modify the configuration of the Event to Trap Translator through an SMS job. It allows the user to provide a data file that creates, deletes, and modifies the configuration of translated events. The tool can also be used to modify trap destinations and communities.

The tool generates an SMS status MIF file after it runs to indicate the overall status of the operation. It also generates a text log file with detailed information on which statements succeeded or failed. If any particular line results in an error, an error is written to a log file and processing continues with the next line in the file.

This tool is called EVENTCM*x*.EXE, where *x* is I for Intel, A for Alpha, and M for MIPS. This tool is located in the MSTEST directory on all SMS logon servers.

The syntax for adding or deleting events using the configuration tool format is:

#pragma {add | delete} *eventlog eventsource eventID* **[count=#] [time=#]**

add
Adds the specified event to the list of events to be translated to traps. If there are any errors in the **add** parameters, the event is not added and an error is returned. If the specified event and event source are already configured, then the count and time values are modified.

delete
Deletes the specified event from the translation list. If the event specified is not in the configuration, an error is returned.

eventlog
The Windows NT event log that contains the event. There are three possible values for this entry: **System**, **Application**, and **Security**.

eventsource
> The source specified in the Windows NT event log. If the event source is more than one word, it should be enclosed in quotation marks.

eventID
> The 32-bit event identification number. This is partially based on the 16-bit event number specified in the Windows NT event log.

count
> The number of times that the event must occur before generating a trap. For example, you can specify that the event must occur 5 times before it is translated.

time
> The time period for the count. For instance, you can specify that the event must occur 5 times in an hour to be translated.

The syntax for modifying SNMP trap destinations is:

#pragma {add_trap_dest | delete_trap_dest} *community address*

add_trap_dest
> Adds the specified address to the list of trap destinations for the specified community. If the community does not exist, it is created and the address is added. If the specified address already exists in the specified community, the statement is ignored.

delete_trap_dest
> Deletes the specified address from the specified community. If the community does not exist or the address is not in the community, an error is written to the log.

community
> The group of computers to which the pragma should be applied.

address
> The trap destination TCP/IP address.

A semicolon in the first column of any line indicates a comment line. A sample CNF file follows:

```
; this is a sample CNF file
;
; the next line configures Rdr event 8003
#pragma Add System "Rdr" 3221227472 1 0
;
; the next line sets up the trap destination address
#pragma Add_Trap_Dest public 198.255.255.255
; end of file
```

Trap Text Format Files

The trap text format is designed to allow a user at an SNMP console to import the configuration of traps into their SNMP console. The format is a comma separated list of the information about the defined traps. The fields in the trap text format are as follows:

Enterprise OID (enterprise object identifier)

A series of numbers that uniquely identifies the trap source.

Source Name

The name of the event source, specified in quotes.

6

A literal number six, indicating that the trap is a specific trap.

Specific ID

The 32-bit specific trap identification number.

Number of VARBinds (variable bindings)

The number of VARBinds specified by the trap. VARBinds are lists of variable elements describing the trap. All traps include at least five VARBinds in addition to the VARBinds specified in the format string.

Format string from DLL

The format string specified for the trap. Any non-printing characters in the format string (such as carriage returns, line feeds, and tabs) must be converted to their escape equivalents.

All of the data for a given event is put on a single line in the text file with no line breaks. A sample exported trap text file line follows:

```
.1.3.6.1.4.1.311.1.4.1.2.65.66, "AB", 6, 1073741824, 8, "The object
called %1%n was %t%2 and %t%3."
```

The number of VARBinds in this example is eight: the five VARBinds that are included in all traps, and the three additional VARBinds for the three substitution strings in the event.

Client Configuration Request Files

The client configuration request (CCR) notifies the Client Configuration Manager that a particular Windows NT-based client needs to be configured. The CCR file is a small text file with an INI file format. The file is named *SMSID*.CCR, where *SMSID* is the 8 character SMS ID assigned to the client.

New CCR files are created by SMS Client Setup for Windows NT (CLI_NT). CCR files are placed in the LOGON.SRV\CCR.BOX directory. CCR files that have failed at least one processing attempt by Client Configuration Manager are moved to the LOGON.SRV\CCR.BOX\RETRY directory.

The CCR file has two sections:

- [NT Client Configuration Request]
- [Request Processing]

Dates and times in the [NT Client Configuration Request] section are relative to the client. The [NT Client Configuration Request] section has the following keys:

Machine Name
The name of the target client. It is used by Client Configuration Manager to locate the computer.

Domain
The name of the SMS domain that the client belongs to, as determined by CLI_NT. Client Configuration Manager uses this field to establish remote administrative access to the system.

Initial Request Date
The date and time when CLI_NT created a new CCR.

Latest Request Date
The date and time that CLI_NT last updated the CCR.

Client Request Count
The number of times that CLI_NT requested configuration work since this CCR was created.

Dates and times in the [Request Processing] section are relative to the server running Client Configuration Manager. The [Request Processing] section has the following keys:

Initial Processing Attempt
The date and time when Client Configuration Manager first attempted to process the request. It is used to determine when to report a delayed error event to the SMS database.

Retry Interval Start

The date and time when Client Configuration Manager first attempted to process the request after a new CCR was received for this computer. It is used to determine when to stop retrying this request and report an event to the SMS database.

Latest Processing Attempt

The date and time when Client Configuration Manager last attempted to process the request.

Number of Processing Attempts

A count incremented each time Client Configuration Manager unsuccessfully attempts to process the request.

Last Error Code

A numeric code indicating the error that prevented Client Configuration Manager from processing the request on the latest attempt.

The keys Machine Name, Domain, Initial Request Date, Latest Request Date, and Client Request Count are written by CLI_NT when the request is created.

The keys Latest Request Date, Client Request Count, and Retry Interval Start are updated by Client Configuration Manager when it finds that a CCR already exists for the specified SMS ID.

The keys Initial Processing Attempt, Latest Processing Attempt, Number of Processing Attempts, and Last Error Code are updated each time Client Configuration Manager encounters an error while attempting to process the CCR.

A sample CCR file follows:

```
[NT Client Configuration Request]
Machine Name=MACHINE01
Domain=SMS_DOMAIN
Initial Request Date=01/01/1996 23:00
Latest Request Date=01/01/1996 23:00
Client Request Count=1

[Request Processing]
Initial Processing Attempt=01/01/1996 23:14
Retry Interval Start=01/01/1996 23:14
Latest Processing Attempt=01/04/1996 3:44
Number of Processing Attempts=8
Last Error Code=5
```

C H A P T E R 5

Working with Systems Management Server

This chapter describes how to work with the following Microsoft Systems Management Server (SMS) components:

- Package definition files
- Network Monitor
- Remote Control
- SNMP traps

For overview information about these topics, refer to the SMS version 1.2 *Administrator's Guide*.

Working with Package Definition Files

A package definition file (PDF) is an ASCII file that contains predefined Workstations, Sharing, and Inventory property settings for a package. When you create a new package, you can use a PDF to specify the properties for the package.

Note When you create a PDF, be sure to include an icon file (.ICO) for the application if it will use Program Group Control, in the SetupIcon entry. (You cannot specify other types of files, such as .EXE, in this entry.)

Using PDFs with SMS Jobs

SMS uses jobs to distribute packages to target systems. There are three primary types of jobs for this purpose: Run Command on Workstation, Share Package on Server, and Remove Package From Server.

There are various job options that you can specify, depending on the type of job that you are creating. The main options that affect distribution software are the specification of targets, the distribution servers where the package will be made available, and the options for the Run Phase.

The most flexible mechanism for specifying job targets is an SMS database query. You can create a query that allows you to target only those clients or servers that meet the criteria for the particular package that you are going to install. Once you have defined and run the query, the resulting set of clients or servers can be specified as the target of the job.

Run Command On Workstation Jobs

Run Command On Workstation jobs are the most common type of job used in SMS. This job is actually run on the target clients in the context of the package share that is associated with the job. It is used to install, remove, and maintain software on target clients.

The following is a sample of a PDF that might be included in a Run Command On Workstation job:

```
[PDF]
Version=1.0

[Simple Server Install Setup]
CommandLine=instsrv.bat Install
CommandName=Automated installation of the Simple Service
UserInputRequired=FALSE
SynchronousSystemExitRequired=FALSE
    SupportedPlatforms = Windows NT 3.5 (Alpha), Windows NT 3.5 (MIPS),
    Windows NT 3.5 (x86), Windows NT 3.51 (Alpha), Windows NT 3.51
    (MIPS), Windows NT 3.51 (x86), Windows NT 4.0 (Alpha), Windows NT 4.0
    (MIPS), Windows NT 4.0 (x86)
```

```
[Simple Server Uninstall Setup]
CommandLine=instsrv.bat Remove
CommandName=Automated deinstallation of the Simple Service
UserInputRequired=FALSE
SynchronousSystemExitRequired=FALSE
SupportedPlatforms = Windows NT 3.5 (Alpha), Windows NT 3.5 (MIPS),
Windows NT 3.5 (x86), Windows NT 3.51 (Alpha), Windows NT 3.51 (MIPS),
Windows NT 3.51 (x86), Windows NT 4.0 (Alpha), Windows NT 4.0 (MIPS),
Windows NT 4.0 (x86)

[Package Definition]
Product=Simple Server
Version=1.0
Comment=Simple Server from the WIN32 samples of VC++ 2.0
SetupVariations=Simple Server Install, Simple Server Uninstall

[Setup Package for Inventory]
InventoryThisPackage=TRUE
Detection Rule Part 1=file 1

[file 1]
FILE=SIMPLE.EXE
COLLECT=FALSE
Checksum=
CRC=
DATE=
SIZE=
TIME=
BYTE=
WORD=
LONG=
TOKEN 1=
TOKEN 2=
TOKEN 3=
TOKEN 4=
```

Share Package On Server Jobs

The Share Package On Server job is used to install an SMS network application on a set of servers. Unlike the Run Command On Workstation job, the Share Package On Server job does not actually run a command on the distribution servers. It simply copies the files and directory structure in the package directory to the specified servers and makes them available as a share. The access permissions for each package can be set in the PDF for that package.

The following is an example of a PDF that might be included in a Share Package On Server job:

```
[PDF]
Version=1.0

[Package Definition]
Product=My Application
Version=1.0
Comment=Sample package for use with Share Package On Server jobs.

[Setup Package for Sharing]
ShareName=MYAPPSHR
ShareAccess=UserRead, GuestRead

[Program Item Properties 1]
Description=My Application
CommandLine=MYAPP.EXE
ConfigurationScript=
RegistryName=MyApp
DefaultINIFile=MYAPP.INI
RunMinimized=TRUE
RunLocalCopyIfPresent=TRUE
DriveMode=UNC
SupportedPlatforms=Windows 3.1
DisplayIconInProgGroup=TRUE
SetupIcon=MYAPP.ICO
```

Remove Package From Server Jobs

Remove Package From Server jobs do not remove packages from clients; that is done with a Run Command on Workstation job. The Remove Package From Server job is used to remove packages from SMS site servers, distribution servers, and servers that have had a package installed using a Share Package on Server job.

There is no specific PDF for this type of job. Any package in SMS can be the basis for a Remove Package From Server job.

Working with SMS Network Applications

SMS provides fault tolerance and load-leveling for SMS network applications by placing application packages on multiple distribution servers and by choosing, at run time, an available server to service a client.

SMS uses a device driver mechanism for Windows 95 clients to choose application servers. This mechanism is completely transparent to both installation and execution of an application. This device driver mechanism depends upon UNC identification of servers. Any references to servers that an application records in the registry, in INI files, in Start menu shortcuts, or program item command lines, must be UNC paths; drive letters are not supported. Any persistent reference to a server location should contain the UNC from which the setup program was activated. At run time, SMS may translate that UNC into an equivalent UNC which represents the same application on a different server.

An application's PDF file should declare a single setup program item to represent a shared SMS network application. The following sample is extracted from the Office for Windows 95 standard PDF file:

```
[Program Item Properties 1]
CommandLine=dummy.exe
Description=Microsoft Office95a Std Install
ConfigurationScript=smsacm32.exe ofs95a+install setup.stf "SETUP.EXE /B4
/Q1" "SETUP.EXE /U /Q1"
RegistryName=ofs95a+install
DefaultINIFile=
RunMinimized=FALSE
RunLocalCopyIfPresent=FALSE
DriveMode=UNC
SupportedPlatforms=Windows95, Windows NT 3.1 (x86)
SetupIcon=OFS95A01.ICO
DisplayIconInProgGroup=TRUE
```

The entries in the application's PDF file should be as follows:

CommandLine

For reasons of backward compatibility, this entry cannot be blank so it should contain some text.

Description

The Start menu shortcut identifier or program item identifier; this entry must not be blank.

ConfigurationScript

Contains the setup program's command line, or, if special preprocessing is desired, the command line of an encapsulation program.

RegistryName

Must be unique to the application and its version.

SupportedPlatforms

See the SMS version 1.2 product documentation for allowable values for this entry.

SetupIcon

Contains the file name of the icon used to represent the setup program. Both the PDF file and the icon file should reside in a package's root directory. This entry is required for Program Group Control, and it only support icon files (.ICO).

The other entries must posses the values indicated in the sample.

You install an SMS network application exactly as you would in the absence of SMS; no changes are made by SMS to Start menu items, program items, registry entries, or INI file entries.

To enable SMS to automatically remove an application upon your request, a setup program or its encapsulation program must record a removal command line in the HKEY_CLASSES_ROOT\SMS\Applications*regname*\Info\Deinstall_App registry key. This must specify a full path to the removal program, including the server and share name.

To enable an encapsulation program to determine the UNC path from which a setup program is initiated, SMS records the installation server's UNC path in the HKEY_CLASSES_ROOT\SMS\Applications*regname*\InstallationServer registry key. An encapsulation program can then prefix the removal command line with this UNC before recording it into the registry. The *regname* component is the name for the program item that was entered into the RegistryName entry within the PDF file.

Creating Setup Command Lines for PDFs

The EXECUTE.EXE program, included in this Resource Kit, is used to run a two-phase setup program under the Package Command Manager or Program Group Control configuration script. A two-phase setup is one that is actually two different programs; the first program starts the second one and then terminates. When the first program terminates, Package Command Manager closes the network connection to the distribution server, leaving the second program without a network connection. EXECUTE.EXE delays Package Command Manager (and Program Group Control) from deleting the distribution server connection too soon.

EXECUTE.EXE runs the command line for a Windows-based program and then polls for its termination. Upon termination, it temporarily pauses and waits until no window possessing a given window title or window class can be found.

EXECUTE.EXE can be used for 16-bit applications running under Windows version 3.1, Windows NT or Windows 95. Use this syntax:

execute *"command-line" "window-caption" "window-classname"*

Where *command-line* is the command line that your setup program will run, *window-caption* is the window title, and *window-classname* is the window class. (Use the SPY.EXE program, distributed with Microsoft Visual C++®, to determine the window class and title.)

The quotation marks around each option are required syntax. The *"window-caption"* and *"window-classname"* options can be empty ("").

For example:

execute "SETUP.EXE /B4" "Microsoft PowerPoint" "PPApplicationClass"

execute "SETUP.EXE /B4" "" "PPApplicationClass"

The EXECUTE.EXE program must reside either in the root directory of the package share, or in the MSTEST directory on the SMS logon server (LOGON.SRV\MSTEST).

Deploying Microsoft Exchange with SMS

The Microsoft Exchange PDF allows you to deploy Microsoft Exchange to clients running Windows 95 and Windows NT on your network, using SMS.

Before you can use the Microsoft Exchange PDF, you must:

- Create the package source directories
- Pre-set various profile defaults such as E-mail name, Microsoft Exchange Home Server, and Personal Address Book (PAB) location.

▶ **To set up package source directories for Microsoft Exchange**

1. Create two directories on your source server: one for Windows NT-based clients and the other for Windows 95 clients.

   In most cases, these directories are located on your SMS server. Once created, they become your package source directories. Use these directory names: EXCHWINNT*xxx* and EXCHWIN95*xxx*, where *xxx* denotes the language, such as USA, GER or FRN.

2. Share the directories with the same names, for example:

   *servername***EXCHWIN95USA**

3. Copy the Microsoft Exchange files into the relevant shares.

   This uses approximately 8–9 MB of disk space.

▶ **To customize the default profile settings for Microsoft Exchange**

1. From a package source directory, start STFEDTR.EXE.

   The Microsoft Exchange Setup Editor window appears.

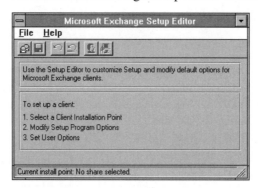

2. From the File menu, choose Select Client Installation Point.

   The Select Client Installation Directory dialog box appears.

3. Select an Exchange installation point and choose OK.

4. From the File menu, choose Set User Options.

   The User Options dialog box appears.

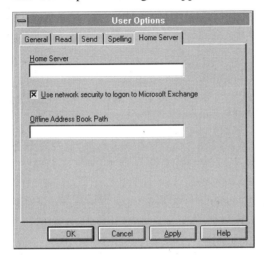

5. Select the Home Server tab.

6. In the Home Server box, type the name of a server in your site where Directory Services are replicated.

   When the user first logs on, the Microsoft Exchange Client computer will query the directory to determine which server to connect to in the future.

7. Choose OK to return to the Microsoft Exchange Setup Editor window.

8. From the File menu, choose Save, and then choose Exit.

Creating the SMS Package

Software is distributed through an SMS package. Before distribution can occur, the package must be created. Since Microsoft Exchange provides a set of PDF files, you don't need to create a package manually. For more information, see your Microsoft Exchange documentation.

▶ **To create a Microsoft Exchange package**

1. In the SMS Administrator, open the Packages window, and from the File menu, choose New.

   The Package Properties dialog box appears.

2. Choose Import.

   The File Browser dialog box appears.

3. Locate the Microsoft Exchange PDF and choose OK.

   The Package Properties dialog box reappears.

4. Choose Workstations.

   The Setup Package for Workstations dialog box appears.

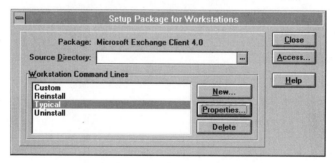

5. In the Source Directory box, type the path to the package source directory.

6. In the Workstation Command Lines box, select the type of installation to view. The Command Line Properties dialog box appears.

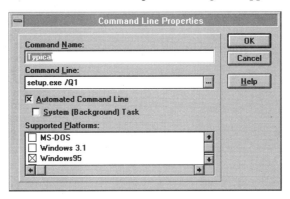

7. Make any necessary changes, then choose OK.

Note If you are creating a Microsoft Exchange package that will use a language other than English, modify the Workstation Command Lines (in the Setup Package for Workstations dialog box, choose Properties). Each language uses different file names for the installation program, for example, French and Swedish use the file name INSTALL.EXE, whereas Spanish uses INSTALER.EXE.

Setting Access Permissions

Setting access permissions allows you to specify user and guest rights to your SMS package directory.

▶ **To set access permissions for the Microsoft Exchange package**

1. In the Setup Package for Workstations dialog box for the Microsoft Exchange package, choose Access.

   The Access dialog box appears.

2. Under Users and Guests, select the Read and Write check boxes.
3. Choose OK.
4. Choose Close.

Sending the Microsoft Exchange Package to a Site

A distribution server is created on your primary site so you can distribute jobs through the SMS package directory.

▶ **To send the Microsoft Exchange package to a site**

1. In the SMS Administrator, open the Packages window and the Sites window.

2. Drag the Microsoft Exchange package from the Packages window to the site in the Sites window.

The Job Details dialog box appears.

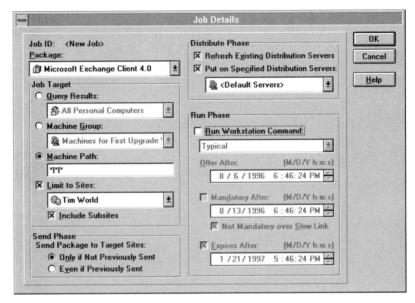

In the Job Details dialog box, confirm the following:

- The correct package, job destination, and SMS site are selected. If you have subsites, please read about creating multiple sites in the SMS version 1.2 *Installation and Configuration.*

- The Distribute Phase check boxes are selected and the correct distribution servers are selected.

- The Run Workstation Command check box is cleared. This ensures that the package is sent only to the distribution server.

3. Choose OK.

4. Choose Schedule.

   The Job Schedule dialog box appears.

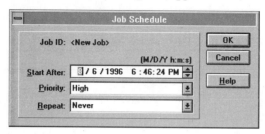

5. Choose OK.

6. Choose OK to start the job.

Setting Up User Names for Clients Running Windows NT

▶ **To set up user names**

1. In the Microsoft Exchange program group, choose the MS Exchange Services icon.

   The Default Exchange Profile Properties dialog box appears.

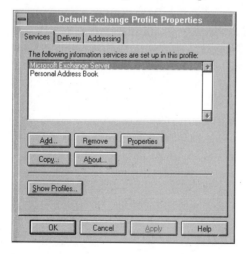

2. Choose Properties.

   The Microsoft Exchange Server dialog box appears.

3. Select the General tab.

4. In Mailbox, type the user's e-mail name.

5. Choose Check Name.

6. When the account appears in Mailbox, choose Apply.

7. Choose OK in all open dialog boxes.

Deploying Windows 95 with SMS

Before you deploy the Windows 95 operating system to SMS clients:

- Use queries to identify which clients have the memory, disk space, and microprocessor required to run Windows 95.
- Use the query results to create a machine group that contains all the computers that you want to upgrade to Windows 95.
- Run ScanDisk on each client that will be upgraded.
- Create a source directory for the Windows 95 operating system files.
- Create a package and a job to distribute Windows 95.
- Run a test to identify any issues in deploying Windows 95 on your network.

For information about queries and machine groups, see the SMS version 1.2 *Administrator's Guide*.

Running ScanDisk

The SCANDISK.EXE program checks for lost chains and clusters on the hard drives of the target clients. Because the Windows 95 Setup program runs ScanDisk and will fail if it detects a problem, you should run ScanDisk before installing Windows 95 on SMS clients.

You can use SCANDISK.PDF to distribute and run the ScanDisk program on clients that you plan to upgrade.

Note If the target client is running Windows for Workgroups version 3.11, use the version of ScanDisk created for MS-DOS version 6.22 rather than the one shipped on the Microsoft Windows 95 compact disc.

For information about using ScanDisk, see the *Microsoft Windows 95 Resource Kit*.

Preparing the Distribution Server

Create a source directory on the distribution server for the Windows 95 operating system files, and share the directory, using a share name that is identical to the directory name. Then copy all relevant files from the Windows 95 compact disc to the new source directory There are two recommended ways to copy the files:

- Use the NETSETUP program (see the *Microsoft Windows 95 Resource Kit* for details) to decompress and copy the necessary files to the source directory. This option will give you maximum flexibility in customizing your installed components. You should use the Netsetup option if you want to create a setup directory that you can use to install shared Windows 95 configurations, where clients run Windows 95 across the network.

- Copy the compressed files directly from the WIN95 directory on the compact disc to the source directory. This method saves disk space, but you lose flexibility in customizing installation options.

From the site server, copy the following files from the LOGON.SRV\MSTEST directory to the source directory:

- WIN95.INF (for automated installs)
- WIN95MIN.INF (for manual installs)
- DOS2W95.EXE (to set up MS-DOS clients)
- WIN2W95.EXE (to set up Windows clients)

Modify the WIN95.INF and WIN95MIN.INF files (Windows 95 setup script files that follow the MSBATCH.INF format) as necessary. The WIN95MIN.INF file is used in manual installs where the user provides or verifies installation choices. The WIN95.INF file is used for automated installations of Windows 95. The WIN95.INF file supports both Microsoft Networks and Netware Networks by default. It also sets clients to validate Windows NT domain logons. You may need to make appropriate changes to the WIN95.INF file to reflect time zone and custom network or installation settings. Be sure to add your Windows 95 product ID to both .INF files.

The automated Windows 95 setup process attempts to determine specific client information when possible. However, you might need to modify the WIN95.INF file for your network attributes or machine group configuration. In particular, you will probably need to modify the product ID and time zone. Eeview the default network client configuration and logon domain settings and add information to the file to override default installation settings. See the *Microsoft Windows 95 Resource Kit* for information about modifying an .INF file for various supported configurations.

The Windows 95 installation process requires the User Name, Domain/Workgroup Name and Computer Name for the targeted client. In the provided WIN95.INF template, these values have been left blank. These values can be provided in one of three ways.

- Edit the WIN95.INF file to provide one or more of the missing values.

- Allow the installation program to fill in the blank items using values in either the client's SMS.INI file or the SYSTEM.INI file. The installation program searches for the User Name in the following manner:

    - Looks in the input Windows 95 script file (usually WIN95.INF).

    - Looks in the SMS.INI on the client.

    - Looks in the MSBATCH.INF file in the Windows directory (Windows 95 clients will have this file from their last installation).

    - Looks in the SERIALNO.INI file in the Windows directory (Windows for Workgroup clients will have this file from their last installation).

    If a User Name cannot be located, the installation program uses the Computer Name as specified in the .INF or the MachineName field in the SMS.INI file. If the client is running NetWare, the installation program uses the logon name of the current user.

- Allow the installation program to prompt the user during the installation process.

Creating a Package to Install Windows 95

Use an SMS package to install Windows 95 on the target clients by running the setup command on each client. Make sure this package points to the proper network location for the Windows 95 source code, including the appropriate .INF files, whether the standard MSBATCH.INF or another version of this file is used.

▶ **To create a package to install Windows 95**

1. Create a source directory for the required installation files and share the directory.

2. In the SMS Administrator, open the Packages window. From the File menu, choose New.

   The Package Properties dialog box appears.

3. Choose Import.

   The File Browser dialog box appears.

4. Select the *servername**sharename*\IMPORT.SRC\ENU\WIN95.PDF file and choose OK.

5. Choose Workstations.

   The Setup Package for Workstations dialog box appears.

6. In the Source Directory box, enter the full UNC name for the source directory (in this case, the directory with the Windows 95 source files), and choose OK.

   If you choose to browse through the list of files, edit the resulting path so that it shows the UNC name (which would begin with *servername**sharename*) rather than the relative name (which would begin with the drive letter you have assigned to the server during the current session).

7. Choose OK in all open dialog boxes.

   When the package has been created and appears in the Packages window, you can use it to create a job.

Running the Package on Clients

Since certain warning and error conditions can pause or terminate automated installations of Windows 95, observe the following guidelines when using SMS to install Windows 95:

- Ensure that all applications have been closed before starting the automated installation. If an application is open, the installation will pause until the user closes the application.

- When you upgrade a client to MS-DOS 6.22, the MS-DOS setup program archives the previous MS-DOS directory as \OLD_DOS*x* (where *x* is a number). If the target computer has this directory, the Windows 95 installation will pause and ask the user if this directory should be deleted. If you want to automatically install Windows 95, make sure that the target clients do not have this directory. Use SMS to query for computers with an old MS-DOS directory and to delete these directories.

For the command in the package to be run on the target clients, you must create a Run Command on Workstation job. You can do this by dragging the package to the Machine Group in the site and filling in the resulting Job Details dialog box.

Once a job is distributed, the associated instructions are kept in the instruction file on each server until the job expires or is canceled, even after the job has completed on all target clients. This consumes about 3K per job per logon server. Use the Expires After setting in the Job Details dialog box to specify an expiration date that is realistic for your organization and for the job.

Testing the Windows 95 Deployment

After you run the test, evaluate the distribution results on the upgraded clients. Note that a Complete job status does not necessarily indicate successful deployment of Windows 95. You must perform additional analysis to determine the results of deployment:

- Make sure that the SMS client inventory has been updated for all clients in the target group.

- Use the following queries to determine whether the upgrade succeeded.

  The following query identifies successful upgrades:

  ```
  Microsoft|Operating_System|1.0:Operating System Name is 'MS
  Windows 95'
  ```

  The following query identifies unsuccessful upgrades:

  ```
  Microsoft|Operating_System|1.0:Operating System Name is 'MS DOS'
  AND
  Microsoft|Operating_System|1.0:Version is not '7.00'
  ```

- Examine the computers that were not successfully upgraded on a case-by-case basis. If you marked the Inventory This Package check box in the Setup Package for Inventory dialog box when you created the package, you can examine a copy of the setup log file created on each target computer. Study this file to determine the cause of any problems. For example, there might have been changes in available disk space or in the availability of some other resource between the time the computer was added to the target group and the time the upgrade was performed.

- Test the clients that were successfully upgraded to ensure that the configuration you specified works as expected on these computers. See the following section for details.

- Check the details of job events to troubleshoot problems. For example, if a job has failed because the .INF file was not available where it was expected, this would be reported in the job events.

- Determine whether any individual clients, which may have failed during the Windows 95 upgrade process, are no longer operational.

  Clients that are no longer operational are not updated in the SMS inventory. You might choose to perform the inventory at more frequent intervals before deployment to make sure that only currently operational computers are targeted. In some cases, you might want to develop an SMS query to identify clients that have not had their inventory updated.

- Determine whether a faulty hardware component caused a failure of the Windows 95 upgrade process.

Testing the Installation

Test the upgraded clients to make sure that the configuration you have installed will serve your organization as expected.

On a client that has been upgraded to Windows 95:

- Connect to and browse through the network.
- Set up a printer and test printing to local and network printers.
- Open, run, and close applications on both the client and the server.
- Shut down completely.

Test all mission-critical applications for proper functioning. If you encounter problems, try removing related features from the proposed configuration as a solution. Document any changes made to the original configuration.

If the preferred client configuration works as expected, you may want to conduct additional testing of the optional software features and components in Windows 95. This can help you determine whether you are running Windows 95 optimally. For this kind of testing, conduct side-by-side evaluations on two clients, changing individual features on each one, to determine the following:

- Performance in terms of responsiveness and throughput
- Ease of use
- Stability
- Compatibility
- Functionality

Testing Installations on Novell Networks

To evaluate network client software for Novell NetWare, run your network performance tests in the following configurations:

- Windows 95 installed with an existing 16-bit, Novell-supplied client (NETX), using ODI drivers.
- Windows 95 added to an existing installation of Windows 3.1 and NetWare, using Client for NetWare Networks and protected-mode networking support components (NDIS adapter drivers).
- Windows 95 as a new installation using all protected-mode components, including both Client for NetWare Networks and Client for Microsoft Networks, plus peer resource sharing support.

Perform several common tasks, such as connecting to the network and administering a remote NetWare server, to test for ease of use. Similarly, you'll want to run any business-specific NetWare applications under Microsoft Client for NetWare Networks to make sure that they run compatibly. Any stability issues should become apparent during this testing.

When you have identified a configuration that performs well during testing, test the same configuration on clients with different types of hardware configurations.

Deploying Microsoft Office for Windows 95 with SMS

Before you deploy Office to SMS clients:

- Review the Office feature set and decide which components to install on the clients.

    You can take advantage of user profiles to require that a mandatory desktop configuration be loaded each time a user logs on. (For more information, see your Microsoft Office for Windows 95 documentation.)

- Decide on configuration and installation options, such as file locations, installation media, and installation method. (For more information, see the *Microsoft Office for Windows 95 Resource Kit*.)

- Decide which existing files, macros, and custom programs you will need to use in the new software, and identify any extra steps that might be required to use the existing files and macros in Office.

- Use SMS queries to identify which clients have the hardware required to run Office.

- Run a test to identify any issues in deploying Office on your network.

The *Microsoft Windows 95 and Office for Windows 95 Evaluation and Migration Planning Kit* (MPK) has several documents that can aid in your review of Office. For a copy of the MPK, contact Microsoft Customer Service.

The *Microsoft Office for Windows 95 Resource Kit*, from Microsoft Press, is a technical supplement to the Office product documentation, written to assist administrators in installing, supporting, and managing Office on corporate networks. The *Microsoft Office for Windows 95 Resource Kit* is available at http://www.microsoft.com/technet/desk/office/orkf/orkftoc.htm.

Defining the Preferred Client Configuration

Before specifying the preferred configuration for clients, you should:

- Understand the current server and client configurations.
- Select the features that will be used in the preferred configuration on clients.
- Select the features that will be used to enable users to work together.
- Decide where Office files will be located and how they will be installed. That is, will Office files be installed on the client's hard disk, or will they be installed on a server and accessed remotely by the client, or a will a combination of both be used?

Researching Current Configuration Variables

To deploy Office successfully, you need to understand your current hardware and software configurations. Your deployment plan will be dictated by your current system environments.

- **Hardware configuration**
    - For minimum hardware requirements, and to determine whether any clients need to be upgraded, see the *Microsoft Office for Windows 95 Resource Kit*.

    Note Microsoft Schedule+ requires a Windows-compatible network and a MAPI 1.0-enabled mail server for scheduling and group functionality.

    - Laptop and desktop users have different configurations, including disk space and access to the network. Installation options will need to be selected with the specific client in mind.
- **Network topology**
    - You can install software on clients from a network server, or you can run Office applications as SMS network applications. You may need to have different configurations for each of these cases.
    - Installing or running Office remotely over the network may not be practical for clients connected over a slow-link network.
    - Use of different network operating systems can create issues such as server file sharing methods and client-server permission schemes.
    - Installing Office over the network and running Office applications over the network place different demands on network bandwidth, both in response time and in length of time connected.

- **Migrating existing configurations**

  Determine whether you need to convert existing files, macros, and custom programs. For more information, see the *Microsoft Office for Windows 95 Resource Kit.*

- **Supporting multiple platforms**

  In many large organizations, users are running Office on a variety of supported platforms. For more information about these issues, see the *Microsoft Office for Windows 95 Resource Kit.*

Selecting Office Standard Features

By reviewing the feature set of Office, you can determine how to configure clients for the needs of your users. Because you can choose which components of Office to install, you have a lot of flexibility in tailoring client installations to include the best set of features for your users, while reducing disk space usage.

Selecting Office Workgroup Features

The workgroup features in Office establish how your users will communicate and work together.

Group scheduling with Schedule+

The group calendaring functions of Schedule+ require an underlying mail client, Microsoft Exchange, which is part of Windows 95. The small-business mail system that comes with Windows 95 allows users to exchange mail and meeting requests through a single post office. Microsoft Exchange also can work with other mail systems as long as the mail system uses a valid MAPI 1.0 driver. Such systems include Microsoft Mail and Microsoft Exchange Server. For more information about Microsoft Exchange with Windows 95, see the *Microsoft Windows 95 Resource Kit.*

Using Word as your e-mail editor

Microsoft Word for Windows 95 can be used to replace the default text editor used in the Microsoft Exchange mail client, which gives the user access to all the Word editing and formatting features. To use this feature, Microsoft Exchange in Windows 95 must be installed first on the client. Then, when Office is installed, choose the Custom Install; WordMail is one of the customization options for Word.

Workgroup templates

Users can share template files for Office documents using the Workgroup Template setting in Office. This setting, maintained in each user's registry, specifies a folder in which Office document templates can be stored for users. By defining this to be a folder on a network server, users in a workgroup can have access to a common set of templates. You can use the Network Installation Wizard to define this setting for your users in a custom installation script rather than having them set it individually.

MAPI and VIM

The Office applications include commands to send and route documents using e-mail. These commands work with Simple MAPI and MAPI 1.0 or later systems, such as Microsoft Mail 3.*x* and the Microsoft Exchange mail client included with Windows 95, and with 16-bit VIM-based mail systems such as cc:Mail and Lotus Notes.

Briefcase support

Office supports the Windows 95 Briefcase, which allows users to synchronize different versions of a file whether or not the files are on the same hard disk drive or on the network. Microsoft Access, specifically, provides individual database replication using Briefcase.

Determining Configuration and Installation Options

When you understand the variables in your organization and how they will affect the manner in which you deploy Office, you can decide on the configuration for the preferred client. You will make decisions in the following areas:

Location of Office files

When deciding where to place Office files, consider how the client will be used and evaluate the benefits of each placement option, including how each option will effect your ability to support these configurations in the future. Office can be local (files installed on the client's hard disk) or shared (files are located on a network server, and users share those files over the network). You can also put some files on the local hard disk and some files on the server.

Installation options

There are several basic installation options available in the Office Setup program when Office Setup is run interactively by the user. You can also create your own customized options if the Office Setup program is to be run in batch mode using a customized script.

Installation method

Three methods can be used to perform the installation on the clients:

- Interactive—allows the user to make all installation decisions.
- Batch—provides a preset installation script for the user.
- Push—initiates the installation for the user without user intervention.

A complete discussion of all these options can be found in the *Microsoft Office for Windows 95 Resource Kit*.

Creating the Administrative Installation Server Share

To install Office over the network, you first create a network installation server share by performing an administrative setup of Office from the Office Installation compact disc or floppy disk set. By using the Network Installation Wizard, you can modify the files in this share to customize the client installations, including whether clients will run Office locally or over the network. For information about creating and customizing a network installation location, see the *Microsoft Office for Windows 95 Resource Kit*.

Preparing the Clients

Make sure that each client has enough hard disk space, RAM, and processing capability to run Office:

- To use Microsoft Office Standard, you need 28 MB of hard disk space for a compact installation, 55 MB for a typical installation, and 89 MB for a custom installation (maximum).
- To use Microsoft Office Professional, you need 40 MB of hard disk space for a compact installation, 87 MB for a typical installation, and 126 MB for a custom installation (maximum).

Note   Office requires 8 MB of memory to run two applications on Windows 95. More memory is recommended to run three or more applications simultaneously on Windows 95.

In addition, before installation run virus detection, disk scanning, and defragmentation programs on the client to prevent any later problems. Although the computer may appear to be operating properly, software upgrades often uncover hardware or software problems because of the way they read and write data to the hard disk. Checking the computer before installing Office will help you stay focused on issues related to the installation process.

Be sure to back up critical data and configuration files for the client, in case the installation fails or you need to revert to the old system for some reason. Also you should create a Microsoft Diagnostics report and copy it to a floppy disk by running MSD.EXE on the hard disk. If you need to automate the restoration, consider using a commercial backup program, instead of copying the files by hand.

Any or all of the following can be used with Office for; however, they are not required:

- Windows-compatible network required for workgroup functionality and WordMail.
- Microsoft Exchange client required for workgroup functionality and WordMail on Windows NT.
- 2400-baud or higher modem (9600-baud modem recommended).
- Audio board with headphones or speaker.

Using SMS to Install Office

Use SMS to distribute an Office installation package to clients and to run the package with or without user interaction.

You can share Office in two ways:

- Install all the main Office components (such as Word and Microsoft Excel) on the client's local hard disk but run the shared components (such as Spelling and ClipArt Gallery) from a network server.
- Install Office using the Run From Network Server installation type and run all Office components from a network server.

The technique for creating each of these sharing environments within the SMS system varies.

How SMS Distributes Office

The following steps give an overview of how to use SMS to distribute Office when all Office components are run from a network server:

1. Create an administrative installation point for Office (run **setup /a** to a server location). See the following section for more information on the **setup /a** command.
2. In the SMS Administrator, create a package using the Office PDF that references the administrative installation point. For more information, see "Creating the Office Package" later in this chapter.

   SMS will pick up all the files in the MSOffice folder on the administrative installation point and copy them to one or more SMS distribution servers.

3. Create a Run Command on Workstation job to distribute the package to selected clients.

4. When the package runs on the client, SMS runs, Office Setup from the copy of MSOffice residing on the distribution server. All the main and shared Office components are accessed from this server.

If Office is installed on a client's hard disk, the work of SMS is completed, and Office has been successfully installed. However, if you want users to share some or all of the Office components, there are more steps to complete.

Using Administrative Setup

Use the administrative setup command to build a source directory. Use the following command to start this setup:

setup /a

This command copies the source files into a directory and creates a SETUP.STF file for use in network installations.

Important Do not use the SETUP.STF file located on the installation disks for a network or customized installation.

▶ **To prepare the administrative installation point**

1. Choose the location for the administrative installation point.

   Make sure that there is sufficient disk space. Office Standard needs about 90 MB for the administrative installation, and Office Professional needs about 130 MB. You need read, write, delete, and create permissions to use these folders while doing the administrative installation.

2. Make sure that all folders are empty.

   If a previous version of Office exists, move any custom templates you want to save, then delete all of the Office files.

3. Create the MSAPPS32 directory for shared files.

4. Lock all folders to prevent network user access during the administrative installation.

5. Disable virus detection software to prevent erroneous virus detection triggers while **setup** is running.

6. Make sure the client on which you will be running SETUP.EXE is running Windows 95 or Windows NT 3.51 or later.

Sharing MSApps Components

When you create an administrative installation point, you define where the shared MSApps folder will be placed on the network; this location is written into the SETUP.STF file. When Office is installed to run shared components from this MSApps folder, the MSApps location defined in the SETUP.STF file is written into the user's registry.

SMS will distribute the Office installation package to the distribution server that is defined for a particular client, but it will not change the shared MSApps location defined in the .STF file. This means that even though a particular package may be sent to multiple distribution servers, all users of that package will share the same MSApps network location definition.

If you want different groups of users to share different MSApps folders, you first need to place copies of the MSApps folder on the servers you want to use for this purpose. You can do this by performing multiple administrative installations, creating the MSApps folder on the different servers. Or, you can do one administrative installation and then copy the MSApps folder to the other servers.

Once you have the MSApps folder on different servers, you can give users access to the appropriate MSApps location in one of two ways: using drive letter mapping and creating one SMS package or using UNC paths and creating multiple packages.

Drive Letter Mapping with One Package

By mapping the same drive letter in every user system to the appropriate MSApps server, you need only one SMS package for all users.

▶ **To use drive letter mapping to define multiple MSApps locations**

1. During administrative setup (**setup /a**) of Office, specify the location of MSApps to be a certain drive letter. For example, drive H.
2. Copy the MSApps folder, with subfolders, to multiple servers, creating the same folder structure on each server.
3. On each client, map the drive letter you specified in Step 1 to the server containing the MSApps folder appropriate for that client.
4. Create a single SMS package for Office using the administrative installation point you created.

   For information about creating this package, see "Creating the Office Package" later in this chapter.
5. Distribute this package to all clients.
6. When Office is installed using the package, Office Setup will define the drive letter you specified to be the location of the MSApps folder, and that drive letter will be mapped to the server appropriate for each client.

UNC Paths with Multiple Packages

If you are using UNC paths to specify the location of the MSApps folder, or if you are using drive letters but cannot define a single drive letter for all clients and all MSApps servers, then you need to create a different SMS package for each MSApps location.

One option is to perform multiple administrative installations and create a separate SMS package for each installation. During each administrative installation, specify a different network location for MSApps so that each package will install Office with a different MSApps location. You then distribute the appropriate package to those clients who need to use a particular MSApps location.

The other option is to perform one administrative installation and make multiple copies of the SETUP.STF file, one for each MSApps location. The location of the MSApps folder is defined in the SETUP.STF file when you do the administrative installation. By using the Network Installation Wizard, you can modify the MSApps definition in each SETUP.STF file to point to a different network location. You then create multiple SMS packages using the same MSOffice folder, but substituting the appropriate SETUP.STF file each time.

▶ **To use multiple STF files to define multiple MSApps locations**

1. Run administrative setup (**setup /a**) for Office.

2. Copy the MSApps folder, and all subfolders, to multiple servers.

3. Make copies of the SETUP.STF file (found in the MSOffice folder)—one copy for each MSApps location.

4. Run the Network Installation Wizard on each SETUP.STF file.

5. In the dialog box in which you define the location of the MSApps folder, specify for each SETUP.STF file a different MSApps location.

6. Copy one of these SETUP.STF files to the MSOffice folder.

7. Create an SMS package for Office using the MSOffice folder.

   For more information, see "Creating the Office Package" later in this chapter.

8. Send this package to those users who will be using the MSApps location defined in the SETUP.STF file.

9. Repeat steps 6 to 8 for each SETUP.STF file.

Creating the Office Package

Microsoft Office for Windows 95 includes a sample PDF for use with SMS: OFF95STD.PDF in the Microsoft Office Standard product, or OFF95PRO.PDF in the Microsoft Office Professional product. The PDF has command definitions in it for the standard types of client setup: Typical, Compact, Custom, Complete (the same as Custom but with all options selected), and Workstation (called Run From Network Server in Setup). Each of these command definitions contains a setup command line that will cause Office Setup to run in batch mode with the specific installation type (except for Custom, for which Office Setup is run interactively).

For example, the command line for Typical is:

```
CommandLine=setup.exe /q1 /b1
```

The **/q1** option directs Office Setup to run with no user interaction, and the **/b1** option directs Office Setup to use the first installation type (Typical). For an explanation of all the available Office Setup command line options, see the *Microsoft Office for Windows 95 Resource Kit*. When this command is run from this SMS package, Office Setup automatically installs Office using the predefined options for the Typical installation type.

Using the Packages window in the SMS Administrator, you can create a new command in the Office package that will run your custom command line for Office Setup.

▶ **To add custom commands to the Office PDF**

1. In the SMS Administrator, open the Packages window, and from the File menu, choose New.

   The Package Properties dialog box appears.

2. Choose Import.

   The File Browser dialog box appears.

3. Select the appropriate PDF (OFF95STD.PDF or OFF95PRO.PDF). It is located in the administrative installation point in the folder containing the main Office application files.

4. Choose OK.

5. Choose Workstation if you want to install Office on the client's hard disk.

   The Setup Package dialog box appears.

6. Specify the location of the administrative installation point for Office as the source folder.

7. To define the new command line, choose New.

8. In the Command Name box, type a name for the new command.

9. In the Command Line box, type the command to run your custom Office Setup.

    For example, to run SETUP.EXE from the administrative installation point with the modified NEWSETUP.STF file, in quiet mode, type:

    setup.exe /t newsetup.stf /qt

10. To indicate that no user input is required to run the package, select the Automated Command Line check box.

11. In the Supported Platforms box, select the appropriate platforms: Windows 95, Windows NT, or both.

12. Choose OK, and then choose Close.

You can now create a Run Command On Workstation job to distribute this package.

Testing the Installation

After you have set up a client with Office, you will need to run a variety of tests to ensure that it runs correctly and that you can still perform all of your usual tasks. Use your own testing methodology or, from a computer on which Office has been installed, test the following to verify correct system operation:

- Open, run, and close Office applications.
- Use the major Office features, including opening, modifying, saving, and printing documents.
- Open existing files in the new Office applications.
- If the client is using shared components on the network, such as spell-checking, test these functions.
- If the client is using a shared Windows 95 installation, test standard Windows 95 functions such as printing.
- Shut down completely.

In addition to ensuring that the preferred client configuration works as expected, you also may want to conduct additional testing of optional software features and components. This can help you determine whether you are running Office optimally. For this kind of testing, conduct side-by-side evaluations on two clients, changing individual features on each one, to determine the following:

- Performance of responsiveness and throughput for local disk and network actions.
- Ease of use for performing common tasks.
- Stability of the two clients under stress.
- Compatibility with applications and hardware.

Deploying Microsoft SQL Server with SMS

You can use SMS to automatically install Microsoft SQL Server version 6.5 on multiple computers running Windows NT Server in your organization.

The Microsoft SQL Server compact disc contains the following files to help you deploy SQL Server with SMS (located at the root of the compact disc).

SQL Server file	Description
SQL65.PDF	Automates the creation of a SQL Server package in SMS. The SQL Server package can then be distributed and installed on SMS computers. The PDF also enables SMS to detect SQL Server on SMS computers and report it in the SMS computer inventory.

(continued)

SQL Server file	Description
SQLFULL*drive*.CMD SQLNOBK*drive*.CMD	Detect the platform of the computer and run the appropriate version of SQL Server Setup with the appropriate parameters, where *drive* indicates the drive letter where SQL Server will be installed. The SQLFULL*drive*.CMD batch file installs the full SQL Server product including the online books. The SQLNOBK*drive*.CMD batch file installs the SQL Server product *without* the online books. The installation scripts product (SQLFULL*drive*.INI and SQLNOBK*drive*.INI) for SQL Server Setup require that the installation drive be specified in the installation script. Batch files and scripts are provided for installation on drives C, D, and E. For example, if you wanted to install SQL Server on drive D, you would use the SQLFULLD.CMD batch file. A custom script (SQLCUSTM.INI) is also provided so that you can change the drive specification to a drive letter that follows E.
SQLFULL*drive*.INI SQLNOBK*drive*.INI	Installation scripts that install SQL Server to a specified drive. *drive* indicates the drive letter where SQL Server will be installed.
SQLCUSTM.CMD SQLCUSTM.INI	The SQLCUSTM.CMD batch file runs SQL Server Setup to install the full SQL Server using the SQLCUSTM.INI initialization file. If you are installing SQL Server on a drive letter after E, you can modify the SQLCUSTM.INI file to specify any drive letter that you want. You need to modify the entries that specify drive locations.

Requirements

The computers where SQL Server will be installed have the following disk space requirements:

- Full installation: 90 MB
- Installation without online books: 75 MB

For other installation requirements for SQL Server, see the Microsoft SQL Server documentation.

On the SMS site server where the job to install the SQL Server is created, the site server must have 180 MB of free disk space.

▶ **To create the Microsoft SQL Server package**

1. Copy all directories and files from the Microsoft SQL Server compact disc to a package source directory.

   To create the package source directory for SQL Server, create the package source directory on a server and share it with the same name. Copy the directories and files from the Microsoft SQL Server compact disc to the package source directory.

2. If you plan to install SQL Server on a drive letter after E (that is, F, G, H, and so on), modify the drive specifications in the custom installation script (SQLCUSTM.CMD and SQLCUSTM.INI).

   You need to modify the following items:

   a. In the [SQLPath] section, set the **LogicalSQLDrive** entry to the drive where you want to install SQL Server. For example, to install SQL Server on drive G,

   LogicalSQLDrive=g:

   b. In the [MasterPath] section, set the **LogicalDBDrive** entry to the drive where you want to create the master database. For example, to create the master database on drive G,

   LogicalDBDrive=g:

    c. In the [Scripts] section, set the CustScPath entry to the custom script path you want to use. For example, if you want to create the master database on drive G, specify:

    CustScPath=g:

    d. If you do not want to install the online books, in the [NewOptions] section of the SQLCUSTM.INI file, set the **BooksOnline** entry to **0**.

For information about the format of the installation script, see the Microsoft SQL Server documentation.

3. In the SMS Administrator, open the Packages window, and from the File menu, choose New.

    The Package Properties dialog box appears.

4. Choose Import, and select the *servername\sharename*\SQL.PDF file.

    The Package Properties dialog box displays SQL Server 6.5 in the Name box.

5. Choose Workstations.

    The Setup Package for Workstation dialog box appears.

6. In the Source Directory box, enter the full UNC name of the SQL Server package source directory (for example, **\\myserver\sql65**).

    You can choose to have SMS inventory this package. If you select this check box, SMS will copy the installation log file from the target computers to the SMS site server.

Important The installation scripts cannot be run by the Package Command Manager service. They can be run only through the Package Command Manager client software. This means that you must leave the System Background Task option disabled in the Command Line Properties of the commands in the SQL Server package.

---

7. Choose Close.

8. Choose OK in all open dialog boxes.

    The SQL Server package now appears in the Packages window. You can now use the SQL Server package to create Run Command On Workstation jobs to install SQL Server.

▶   **To distribute the Microsoft SQL Server package**

1. In the SMS Administrator, open the Queries window, and from the File menu, choose New.

   Define a query to find the computers where you want to install SQL Server.

   Because the installation scripts are based on the installation drive, you should use a query to identify the computers that have the specified installation drive and also have enough free disk space on those drives. You can also create queries that impose other requirements such as amount of RAM or an existing SQL Server.

   For example, the following query is designed to find all computers running Windows NT Server that have enough free space on drive D for a full installation of SQL Server:

```
(
    MICROSOFT|DISK|1.0:Disk Index is 'D'
    AND
    MICROSOFT|DISK|1.0:Free Storage (MByte) is greater than or equal
        to '90'
)
AND
(
    MICROSOFT|OPERATING_SYSTEM|1.0:Operating System Name is
        'Microsoft Windows NT'
    AND
    MICROSOFT|OPERATING_SYSTEM|1.0:Version is same as or comes after
        '3.51'
)
```

Note   The installation drive has these disk space requirements:

Full installation: 90 MB

Installation without online books: 75 MB

For other requirements for SQL Server such as RAM, see the Microsoft SQL Server documentation.

---

2. To run the query, from the File menu, choose Execute Query.

3. Use the query results to add the selected computers to a machine group.

4. Use the new machine group to specify the target computers where you want to install SQL Server.

   You can also specify the query as a target—SMS will evaluate the query when it activates the job used to install the SQL Server package and use that result as the list of target computers.

5. In the SMS Administrator, open the Jobs window, and from the File menu, choose New.

6. Choose Details.

7. In the Job Target box, specify the query or machine group.

8. Select the Run Workstation Command check box.

9. Select the command that specifies the drive where you want to install SQL Server (for example, select Complete Install on D: Drive if you want to install the full installation of SQL Server on drive D of all the target computers).

   Note that if you set up the SQLCUSTM.INI setup script, you must select the Custom Install command to use that script.

10. Choose OK in all open dialog boxes.

   When the job completes, SQL Server will be installed on all target computers.

Working with Network Monitor

This section describes the Network Monitor initialization file and how to set a server-down trigger.

Editing Parser Initialization Files

Each Network Monitor protocol parser uses an initialization (.INI) file. This section explains the sections of parser .INI files and situations in which you might need to modify these files.

The [ETYPES] Section

An Ethertype is a four-digit hexadecimal number that uniquely identifies a protocol implementation. If you write a new implementation for an existing protocol, you register the implementation with the Xerox Corporation, and you are assigned an Ethertype. This Ethertype appears in any frame that uses the new implementation, and enables software that receives the frame to distinguish the frame from any frame that does not use the new implementation.

The ETYPES section of a parser .INI file lists protocols and their associated Ethertypes. This information is used by the Network Monitor application programming interface (NMAPI) to ensure that a frame is passed to the correct parser for processing.

For example, the MAC.INI file contains the following entry:

```
0x600   =   XNS
```

If the media access control (MAC) protocol parser for Network Monitor encounters 0x600 in a frame, the parser reads its .INI file to identify the protocol associated with this Ethertype. It passes this protocol name to the NMAPI. The NMAPI passes the frame to the correct XNS parser.

If you add a parser to Network Monitor, or replace a Network Monitor parser with an implementation of your own, you must add the protocol name and the associated Ethertype to the ETYPES list in the Network Monitor .INI files. Make appropriate additions to the .INI file for every parser that can pass frames to your parser.

The [FORCE_RAW_IPX] Section

The information in this section applies only to the MAC.INI file.

Use the FORCE_RAW_IPX section of the MAC.INI file to specify how Network Monitor should respond when it receives an Ethernet or Fiber Distributed Data Interface (FDDI) frame that contains ambiguous data in the first two bytes after the frame's Length field.

An Institute of Electrical and Electronics Engineers (IEEE) 802.3 frame contains the following components:

Destination Address
Identified in the first six bytes of the frame.

Source Address
Identified in the second six bytes of the frame.

Length
Identified in the thirteenth and fourteenth bytes of the frame.

LLC Header
Identified in the next three bytes of the frame. Contains the destination service access point (DSAP), source service access point (SSAP), and control information.

All implementations of the IEEE 802.3 standard use the first three fields described in the preceding list to store the same types of information. However, implementations of IPX differ in their use of the bytes that follow the Length field. Differences in implementation can render the IPX protocol parser unable to interpret the first two bytes following the Length field.

For example, in a raw IEEE 802.3 frame, the bytes following the Length field always contain the hexadecimal numbers FFFF, which marks the beginning of the IPX frame. Because IPX frames currently do not use the checksum field, these two bytes are always FFFF and constitute the IPX header.

A true IEEE 802.3 frame, on the other hand, uses these bytes to store the DSAP and the SSAP. In the event that the DSAP and SSAP fields both equate to FF, the IEEE 802.3 frame cannot be distinguished from the IPX header in a raw IEEE 802.3 frame.

In most cases in which the number FFFF appears in the first two bytes following the Length field, it indicates that the frame is a raw IEEE 802.3 frame. Therefore, the FORCE_RAW_IPX field of the parser MAC.INI file is set to Yes for both Ethernet and FDDI frames. This setting notifies Network Monitor to interpret a frame containing FFFF in the first four bytes following the Length field as a raw IPX frame. If you set these entries to No, such frames are interpreted as true IEEE 802.3 frames.

Setting a Server-Down Trigger

This section explains how to set a server-down trigger. The trigger stops a capture on a computer running Network Monitor when another computer stops functioning. A third computer, running the Windows NT platform, runs a batch file that uses the **net view** command to query the network for the monitored server. If the server goes down, the computer running the Windows NT platform uses the **net send** command to notify the computer running Network Monitor, and the running capture is stopped.

Throughout this example, the computers will be referred to by the following names:

- NM_HOST: The computer running Network Monitor.

- NM_ASSIST: The computer running the Windows NT platform that notifies NM_HOST if the server goes down. Network Monitor on NM_HOST will be set up to stop capturing if it captures a frame that contains a particular data pattern. NM_ASSIST is set up to send NM_HOST a frame containing this pattern if a server goes down.

  This computer does not have to be running the Windows NT platform, but it must be a computer on which the **net send** command is available. This command is available for Windows version 3.*x* running LAN Manager version 2.*x*. This command is not available for Windows for Workgroups version 3.*x*.

- SOME_SERVER: The server being monitored. This computer can be running either Windows or the Windows NT platform.

The following figure illustrates the relationship among these three computers.

1. Network Monitor captures frames from the network with a server-down trigger set.

2. Computer running Windows NT and WATCH.BAT repeatedly executes **net view** command with the server name as a parameter.

3. If the server returns an error to the computer running WATCH.BAT, that computer then executes a **net send "serverdown"** to the computer running Network Monitor.

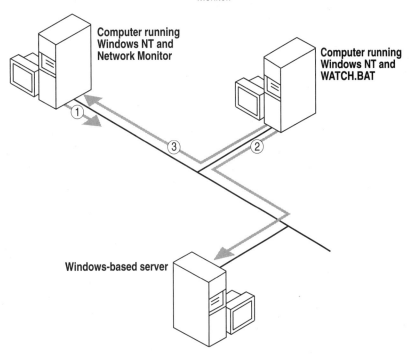

This example is designed so that you can work through it simply by substituting the computer names on your network for the computer names used in the example.

Implementing a Server-Down Trigger

To set the server-down trigger illustrated in this example, perform the following procedures:

1. On NM_HOST, set a capture filter that captures frames sent from any computer to the computer running Network Monitor, and then start a capture.

2. On NM_ASSIST, use the **net send** command to send a text string (**serverdown** in this example) to NM_HOST.

3. Use Network Monitor to capture and display the frame that contains the **serverdown** test string. Use this frame to determine the offset at which **serverdown** appears in the frame.

Note The first three steps are intended simply to provide NM_HOST with a test frame. This frame's attributes are used later to provide necessary trigger specifications, and step 5 ensures that if SOME_SERVER stops functioning, a frame identical to the test frame is sent to NM_HOST.

---

4. On NM_HOST, set the capture trigger, set the same filter you used in step 1, and then start a capture.

5. Run a batch file on NM_ASSIST that uses the **net send** command to send the **serverdown** string to NM_HOST if the server goes down.

The following sections explain how to perform each of these steps.

Step 1: Filtering and Capturing

The server-down trigger requires two pieces of information: a pattern and an offset. A pattern is a particular arrangement of hexadecimal or ASCII data within a captured frame. The offset designates how many bytes into a frame the pattern occurs; this number is always hexadecimal.

The pattern in this example is arbitrary; when the trigger is set, the computer running Network Monitor stops capturing if it detects the text string **serverdown** within a frame. The text string, **serverdown**, represents the trigger's data pattern.

The offset is not arbitrary; because it measures how far into the frame the pattern appears, it can possibly distinguish between two frames containing an identical text string.

To determine the pattern offset, set up a Network Monitor filter to capture a frame containing the specified pattern.

▶ **To filter for the serverdown pattern**

1. From the Network Monitor Capture menu, choose Filter.

   The Capture Filter dialog box appears.

2. Select the Address Pairs line.

3. Under Add, choose Address. ·

   The Address Expression dialog box appears.

4. In the Station 1 box, select the local computer name.

5. In the Direction box, select <-->.

6. In the Station 2 box, select ANY.

7. Select Include.

8. Choose OK in all open dialog boxes.

9. In the Capture window, from the Capture menu, choose Start.

Step 2: Sending a Test String

When a capture has been started on the computer running Network Monitor, a test frame must be sent to this computer. This frame, when captured, provides the pattern offset that is necessary for the server-down trigger to function correctly.

To provide the running capture with a test frame, on NM_ASSIST, use the **net send** command to send **serverdown** to NM_HOST. The **net send** command takes two parameters—the name of a computer and an ASCII text string—and has the following syntax:

net send *computername string*

In this example, *string* is **serverdown**. Remember that on NM_HOST, a filter has been set that captures all frames sent to that computer. This filter will capture the frame that contains **serverdown**, and you will use this frame to determine the offset of **serverdown**. In later steps, you'll need this offset to set up the trigger.

Step 3: Capturing and Displaying the Test String

In this step, identify the offset of **serverdown**—that is, how many bytes into the frame the first character in **serverdown** appears. This is the offset that you provide later when you set the server-down trigger.

▶ **To determine the offset of the serverdown test string**

1. In the Network Monitor Capture window, from the Capture menu, choose Stop and View to display the Frame Viewer window.

2. In the Detail pane of the Frame Viewer window, expand the displayed protocol headers until the string SERVERDOWN appears in the lower-right corner of the Hex pane.

Tip In the Detail pane, you need to expand only levels containing the SMB protocol header. If a plus sign (+) appears to the left of a level, the level can be expanded.

---

3. In the Hex pane, click the S in SERVERDOWN.

The pattern offset appears in parentheses in the status panel of the Frame Viewer window to the right of the word Offset. This is the hexadecimal number you use when you set the trigger.

Step 4: Setting the Capture Trigger

Once you have determined the offset of the test string, you can actually set the trigger and begin capturing.

▶ **To set the server-down trigger**

1. In the Network Monitor Capture window, from the Capture menu, choose Trigger.

   The Capture Trigger dialog box appears.

2. Under Trigger On, select Pattern Match.

3. In the Pattern box:

   - Select From Start of Frame.
   - Select ASCII.
   - In the Offset (In Hex) box, type the offset that you obtained in the preceding section.
   - In the Pattern box, type **serverdown**.

4. In the Trigger Action box, select Stop Capture.

5. Choose OK.

6. From the Capture menu, choose Start.

Step 5: Running the Batch File

Network Monitor monitors the server with the help of a computer running the Windows NT platform and a batch file. This computer running the Windows NT platform is the one that you used in "Step 2: Sending a Test String" to send the **serverdown** text string to the computer running Network Monitor.

The following is an example of a batch file that you might use:

```
:TOP
NET VIEW \\SOME_SERVER
If errorlevel 1 GOTO FAIL
GOTO TOP
:FAIL
NET SEND NM_HOST serverdown
```

This batch file contains a simple loop and two labels: TOP and FAIL. When the file begins processing, it runs the **net view** command, specifying the server name as a parameter, then processes the IF statement. If the **net view** command locates the server, the batch file returns to the TOP label and runs the **net view** command again. This process repeats until the **net view** command returns ERROR LEVEL 1, which indicates that **net view** was unable to locate the server and that the server is probably no longer functioning.

If the **net view** command returns ERROR LEVEL 1, the batch file runs the **net send** command, with **serverdown** as a string parameter, on the computer running Network Monitor. Network Monitor captures the frame containing **serverdown** as the offset specified in the trigger, and the trigger action is implemented; a message appears to indicate that the capture has stopped.

Note This example uses one batch file to monitor one server. Because you can run multiple MS-DOS sessions under Windows NT, you can run the batch file in multiple sessions, monitoring multiple servers. You need only to specify a different test string for each server, as well as the appropriate computer name for each instance in which the **net view** command appears.

Configuring SMS Clients for Remote Control

Each time an SMS client runs the SMS Client Setup program, the settings on the client can be changed. To make permanent changes, the user must use the Client Setup Options (CLIOPTS.EXE) utility, included in this Resource Kit.

The syntax for CLIOPTS.EXE is as follows:

cliopts /set *optionname optionvalue*

or

cliopts /list *optionname*

where *optionname* is either **usertsr, useripx,** or **wuser**, and *optionvalue* is any legal switch that can be passed to the named option. These are documented in the SMS version 1.2 *Administrator's Guide*.

For example, to see the current configuration of **useripx**, type:

cliopts /list useripx

To set USERTSR.EXE to use Lana number 1, type:

cliopts /set usertsr /L1

Changes do not take affect until the user restarts the computer, restarts the Windows operating system, or both, depending on which values are set.

Note The **cliopts** program is recommended for clients whose options differ from the norm. If you want to change properties for all clients, use the Client button in the Site Properties dialog box in the SMS Administrator. Send **cliopts** in a package only to those clients that require changes to the default client settings.

Configuring the Event-to-Trap Translator

You can remotely modify the event to SNMP trap configuration on clients, using a job that uses EVENTCM*x*.EXE. You can run any of the following remote event configuration tools from the SITE.SRV\MAINCFG.BOX\MSTEST directory:

Executable file name	Supported platform
EVENTCMA.EXE	Alpha
EVENTCMI.EXE	Intel (x86)
EVENTCMM.EXE	MIPS

The remote event configuration tool uses the following syntax:

eventcm[i|a|m] *filename options*

Where *filename* is a .CNF configuration file that contains the event configuration to run on the client, and *options* can be one or more of the following:

/nolog
No logging.

/nomif
No MIF file generation.

/default
The configuration is modified only if the current configuration type is not CUSTOM.

/setcustom
Sets the current configuration type to CUSTOM.

/nostopstart
Do not stop and start the SNMP service.

For more information about the syntax of the configuration files (.CNF), see Chapter 4, "File Formats."

Debugging SNMP Traps

The Event to Trap Translator converts selected Windows NT events, from the three Windows NT event logs, to SNMP traps and sends them to a site. At the site, SNMP traps are filtered for specific traps, and these are written to the database. Also, the traps can be sent to other network management consoles besides the SMS Administrator.

To use the SNMP traps functionality, complete the following steps.

On the client that will be used to send traps:

- Install TCP/IP and SNMP.
- Use the Windows NT Control Panel to configure the SNMP client.
- Install the SMS SNMP and translation agent files.
- Use the Personal Computer Properties in the SMS Administrator to configure the SNMP clients.
- If you want to use security traps from the client, use the Windows NT User Manager to enable security logging on the client.
- If you are going to trap file activity on the client, use the Windows NT File Manager to enable security auditing for those directories.

At the site to receive traps

- Install TCP/IP and SNMP.
- Configure a filter for incoming traps.

Installing TCP/IP and SNMP

If the Windows NT-based client that will generate traps is running Windows NT version 3.51, SP4 must be installed. For detailed installation procedures, see the SMS version 1.2 *Administrator's Guide*, Chapter 14.

You must configure the SNMP service and add at least one community name containing at least one address to send traps to.

▶ **To add a community name**

1. On the client that will receive the traps, run **ipconfig** to display the IP address for the local computer.
2. On the client that will send traps, make sure the SNMP service is running.

3. On the client that will send traps, configure the SNMP service (in the Networks control panel) and add the address of the receiving client to the community.

4. Stop and then start the SNMP service so that all the settings will be active.

If SNMP is installed after the SMS client is installed, you might need to manually set the TranslatorEnabled value in the HKEY_LOCAL_MACHINE\Software \Microsoft\SNMP_EVENTS\EventLog registry key. This value is created by SNMP Setup and set to Yes by the **cli_nt** program the next time the user logs on or runs RUNSMS.BAT. Ensure that this value is Yes so that the event to SNMP trap translation will occur.

▶ **To start the Event to Trap Translator**

1. In the SMS Administrator, open the Personal Computer Properties for the client that will be sending SNMP traps.

2. In the Windows NT Administrator group, select Event to Trap Translator.

   The EVENTRAP.EXE program starts, using the client as the target. The Event to Trap Translator window appears.

   Unless you use this tool to specify events to be converted to SNMP traps, no Windows NT events will be translated and sent. A few traps are sent by default.

3. Choose Custom.

4. Choose Edit.

5. In the Event Source list, choose Security.

6. Choose Security to list the Windows NT security events. One at a time, select an event, and choose Add to add it to the configuration.

7. When you are finished, choose Close.

The following event IDs can be quite useful: 560, 561, 562, 592, and 593. The $56x$ events are for the directory where you can test bursts of traps, and the $59x$ events can be used to tell if a process has a general protection fault and gets restarted. (It had a general protection fault if you weren't the one to start it.)

The LOGON.SRV\MSTEST\EVENTCM$x$.EXE program can be sent as a job to configure SNMP on a group of clients. For details on this program, see "Configuring the Event to Trap Translator" earlier in this chapter.

▶ **To audit Windows NT events**

1. Start the Windows NT User Manager.

2. From the Policies menu, choose Audit.

   The Audit Policy dialog box appears.

3. Choose Audit These Events, and then select all events to be audited.

4. Choose OK.

5. If you want to audit file and object access, open the File Manager and select the directory to be audited.

6. From the Security menu, choose Auditing.

7. Select the events to audit.

   If you select the name *after* the events, nothing gets audited.

Note Auditing is available only on NTFS partitions.

Do not use the domain\smsadmin and local\smsadmin accounts because Windows NT will never activate the local admin account for auditing.

Now go to the SMS Administrator for the site that the client is sending SNMP traps to, and set it to write some of these traps to the database. For details, see the SMS version 1.2 *Administrator's Guide*.

How SNMP Works in SMS

Client services related to SNMP:

- SNMP service (process name SNMP)
- TCP/IP NetBIOS helper (not a separate process, part of the network)

Site services related to SNMP:

- SMS_CLIENT_CONFIG_MANAGER (process name Clicfg)
- SMS_EXECUTIVE (process name SmsExec)
- SNMP service (process name SNMP)
- TCP/IP NetBIOS helper (not a separate process, part of the network)

Site processes not running as a service related to SNMP:

- SNMPTRAP

SmsExec thread components related to SNMP:

- TRAPFLTR

The **net start** command will display the service name SNMP Service, but it will also respond to the simpler SNMP when you are controlling it from the command line.

The SMS functionality for Windows NT event to trap translation is a DLL extension (SNMPELEA.DLL) to the SNMP service with the process name of SNMP and service name of SNMP service. The SMS extension to the SNMP service uses the Windows NT file SNMPAPI.DLL. As one thread reads the Windows NT event log, translates events, and adds SNMP traps to a list to be sent, another thread reads the list and has the SNMP service send the trap, and deletes it from the list. This second thread is sometimes called the trap sender. As the list grows, more memory is allocated to the SNMP service. After all the traps have been sent, the memory allocation will return to the original level, and the SNMP service idles. Since the Event to Trap Translator adds traps to the list faster than it sends them, a big burst can add quite a bit of memory allocation to the SNMP service.

The SMS feature trap translator is the TRAPFLTR thread component in SmsExec. TRAPFLTR starts SNMPTRAP.EXE after SmsExec starts TRAPFLTR. SNMPTRAP.EXE receives SNMP traps sent to that client, and passes them to the thread component TRAPFLTR in SmsExec. As the client receives traps, SNMPTRAP.EXE shows CPU activity. TRAPFLTR decides whether to write the trap to the database, or discard it. If it is a burst of traps, TRAPFLTR will get behind, and the memory allocation for SmsExec will grow. As the traps are discarded or written to the database, the memory allocation for SmsExec will be released and return to the original level.

If the Windows NT event log is set to a small size and to overwrite events as needed, and there is a burst of events, the Event to Trap Translator can fall behind and lose traps if they are overwritten before it translates the event.

If a client is sending traps to itself, use Network Monitor (running on a separate computer) to monitor the activity.

Testing the SNMP Client Setup

When testing the translation of events to SNMP traps on clients running Windows NT, remember:

- If the events are not being written to the Windows NT event log, they can't be translated.
- If the traps are not going out on the network, the site can't receive them.

To test whether security logging and auditing is working, add user permissions for a file or directory and see if security events show up in the Windows NT event log. Every time a file has its permissions changed, event IDs 560 and 562 should be created.

Next, test the trap sending on the client. In a directory that contains at least 50 files, set auditing for your user name. Add or remove a user from the permissions for the directory, subdirectories, and files. In the Performance Monitor, you should see CPU activity for SNMP. Private bytes for SNMP should slope up, then slope down, and then CPU activity should stop. This sequence means the Event to Trap Translator converted some events to traps, put them in the list, and sent them somewhere.

Network Monitor allows you to view whether events that have been translated into traps are sent to the destination.

At the site receiving the traps, SmsExec should grow in size and show an increase in CPU usage. The TRAPFLTR thread in SmsExec should show the increase in CPU usage. The TRAPFLTR log should show traps being written to the database, and the SNMP traps window should show new traps, after being refreshed.

For information about using the following tools, see the *Microsoft Windows NT Resource Kit*:

- SNMP Monitor (SNMPMON.EXE)
- SNMP Browser (SNMPUTIL.EXE)

Loading the SNMP Traps' Functionality and Sizing Hardware

Trapping for file activity is a good way to size the hardware for SNMP traps. Create several bursts of traps by changing the file permissions in large groups of files. By timing how long it takes to process the traps, you can calculate the trap throughput.

Caution   There is a large amount of file activity in all SMS directories on all SMS servers and clients. Trapping file activity in these locations will cause a flood of traps.

If the Automatically Configure Logon Scripts option is enabled, by default the Site Configuration Manager will check each user account for correct logon script configuration every 24 hours. This will produce two events for each user account in each SMS domain in the site.

Changing permissions on a group of files can cause bursts of traps. If the bursts are too large or too frequent, SNMP might stop responding. If so, stop and then start the SNMP service.

If you use the default of enabling the trap throttle, remember that if the throttle gets tripped, you have to manually reset it before any more traps are sent.

Backing Up and Restoring the SMS System

The SMS version 1.2 *Administrator's Guide* describes how to back up and restore an SMS site. This section provides more details about these processes.

Every time a database is expanded, it creates another fragment. The SMS database typically expands occasionally as the number of inventoried machines grows. To completely restore the database, the new device(s) have to have the same fragment pattern. If the database was created with 20 MB data and a 10 MB log, and then the data expanded by 30 MB and the log expanded by 5 MB, to restore data to the new database the first four fragments need to be the same type and size and in the same order. The new database can be bigger with more fragments, but the first four fragments have to match the four from the backed up database. Along with this, the SQL server must use the same sort order and code page that was in use by SQL server when the backup was made.

There is a SQL limit of 32 fragments in a database. Once this limit is reached, the database cannot be expanded any more. If the fragments are not contiguous, the only way to reduce the number of fragments and save the data is to transfer the whole database to a new database that uses one large data fragment and one large log fragment. (See the SQL Server documentation for more information.) After that, SMS must be pointed at the new database.

▶ **Before backing up the database**

1. Start the MSSQL\BINN\ISQLW.EXE program and select the SMS database as the default.

2. Stop all other processes that might access the SMS database.

3. Run the following data integrity checks:

   dbcc checkdb
   go
   dbcc newalloc
   go
   dbcc checkcatalog

   Note Errors that are not corrected before backup might prevent the restore.
   ---

4. Save a copy of the files in the \MSSQL\LOG\ERRORLOG directory, which will contain the SQL version, sort order, and code page being used at that time.

5. To consolidate any contiguous fragments, select the SMS database as the default in **isqlw**, and run the following command:

   sp_coalesce_fragments *SMSdatabase*

   Where *SMSdatabase* is the name of your database.

   Note If the fragments are not contiguous, this command will not help. If the database was created with a data then log fragment, and data was expanded then log expanded, there will be four noncontiguous fragments, this command will not help.

   ---

6. Select the SMS database as the default in **isqlw** and run the following command to display basic information about the database including the name, options selected, and a list of the fragments:

   sp_helpdb *SMSdatabase*

7. Save the results for future reference.

Now back up the database.

You can create a script that will create the correct fragment pattern. If the database name or physical device names will be changed, you must edit the script to reflect these changes.

▶ **To generate the fragment correction script**

1. Select the SMS database as the default in **isqlw**.

2. Run the following command:

   sp_help_revdatabase *SMSdatabase*

3. Save the results.

   Be sure to verify that the database is still intact after completing these tasks. If there were errors interjected into one of the steps, the restore might not be completely successful.

4. Select the SMS database as the default in **isqlw**, and run the following commands:

   dbcc checkdb
   go
   dbcc newalloc
   go
   dbcc checkcatalog

5. Create the data devices for the SMS database: one for data and a separate one for log. Even if there are several fragments, all the data fragments can go on the data device and all the log fragments on the log device.

6. If necessary, edit the database name and device names in the script produced by **sp_help_revdatabase**, and run the script from **isqlw**.

7. Restore the SMS database.

8. In SMS Setup, run Operations/SMS Database and change the SQL Server name and the database name, if appropriate. This points SMS services to the new server and database.

Note The REGEDT32.EXE program can save registry information in both binary and ASCII format. Be sure you are saving the SMS registry keys in a format that **regedt32** can restore (binary).

C H A P T E R   6

Tuning

Microsoft Systems Management Server (SMS) is a complex and powerful tool. For SMS, as with most complex systems, performance monitoring and tuning is an important part of system maintenance to ensure optimum system performance. This chapter discusses methods for identifying and fixing tuning problems— problems that occur when the system is performing properly, but not efficiently.

To help you find and eliminate tuning problems, this chapter provides information about the following:

"Tuning and Bottlenecks" A single component can degrade system performance. When this happens, the limiting component is called a *bottleneck*. This section discusses bottlenecks and how to find them.

"Performance Monitor" Performance Monitor is a Windows NT administrative tool for monitoring the performance of computers running Windows NT. This section describes Performance Monitor and how to use it to find bottlenecks in an SMS system.

"Task Manager" Task Manager is a new tool introduced with Windows NT 4.0. It lets you start, stop, and monitor applications and processes on your computer. It also provides basic performance-monitoring capabilities. This section describes how to use Task Manager to find bottlenecks.

"Tuning Tips" This section describes ways to tune your SMS system once you have found bottlenecks that are impairing system performance.

Tuning and Bottlenecks

Tuning a system means locating the reason why the system is not performing up to expectations. Frequently, there is a single system component that is causing the system to perform poorly. The condition in which the limitations in one component prevent the whole system from operating faster is known as a *bottleneck*. The primary indicator of a bottleneck is an extended high rate of use on one hardware resource and resulting low rates of use on related components. It is accompanied by sustained queues for one or more services, and slow response time.

If a computer handles many different types of tasks, different components may become bottlenecks at different times. For instance, the CPU may become the bottleneck when a compute-intensive application is running; the disk may become the bottleneck if several applications are attempting to read and write data simultaneously. However, in general, the device with the lowest maximum throughput is the most likely to become a bottleneck if it is in demand. This is especially true of server applications that tend to run only a few demanding applications (like SMS or SQL Server). If a component is acting as a bottleneck, making other components faster can never yield more throughput; it can only result in lower utilization of the faster components.

Although 100 percent utilization of a resource is a clear warning of a bottleneck, it is neither a necessary nor sufficient condition. You can have bottlenecks on devices with utilization well below 100 percent and you can, at least in theory, have a device running at nearly 100 percent utilization that is not a bottleneck. That is, the device is not preventing any other resource from getting its work done, nothing is waiting for it, and even if it were infinitely fast, things wouldn't happen any sooner.

The following list describes some of the most obvious and common signs that can be observed and that may indicate a bottleneck:

Server hard disk is always busy.
Frequently, you can observe how busy a server's hard disk is by watching and listening to the server. If the server's disk is always busy, then there is a good chance that the server is not performing optimally.

Server applications run very slowly.
You may notice that the SMS Administrator (or other applications) runs very slowly on the server.

Clients cannot access server (or server responds very slowly).

SMS servers are used to perform a number of different functions. For instance, servers log clients on to the network, configure the clients to run SMS, collect the inventory data from the clients, and provide distributed packages to the clients. You may observe that some servers are so busy that they stop processing log ons, or process the logon requests very slowly. Users may notice that their logon scripts take much longer than they used to, or that SMS Client Setup or inventory is much slower. Additionally, users may not be able to install packages, or may not be able to gain access to shared packages.

SMS stops processing system files.

You should routinely check the SMS system directories to be sure that files are being processed correctly. The following table lists some of the directories that should be monitored; a backlog of files in these directories may indicate that the system is not performing optimally.

Directory	Comment
LOGS	Used by the SMS services and components to store logs. Contains primary and backup logs for up to 19 components. By default, each log uses up to 128K. Logging can take a great deal of disk space and can degrade system performance. Use the SMS Service Manager to change the log size or to disable logging.
SITE.SRV\INVENTRY.BOX	The location where Maintenance Manager puts client inventory files that it collects from SMS logon servers. The Inventory Processor monitors this directory. The files in this directory are deleted when the inventory data is written to the SITE.SRV\DATALOAD.BOX\DELTAMIF.COL directory. A backlog might indicate that the Inventory Processor is not running or is too busy to process the files.
SITE.SRV\INVENTRY.BOX \BADMIFS	The location where the Inventory Processor places .MIF files that cannot be processed. This directory should always be empty.
SITE.SRV\INVENTRY.BOX \BADRAWS	The location where the Inventory Processor places .RAW files that cannot be processed. This directory should always be empty.
SITE.SRV\DATALOAD.BOX \DELTAMIF.COL	Used by the Inventory Processor to store MIF files that are ready to be processed by the Data Loader. When the Data Loader is ready to process the files, it moves them to the PROCESS subdirectory. A backlog in this directory might indicate that the SQL Server is unavailable, or that the Data Loader is too busy to process the files.
SITE.SRV\DATALOAD.BOX \DELTAMIF.COL\PROCESS	Used by the Data Loader to store MIF files that it is ready to process. Once these files are processed, they are moved to the SITEREP.BOX directory. If the Data Loader is unable to process some files, they are moved to the BADMIFS directory. A backlog might indicate that the SQL Server is unavailable, or that the Data Loader is too busy to process the files.

(continued)

Directory	Comment
SITE.SRV\DATALOAD.BOX \DELTAMIF.COL\BADMIFS	Used by the Data Loader to store MIF files that cannot be processed. Under ideal conditions, this directory is empty. Any files here indicate a problem.
SITE.SRV\SITEREP.BOX	Used by the Data Loader to store files that should be sent to a parent site. When the Site Reporter detects a queue of MIF files in this directory, it creates a system job that sends these MIF files to the parent site. A backlog might indicate that Site Reporter is not running or is overloaded, or that the site cannot connect to the parent site.
SITE.SRV\SCHEDULE.BOX	Used by the SMS components to store system job instructions for the Scheduler. The Scheduler monitors this directory and uses the instructions to start the specified system jobs. A backlog might indicate that the Scheduler is not running or is too busy to process the jobs.
SITE.SRV\SENDER.BOX \REQUESTS	The location where the Scheduler places send request files for the sender. The specific sender assigned to each subdirectory (outbox) monitors its directory and processes the requests. Files remain in this directory until the sender successfully sends the job. A backlog might indicate that the sender is busy or not running, or that it cannot connect to the target site.
SITE.SRV\SENDER.BOX \TOSEND	The location where the Scheduler places compressed packages and despooler instruction files to be sent to another site. When the sender processes a send request for a job, it sends the job's files from this directory to the target site. A backlog might indicate that the sender is busy or not running, or that it cannot connect to the target site.
SITE.SRV\DESPOOLR.BOX \RECEIVE	The location where the sender places despooler instruction files and compressed packages that are targeted for the site. The Despooler monitors this directory and processes the instruction files. The packages should be moved to the STORE directory as soon as the Despooler verifies that the package and instructions have been completely and correctly received. A backlog might indicate that the Despooler is too busy to process the packages.

In these cases, it may or may not be reasonably easy to determine the cause of the problem and to find a solution. For instance, if MIF files are backing up in the DELTAMIF.COL directory, you can be reasonably sure that the Data Loader is the bottleneck. A quick look may show that the Data Loader is not running, in which case you simply need to restart it. If the Data Loader is running, you may need to increase the capacity of the site server, or move the Data Loader to another server, in order to get better results. To specifically determine the reason that the Data Loader is not keeping up, you should use one of the troubleshooting tools or techniques described later in this chapter.

Performance Monitor

Performance Monitor is a Windows NT administrative tool for monitoring the performance of computers running Windows NT. It uses a series of counters to track data, such as the number of processes waiting for disk time, the number of network packets transmitted per second, and the percentage of microprocessor utilization. You can watch this data in real time, log it for future study, use it in charts and reports, and set alerts to warn you when a threshold value is exceeded.

Performance Monitor lets you:

- View data from multiple computers simultaneously.
- See how changes you make effect the computer.
- Change charts of current activity while viewing them.
- Export Performance Monitor data to spreadsheets or database programs, or use it as raw input for C programs.
- Trigger a program or procedure, or send notices when a threshold is exceeded.
- Log data about various objects from different computers over time. You can use these log files to record typical resource use, monitor a problem, or help in capacity planning.
- Combine selected sections of several log files into a long-term archive.
- Report on current activity or trends over time.
- Save different combinations of counter and option settings for quick starts and changes.

Performance Monitor shows a broad view of the computer's performance. In some cases, you can use Performance Monitor to fully identify and fix a problem. In other cases, you may need to use a more specialized tool, such as a profiler, a working set monitor, or a network analyzer. The usage of those tools is beyond the scope of this chapter; for more information about specialized troubleshooting tools, contact the vendor of the tool.

The next sections provide some tips for using Performance Monitor. The sections assume you are using Windows NT Server 4.0 and SQL Server 6.5.

For more specific instructions about using Performance Monitor, see Performance Monitor Help, or see the detailed description in the *Microsoft Windows NT Resource Kit*.

Starting Performance Monitor

You can start the Windows NT Performance Monitor from the Administrative Tools menu on the Start menu or from the command line.

When you use Performance Monitor, you select object counters and options to customize each of the four Performance Monitor views: Chart, Log, Report, and Alert. You can save these counter and option settings to a file and design different settings files for all of your monitoring tasks.

You can save settings for one view or save a group of view settings in a workspace. The following table shows the file extensions associated with each view.

View	Settings file extension
Alert	.PMA
Chart	.PMC
Log	.PML
Report	.PMR
Workspace	.PMW

You can start Performance Monitor with a settings file or open the settings file after you start. You can use only one settings file of each type at a time, but you can open multiple copies of Performance Monitor and use a different settings file or workspace with each copy.

When you start Performance Monitor from a batch file or from the command line, you can specify a settings file listing the counters and options for each view. For example:

```
C:\> perfmon settings.pmw
```

To configure Performance Monitor to start automatically when a user logs on to the system, copy the Performance Monitor icon to the Startup program group, with the command line **perfmon.exe** *my.pmw*, where *my.pmw* is the name of a workspace file that exists on the computer.

To configure Performance Monitor to run on system startup (so it's running even if nobody logs on), use the MONITOR.EXE program provided in the *Microsoft Windows NT Resource Kit*. MONITOR is the configuration tool for installing and controlling the Data Logging service (DATALOG.EXE). The Data Logging service is a Windows NT service that performs alert and log view functions. For more information on remote logging and automatically starting and stopping the service, see the *Microsoft Windows NT Resource Kit*.

Performance Monitor Views

Performance Monitor lets you set up views for charts, alerts, logs, and reports. When you start using Performance Monitor to find bottlenecks in the system, you may find it useful to set up more than one type of view. Using multiple views at the same time gives you a better representation of what is actually happening in your system. For instance, Log view (which occurs over a long period of time) may show you trends which you would not notice in Chart view.

When you set up multiple views, you create a workspace. You can preserve the workspace, thus preserving the complete configuration of all views you are using. To preserve a workspace, save the view configurations in a workspace settings (.PMW) file.

Chart View

When you begin troubleshooting a performance problem, you will most likely want to start with Chart view. Chart view shows you the current activity of the selected counters and instances. You can customize each chart (by adding or deleting objects, counters, and instances) to create a chart that lets you monitor many different types of performance. You can change chart selections, such as chart scale or counter display colors, to make your charts more readable.

When you add objects to a chart, you can use the Explain button to learn more about what each counter is used for. You can use the Chart Options dialog box to change the update time, to display in histogram mode, or to change many other Chart view options.

Log View

You can use Log view to document activity and trends over a long period of time. Log view takes whole objects with all their counters for all instances, and it writes all of this data to a log file. These log files can get very large, so use caution when setting up logging.

It is often a good idea to begin by logging the Logical Disk, Memory, Process, Processor, System, and Thread objects. You configure the log in the Log Options dialog box. You must specify the log file name and update interval before you can start logging. When you are ready to start logging, select the Start Log button.

The Log View window displays the log file, file size, logging status, and log interval while logging is enabled. Monitor the size of the log file to ensure that it does not become too large. When you want to stop logging, go back to the Log Options dialog box and select the Stop Logging button.

To view the log, select Options, Data From, and specify the log file name.

The log can be exported with comma or tab delimited columns for analysis in a spreadsheet or database.

Alert View

You can configure Performance Monitor alerts to notify you if the system seems to be reaching a critical state in a key area. For instance, you can set alerts to be generated if Logical Disk: % Free Space, or Memory: Available Bytes falls below 20 percent, or if System: Processor Queue Length exceeds 3.

You can configure Performance Monitor to carry out one or more of the following actions when an alert is generated:

- Run a program.
- Log an event to the Windows NT application log on the system where Performance Monitor is running.
- Send a network alert message to another computer.

Objects and Instances

Performance Monitor uses objects, counters, and instances to describe the components of a computer that can be monitored. *Objects* represent threads and processes, sections of shared memory, and physical devices in the computer. For instance, a computer has at least one object known as microprocessor. In some cases, computers have more than one *instance* of an object; for example, a computer may have multiple microprocessors. *Counters* are the things about an object that can be measured (or counted). When you specify what you want to monitor in Performance Monitor, you must always specify the object, counter, and instance that you want to monitor.

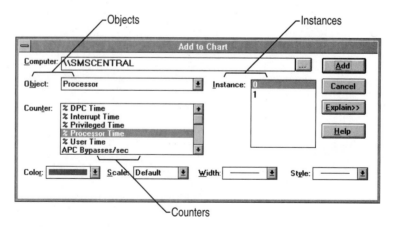

Performance Monitor collects data on activity, demand, and space used by the objects in your computer. Some objects always appear in Performance Monitor; others appear only if the service or process is running. The following table shows the objects that always appear when you run Windows NT 4.0.

Object name	Description
Cache	The file system cache is an area of physical memory that holds recently used data.
Logical Disk	Disk partitions and other logical views of disk space.
Memory	RAM used to store code and data.
Objects	Certain system software objects.
Paging File	File used to back up virtual memory allocations.
Physical Disk	Hardware disk unit (spindle or RAID device).
Process	Software object that represents a running program.
Processor	Hardware unit that runs program instructions.
Redirector	File system that diverts file requests to network servers.
System	Counters that apply to all system hardware and software.
Thread	The part of a process that uses the CPU.

Each *instance* of an object represents a component of the system. When the computer being monitored has more than one component of the same object type, Performance Monitor displays multiple instances of the object in the Instance box of the Add to Chart (View, Log, or Report) dialog box. It also displays the **_Total** instance, which represents a sum of the values for all instances of the object.

For example, if a computer has multiple physical disks, there will be multiple instances of the Physical Disk object in the Add to Chart dialog box. This dialog box shows two instances of physical disks and a **_Total** instance. You can monitor the same or a different set of counters for each instance of an object.

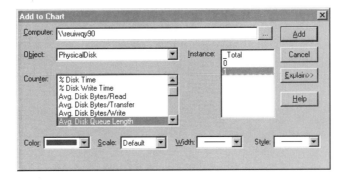

All counters for an object have the same instances. But, sometimes, the instances just don't make sense for a particular counter. For example, the totals of ordinal numbers, like _Total of Process: Process ID or Thread: Thread State, have no meaning. If you add them to you view, Performance Monitor displays the values as zeros.

Only 32-bit processes appear in the Instances box. Active 16-bit processes appear as threads running in a Windows NT Virtual DOS Machine (NTVDM) process. However, you can run each 16-bit application in a separate NTVDM process to make monitoring easier. For more information, see the *Microsoft Windows NT Resource Kit.*

Some objects are parts of other objects or are dependent upon other objects. The instances of these related objects are shown in the Instances box in the following format:

Parent object = => Child object

The *child object* is part of or is dependent upon the *parent object*. This makes it easier to identify the object.

For example, each logical partition of a disk is shown as the child of a parent physical disk.

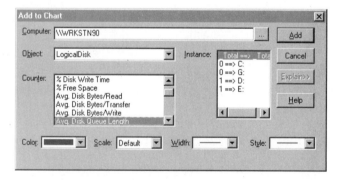

In this example, two physical disks, 0 and 1, are each divided into two logical disks. The Instances box shows that logical disks C and G are partitions of physical disk 0, and logical disks D and E are partitions of physical disk 1.

Counters

Performance Monitor provides counters that collect, average, and display data about computers running Windows NT. Performance Monitor collects data on various aspects of hardware and software performance, such as use, demand, and available space. You activate a Performance Monitor counter by adding it to a chart or report or by adding an object to a log. Performance Monitor begins collecting data immediately.

In this chapter, counters are associated with an object in the following format:

Object: *Counter*

For example, the % Processor Time counter of the Process object would appear as Process: % Processor Time to distinguish it from Processor: % Processor Time or Thread: % Processor Time.

Tip To display the definition for each counter, choose the Explain button in the Add To dialog box. The Explain button works only when you are monitoring current activity, not logs.

There are three types of counters:

- *Instantaneous* counters display the most recent measurement.

  For example, Process: Thread Count displays the number of threads found in the most recent measurement.

- *Averaging* counters, whose names include per second or percent, measure a value over time and display the average of the last two measurements. When you start these counters, you must wait for the second measurement to be taken before any values are displayed.

  For example, Memory: Pages/sec, shows the average number of memory pages found in the last two reads during the second measured.

- *Difference* counters subtract the last measurement from the previous one and display the difference if it is positive. If it is negative, they display a zero.

  Performance Monitor doesn't include any difference counters in its basic set, but they might be included in other applications that use Performance Monitor, and you can write them yourself. For information on writing performance counters, see the *Microsoft Windows NT 4.0 Software Developer's Kit*.

Performance Monitor includes default counters for each object. For instance, when you open the Add To dialog box, the Processor: % Processor Time counter is selected because this counter is used most often. Each object has a default counter which is highlighted when you select the object. These counters were selected as defaults because they are excellent indicators of the object's activity.

Some hardware and applications designed for Windows NT come with their own counters. Many of these *extensible* counters are installed automatically with the product, but some are installed separately. In addition, there are a few specialized counters on the compact disc in the *Microsoft Windows NT Resource Kit*. See your product documentation and Performance Monitor Help for detailed instructions on adding extensible counters.

Using Performance Monitor to Tune SMS

This section describes the objects and counters that should be used with SMS. In many cases, you can use a small subset of these counters to determine the status of an SMS system. The counters that are most useful to monitor in an SMS environment are:

Object	Counter	Measure on
Memory	Committed Bytes	Site server
PhysicalDisk	% Disk Time (for all physical disks)	Site server and SQL Server
Processor	% Processor Time (for all processors)	Site server and SQL Server
Redirector	Current Commands	Site server and SQL Server
SQLServer	User Connections	SQL Server
SQLServer	Cache Hit Ratio	SQL Server

These counters (and other useful objects and counters) are described in the following sections.

Cache Object

Data Map Hits %

The percentage of data maps in the cache that could be resolved without having to retrieve a page from the disk, meaning that the page was already in physical memory. This is an indicator of application I/O.

Higher is better. A poor cache hit rate may indicate a memory shortage.

LogicalDisk Object

Avg. Disk Queue Length

A measure of the activity of each logical partition of the disk. An Avg. Disk Queue Length of 1.0 indicates that the logical disk was busy for the entire sample time. Busy time includes all processing time for a disk I/O request, including driver time and time in the queue, so values for a single logical disk may exceed 1.0.

Sustained high values over time indicate a possible disk bottleneck.

% Free Space

The ratio of the free space available on the logical disk to the total usable space provided by the selected logical disk drive.

Higher is better. Free space should not go below 10 percent, or disk performance will suffer. If the drive that SMS is installed on runs out of free space, SMS will stop all processing and SMS won't be able to send events warning that all processing has stopped.

Memory Object

Committed Bytes

The size of virtual memory that has been committed (rather than reserved). Committed memory must have disk storage available, or there must be enough memory available so that it doesn't need to use. Notice that this is an instantaneous count, not an average over the time interval.

Lower is better. If the value is consistently less than the amount of physical RAM, then additional RAM is not needed. If the value is consistently more than twice the amount of physical RAM, and the system is paging frequently, then more RAM may be needed.

Page Faults/sec

A count of the page faults in the microprocessor. A page fault occurs when a process refers to a virtual memory page that is not in its Working Set in main memory. A page fault will not cause the page to be retrieved from disk if that page is on the standby list, and already in main memory, or if it is in use by another process that shares the page.

Lower is better.

Pages/sec

The number of pages read from the disk or written to the disk to resolve memory references to pages that were not in memory at the time of the reference. This is the sum of pages input/sec and pages output/sec. This counter includes paging traffic on behalf of the system cache to access file data for applications. This is the primary counter to observe if you are concerned about excessive memory pressure (thrashing), and the excessive paging that can result.

Lower is better. If this counter is consistently high, memory is in short supply. Sustained paging degrades performance.

Pool Non-Paged Bytes

The number of bytes in the non-paged pool. The non-paged pool is a system memory area where space is acquired by operating system components as needed. Non-paged pool pages cannot be paged out to the paging file; they remain in main memory as long as they are allocated.

Lower is better. If this level approaches the amount of physical RAM, the system can stall.

Transition Faults/sec

The number of page faults resolved by recovering pages that were in transition, that is being written to disk at the time of the page fault. The pages were recovered without additional disk activity.

Lower is better. As the number of transition faults approaches the number of page faults, the applications running will approach a state where they produce little results other than thrashing the disk. You can add more RAM to reduce this problem.

Objects Object

Processes

An instantaneous count of the number of processes running. When charted with Processor: % ProcessorTime, it shows the effect on the microprocessor of adding and removing processes.

Paging File Object

%Usage Peak

The peak usage of the page file instance in percent.

Lower is better. If it is over 80 percent, increase the size of the paging file or add more RAM.

PhysicalDisk Object

Numbers are shown for an array as a group. The first disk shows numbers, the others show zeros. Note that you must run **diskperf -y** and restart the computer before you can use this counter. For Pentium-class computers, the impact of enabling these counters is negligible.

Avg. Disk Queue Length

A measure of the activity of the disk subsystem. It is the sum of Avg. Disk Queue Length for all logical partitions of the disk.

This is a good measure of disk activity when measuring multiple physical disks in a disk set.

%Disk Time

The percentage of elapsed time that the selected disk drive is busy servicing read or write requests.

Lower is better. Recommended range is 50% or below. Avoid averaging over 80 percent. This is a good counter to check to determine if the disk is acting as a system bottleneck. A high value may indicate the need for a faster disk, or it may indicate system configuration problems.

Disk Bytes/sec

The rate bytes are transferred to or from the disk during write or read operations.

Lower is better. The throughput for most disks is in the range of 1 to 4 MB per second. To get a feel for the upper limit for a specific disk, start several file copy operations from other physical disks, RAM, or the network. Keep in mind that reading and writing have different limits and that file size, block size, and other factors will effect disk throughput. The whole point to an array is to multiply the throughput by increasing the number of disks. If the throughput for a single disk is 3 MB per second, and 4 disks are used for an array, the total throughput should approach 12 MB per second. There is overhead with arrays that will prevent the actual throughput from reaching this point.

Disk Queue Length

The rate that bytes are transferred to or from the disk during write or read operations.

Lower is better. More than two is not recommended. This is two per disk, in an array, that divide the disk queue length by the number of disks.

Process Object

These are the key processes to monitor in an SMS environment:

- Idle (unused system resources)
- PERFMON
- PREINST
- SITEINS
- SMS
- SMSEXEC
- SQLSERVER (version 4.*x*)
- MSSQLSERVER (version 6.*x*)

For each process, you can monitor the following counters:

% Processor Time

The percentage of elapsed time when all the threads for a process are used by the microprocessor to execute instructions. An instruction is the basic unit of execution in a computer. A thread is the object that executes instructions. A process is the object created when a program is run. Code executed to handle certain hardware interrupts or trap conditions may be counted for this process.

Lower is better. If a single process is using close to 100 percent of the microprocessor time for extended periods, then it is causing a microprocessor bottleneck.

Private Bytes

The current number of bytes this process has allocated that cannot be shared with other processes.

Lower is better. If this number shows a steady upward climb, that could suggest a memory leak. Monitor this value over a period of several hours to be sure it is not a one time increase, as many processes will allocate a great deal of memory on startup.

Processor Object

% Interrupt Time

The percentage of elapsed time that the microprocessor spent handling hardware interrupts. When a hardware device interrupts the microprocessor, the interrupt handler manages the condition, usually by signaling I/O completion and possibly issuing another pending I/O request. Some of this work may be done in a deferred procedure call (DPC). However, time spent in DPCs is not counted as time in interrupts. Interrupts are executed in privileged mode, so this is a component of Processor: % Privileged Time. Use this counter to determine the source of excessive time for Privileged Mode.

Lower is better.

% Processor Time

Expressed as a percentage of the elapsed time that a microprocessor is busy executing a non-idle thread. It is viewed as the fraction of time spent doing productive work. Each microprocessor is assigned an idle thread in the idle process that consumes those unproductive microprocessor cycles not used by any other threads.

Lower is better. Recommended range is 50% or below. This value is a good indicator of the demand for and efficiency of a microprocessor.

Interrupts/sec

The number of device interrupts that the microprocessor is experiencing. A device interrupts the microprocessor when it has completed a task or when it requires attention. Normal thread execution is suspended during interrupts. An interrupt may cause the microprocessor to switch to another, higher priority thread. Clock interrupts are frequent and periodic and create a background of interrupt activity.

Lower is better. A high level indicates a type of microprocessor thrashing. On a Pentium computer, 500 interrupts per second might be normal. High can be as much as 1,000 interrupts per second.

Redirector Object

Bytes Total/sec

The rate at which the Redirector is processing data bytes. This includes all application and file data in addition to protocol information such as packet headers.

Lower is better.

Current Commands

Counts the number of requests to the Redirector that are currently queued. If this number is much larger than the number of network adapter cards installed in the computer, then the network(s) and/or the server(s) being accessed are a bottleneck.

Lower is better.

File Data Operations/sec

The rate at which the Redirector is processing data operations. One operation includes many bytes because each operation has overhead. You can determine the efficiency of this path by dividing the bytes per second by this counter to determine the average number of bytes transferred per operation.

Lower is better.

Network Errors/sec

Counts unexpected errors that generally indicate the Redirector and one or more servers are having communication difficulties. For example, an SMB (Server Manager Block) protocol error will generate a network error. This results in an entry in the system event log, so look there for details.

Lower is better.

Packets/sec

The rate at which the Redirector is processing data packets. One packet includes many bytes. You can determine the efficiency of this path by dividing the bytes per second by this counter to determine the average number of bytes transferred/packet. You can also divide this counter by operations per second to determine the average number of packets per operation, which is another measure of efficiency.

Lower is better.

Server Sessions Hung

Counts the number of active sessions that are timed out and unable to proceed due to a lack of response from the remote server.

Lower is better.

Server Object

Bytes Total/sec

The number of bytes the server has sent to and received from the network. This value provides an overall indication of the server's activities.

Lower is better.

Context Blocks Queued/sec

The rate that work context blocks had to be placed on the server's FSP queue to await server action.

Lower is better.

Pool Non-paged Bytes

The number of bytes of non-pageable computer memory that the server is currently using. Use this counter to determine usable values for **maxnonpagedmemoryusage**.

Lower is better.

Pool Non-paged Failures

The number of times allocations from non-paged pool has failed. Use this counter to determine if the computer's physical memory is too small.

Anything other than zero is not recommended.

Pool Non-paged Peak

The maximum number of bytes in a non-paged pool that the server has had in use at any point. Use this counter to determine how much physical memory the computer should have.

Lower is better, and should leave a buffer of available RAM. Depending on the applications, additional space might be needed to page data and code.

Pool Paged Bytes

The number of bytes of pageable computer memory that the server is currently using. Helps determine good values for **maxpagedmemoryusage**.

Lower is better.

Pool Paged Failures

The number of times that allocations from the paged pool have failed. Use this counter to determine if the computer's pagefile physical memory is too small.

Anything other than zero is not recommended.

Pool Paged Peak

The maximum number of bytes of paged pool that the server has allocated. Use this counter to determine the proper sizes for the page file(s) and physical memory.

Lower is better. The total for RAM and page file should be at least 20 percent larger than this number.

Sessions Errored Out

The number of sessions that have been closed due to unexpected error conditions. Use this counter to determine how frequently network problems are causing dropped sessions on the server.

Lower is better.

Server Work Queues Object

Bytes Transferred/sec

The rate at which the server is sending and receiving bytes with the network clients on this CPU. Use this counter to determine how busy the server is.

Lower is better.

Queue Length

The current length of the server work queue for this CPU. A sustained queue length greater than four can indicate microprocessor congestion. This is an instantaneous count, not an average over time.

Lower is better.

Total Bytes/sec

The rate at which the server is reading and writing data to and from the files for the clients on this CPU. Use this counter to determine how busy the server is.

Lower is better.

Total Operations/sec

The rate at which the server is performing file read and file write operations for the clients on this CPU. This value will always be zero (0) in the Blocking Queue instance. Use this counter to determine how busy the server is.

Lower is better.

Work Item Shortages

Each request from a client is represented on the server as a work item, and the server maintains a pool of available work items per CPU to speed processing. A sustained value greater than zero indicates the need to increase **MaxWorkItems** for the Server service. This value will always be zero (0) in the Blocking Queue instance.

Anything other than zero is not recommended.

SQLServer Object

Cache Hit Ratio

The percentage of time that a requested data page was found in the data cache (instead of being read from disk).

Higher is better. 99% is desirable. If the percentage consistently averages below 97%, you should increase the amount of memory allocated to SQL Server.

I/O - Outstanding Reads

The number of pending physical reads.

Averaging more than two is not recommended.

I/O - Outstanding Writes

The number of pending physical writes.

Averaging more than two is not recommended.

Max Tempdb Space Used (MB)

The maximum amount of tempdb RAM used (in MB).

Max Users Connected

The maximum number of user connections used.

NET - Command Queue Length

The number of client requests that are waiting to be handled by the SQL Server working threads.

Averaging more than two is not recommended.

User Connections

The number of open user connections.

Lower is better. This number should always be at least 10 lower than the maximum limit set in SQL Server. Running out can cause SMS to stall, and also prevents remote access.

SQLServer-Locks Object

Total Locks

A count of all locks being used by SQL Server.

Lower is better. This number should be lower than the maximum limit set in SQL Server.

SQLServer-Log Object

Log Space Used (%)

The amount of space allocated to the transaction log.

Lower is better. If the log space used exceeds 60 percent, the logical log device needs to be increased in size. This should be monitored for both the tempdb and the SMS database log device.

System Object

% Total Interrupt Time

The sum of % Interrupt Time of all microprocessors divided by the number of microprocessors in the system.

Lower is better.

% Total Processor Time

Include this counter to monitor systems with multiple microprocessors. It combines the average microprocessor usage of all microprocessors into a single counter. It can be viewed as the fraction of time spent doing productive work. Each microprocessor is assigned an idle thread in the idle process, which consumes unproductive microprocessor cycles not used by any other threads.

Lower is better.

Processor Queue Length

The instantaneous length of the microprocessor queue in units of threads. This counter is always 0 unless you are also monitoring a thread counter. All microprocessors use a single queue for threads to wait for microprocessor cycles. This length does not include the threads currently running. A sustained microprocessor queue length greater than two generally indicates microprocessor congestion. This is an instantaneous count, not an average over the time interval.

Averaging more than two is not recommended.

System Up Time

> The total time (in seconds) that the computer has been operational since it was last started. Use this counter to determine how often to restart the server.

Total Interrupts/sec

> The rate at which the computer is receiving and servicing hardware interrupts. The devices that generate interrupts are the system timer, the mouse, data communication lines, network interface cards, and other peripheral devices. This counter provides an indication of how busy these devices are on a computer-wide basis.
>
> Lower is better.

Thread Object

The thread object is typically used during debugging when looking for the source of a problem, and particularly when tracking SMSEXEC thread components.

% Processor Time

> Threads are the components of a process that execute its code on the microprocessor. This counter indicates which threads are getting microprocessor time.
>
> Lower is better.

Elapsed Time

> The total elapsed time (in seconds) that this thread has been running.
>
> Lower is better. Some threads may need several minutes to initialize. The longer the thread has been running, the greater the chance for a memory leak, or for corruption to occur.

ID Process

> The unique identifier of this process. ID process numbers are reused, so they only identify a process for the lifetime of that process.

ID Thread

> The unique identifier of this thread. ID thread numbers are reused, so they only identify a thread for the lifetime of that thread.

Priority Base

> The current base priority of this thread. The system may raise the thread's dynamic priority above the base priority if the thread is handling user input, or lower it towards the base priority if the thread becomes compute bound.

Priority Current

The current dynamic priority of this thread. The system may raise the thread's dynamic priority above the base priority if the thread is handling user input, or lower it towards the base priority if the thread becomes compute bound.

Thread State

The current state of the thread:

Value	State	Meaning
0	Initialized	Thread has just initialized.
1	Ready	Thread is waiting for a microprocessor because none are free.
2	Running	Thread is using a microprocessor.
3	Standby	Thread is about to use a microprocessor.
4	Terminated	Thread has been terminated.
5	Wait	Thread is waiting for a peripheral operation to complete or a resource to become free.
6	Transition	Thread is waiting for a resource in order to run (such as waiting for its execution stack to be paged in from disk).
7	Unknown	Thread is in an unknown state.

Thread Wait Reason

This counter only applies when the thread is in Wait state. It is:

Value	The thread is waiting for
0 or 7	Executive
1 or 8	Free page
2 or 9	Page in
3 or 10	Pool allocation
4 or 11	Execution delay
5 or 12	Suspended condition
6 or 13	User request

(continued)

Value	The thread is waiting for
14	Event pair high
15	Event pair low
16	LPC receive
17	LPC reply
18	Virtual memory
19	Page out

Network Performance Objects

You should also include counters to monitor network throughput. The counters you choose depend upon your network protocol and whether the computer is primarily a client, a server, or both. NetBios: Bytes Total/sec for NWLink and Network Interface: Bytes Total/sec for TCPIP/SNMP are good overview counters.

Locating Bottlenecks in the SMS Executive

The SMS Executive is an SMS service that controls multiple SMS components. Because these components all run as threads under SMSEXEC, it can be quite difficult to determine what each component is doing. This section explains how to determine which SMS component thread is causing a bottleneck. The section assumes a problem with CPU utilization, but the technique discussed can be applied to other tuning concerns as well.

To determine if you have a CPU bottleneck, you might start by monitoring the Process: %Processor Time for the Idle process. If this counter is less than about 15 percent, you probably have a CPU bottleneck. Monitor the other system processes to determine which one is using the most CPU time. If the bottleneck is in SMSEXEC, use the following procedure to determine which thread in SMSEXEC is causing the problem:

1. For all instances of SMSEXEC, add counters for THREAD: %Processor Time and THREAD: ID Thread.

2. Determine which thread is taking the most processor time. Note the instance number (decimal) reported in the Instance column in the chart.

3. Determine which ID Thread counter has the same instance number. Note the value that is reported in decimal and convert this number to hexadecimal.

4. Start the Registry Editor (**regedt32**).

5. Locate the thread ID that matches the ID Thread counter under HKEY_LOCAL_MACHINE\SOFTWARE\Microsoft\SMS\COMPONENTS \SMS_EXECUTIVE\Threads. This thread is taking the CPU time.

6. If the ID Thread is a SQL Server thread, consider turning on SQL Server tracing. This will provide a log of the exact SQL statement that is being run. SQL Server tracing is set in following key:

   HKEY_LOCAL_MACHINE\SOFTWARE\Microsoft\SMS\TRACING SQLEnabledc

   Use 1 to enable tracing and 0 to disable tracing. To activate this change, stop and restart the SMS Executive.

Note If you suspect that a certain SMS component is causing performance problems, and you want to see the log for the component, you can run the SMSTRACE or the TRACER program against the log file for the component. These programs display the component logs in real-time. The SMSTRACE program has a graphical user-interface and is therefore preferred. For more information, see the SMSTOOLS.HLP file.

If the interface to SQL Server is causing the bottleneck, you can use the SQLTRACE utility provided with SQL Server to monitor SQL Server activity. The SQLTRACE utility is located in the SQL Server program group.

Task Manager

Task Manager is a new tool introduced with Windows NT 4.0. It lets you monitor active applications and processes on your computer, and start and stop them. It also has basic performance-monitoring capabilities.

Task Manager offers the following features:

- It displays running applications and processes, including 16-bit processes.
- It displays the most commonly used performance measures for processes, including microprocessor time, main memory size, virtual memory size, page faults, base priority, and number of threads.
- It displays line graphs and instantaneous values of microprocessor and memory use for the computer.
- It lets you set microprocessor affinity for a process, change the base priority class of a process and activate a debugger, if you have one.

Task Manager gets its data from the same functions used by Performance Monitor. However, it calls these functions directly, bypassing the Performance Library and the registry. Thus, it cannot log data to a file and it cannot monitor remote computers. However, it is a useful tool for quick checks of basic counters and for training users to monitor their own computer.

Starting Task Manager

Task Manager is integrated into Windows NT 4.0 and does not need to be installed separately. This section explains how to use Task Manager as a performance monitoring tool. For more general information, see Task Manager Help or the Windows NT documentation.

To start Task Manager, use any of these methods:

- Press CTRL+SHIFT+ESC.
- Use the right mouse button to click the Task Bar, then click Task Manager.
- Press CTRL+ALT+DELETE, then click Task Manager.

You can also start Task Manager from the command prompt or the Run command, and you can create a shortcut to TASKMGR.EXE.

The following window is displayed when you start the Task Manager:

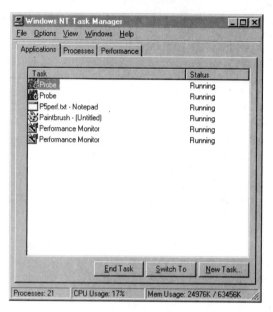

Task Manager has three tabs, but the status bar always displays the total number of processes, CPU use, and virtual memory use for the system. When Task Manager is running, an accurate miniature CPU usage gauge appears on the taskbar on the end opposite the Start button.

Monitoring Processes with Task Manager

Select the Task Manager Processes tab to see a list of running processes and measures of their performance. The Task Manager process table includes all processes that run in their own address space, including all applications and system services. From the Options menu, choose Show 16-bit Tasks to include those in the display.

Note Task Manager displays its values in kilobytes, which are units of 1024 bytes. Performance Monitor displays the full number values. When comparing Performance Monitor and Task Manager values, multiply Task Manager values by 1024 (and drop the K). For example, in the following illustration, Task Manager shows the PERFMON.EXE process using 28K bytes of memory. In Performance Monitor, this value would be displayed as 28,672 bytes.

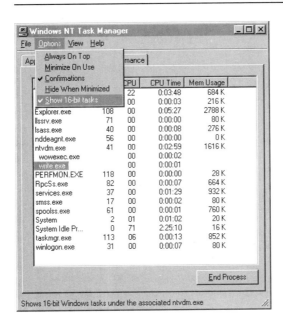

From the View menu, choose Select Columns to add to or remove performance measures from the display. The following table briefly describes the measures and their Performance Monitor counterparts, if any.

Process measure	Description	Performance Monitor Process counter
Image Name	Name of the process.	The process name in the Instances box.
PID (Process Identifier)	Numerical ID assigned to the process while it runs.	ID Process.
CPU Usage	The percentage of time the threads of the process used the microprocessor since the last update.	%Processor Time.
CPU Time	The total microprocessor time used by the process since it was started, in seconds.	None.
Memory Usage	The amount of main memory used by the process, in kilobytes.	Working Set.
Memory Usage Delta	The change in memory use since the last update, in kilobytes. Unlike Performance Monitor, Task Manager displays negative values.	None.
Page Faults	The number of times data had to be retrieved from disk for this process because it was not found in memory. This value is accumulated from the time the process is started.	None. Page faults/sec is the rate of page faults over time.
Page Faults Delta	The change in the number of page faults since the last update.	None.
Virtual Memory Size	Size of the process's share of the paging file, in kilobytes.	Page File Bytes.
Paged Pool	Amount of the paged pool (user memory) used by the process, in kilobytes. The paged pool is virtual memory available to be paged to disk. It includes all of user memory and a portion of system memory.	Pool Paged Bytes.

(continued)

Process measure	Description	Performance Monitor Process counter
Nonpaged Pool	Amount of the non-paged pool (system memory) used by the process, in kilobytes.	Pool Nonpaged Bytes.
	The non-paged pool is operating system memory, which is never paged to disk.	
Base Priority	The base priority of the process, which determines the order in which its threads are scheduled for the microprocessor.	Priority Base.
	The base priority is set by the process code, not the operating system. The operating system sets and changes the dynamic priorities of threads in the process within the range of the base.	
	Use Task Manager to change the base priority of processes.	
Handle Count	The number of object handles in the process's object table.	Handle Count.
Thread Count	The number of threads running in the process.	Thread Count.

Setting the Update Speed

You can control the rate at which Task Manager updates its counts. This will reduce Task Manager overhead, but might miss some data. You can force an update at any time by choosing Refresh Now from the View menu or by pressing F5.

Task Manager Update Speed options:

Option	Description
High	Updates every half-second.
Normal	Updates once per second.
Low	Updates every four seconds.
Paused	Does not update automatically. Press F5 to update.

Using Task Manager to Monitor System Performance

Select the Task Manager Performance tab to see a dynamic overview of system performance, including a graph and numeric display of microprocessor and memory usage.

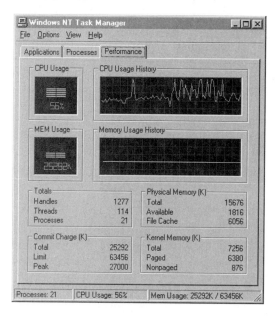

To graph the percentage of microprocessor time in privileged or kernel mode, from the View menu, choose Show Kernel Times. This is a measure of the time applications are using operating system services. The remaining time, known as user mode, is spent running threads within the application code.

If you are monitoring a computer with multiple microprocessors, from the View menu choose CPU History, and then choose to graph the non-idle time of each microprocessor in a single graph or in separate graphs.

The following table briefly describes the counts on the Performance tab and their Performance Monitor counterparts, if any.

Task Manager counts	Description	Performance Monitor counters
CPU Usage	The percentage of time the microprocessor is running a thread other than the Idle thread.	Processor: % Processor Time and System: % Total Processor Time

(continued)

Task Manager counts	Description	Performance Monitor counters
MEM Usage	The amount of virtual memory used, in kilobytes.	Memory: Committed bytes
Total Handles	The number of object handles in the tables of all processes.	Process: Handle Count: _Total
Total Threads	The number of running threads, including one Idle thread per microprocessor.	Process: Thread Count: _Total
Total Processes	The number of active processes, including the Idle process.	Object: Processes is the same, but excludes the Idle process
Physical Memory: Total	Amount of physical, RAM installed in the computer, in kilobytes.	None
Physical Memory: Available	Amount of physical memory available to processes, in kilobytes. It includes zeroed, free, and standby memory.	Memory: Available Bytes
Physical Memory: File Cache	Amount of physical memory released to the file cache on demand, in kilobytes.	Memory: Cache Bytes
Commit Charge: Total	Size of virtual memory in use by all processes, in kilobytes.	Memory: Committed Bytes
Commit Charge: Limit	Amount of virtual memory, in kilobytes, that can be committed to all processes without enlarging the paging file.	Memory: Commit Limit
Commit Charge: Peak	The maximum amount of virtual memory used in the session, in kilobytes. The commit peak can exceed the commit limit if virtual memory is expanded.	None

(continued)

Task Manager counts	Description	Performance Monitor counters
Kernel Memory: Total	Sum of paged and non-paged kernel memory, in kilobytes. *Kernel* refers to memory available to operating system components running in highly privileged kernel mode.	None (Sum of Pool Paged Bytes and Pool Nonpaged Bytes)
Kernel Memory: Paged	Size of the paged pool allocated to the operating system, in kilobytes. The paged pool is an area of operating system memory that can be paged to disk as applications demand more memory.	Memory: Pool Paged Bytes
Kernel Memory: Nonpaged	Size of the non-paged pool allocated to the operating system, in kilobytes. The non-paged pool is the part of operating system memory that remains in physical memory as long as it is allocated.	Memory: Pool Nonpaged Bytes

Tuning Tips

Once you have determined that your SMS system has a bottleneck, you need to tune the computer so that the bottleneck does not impair system performance. You can do this by decreasing the load on the component, or by increasing the capacity on the component. For instance, if you find that the CPU is the bottleneck, you can reduce the number of applications running on the computer (thus reducing the load on the CPU), or you can add faster or multiple CPUs (thus increasing the processing capacity).

The following sections contain information about things you can do to prevent or fix bottlenecks once you have identified them.

Perform the Recommended Maintenance Tasks

Chapter 15 in the SMS version 1.2 *Administrator's Guide* includes a section called "Common Administrative Tasks." This section outlines the tasks that you should perform on a regular basis to keep the SMS system, services, and database functioning efficiently.

Ensure Computers Have Adequate Capacity

Capacity planning is the process of ensuring that a system has enough resources to perform optimally. Ideally, capacity planning should be done before you implement SMS, however it is often a good idea to review your planning assumptions after you have deployed SMS. To review the guidelines for capacity planning, see the SMS version 1.2 *Concepts and Planning*, Chapters 10 and 11.

Capacity planning guidelines generally focus on computer CPU, disk, memory, and networking capabilities. The following guidelines should be observed for SMS site servers:

A fast CPU is required.
The site server requires a fast Pentium, Alpha, or MIPS CPU. In certain cases, multiple CPUs are recommended.

A large, fast, NTFS disk is required.
The site server should have a fast disk formatted as NTFS. Multiple drives or drive arrays are recommended. The disks should have at least 500 MB free; 1 GB free space is recommended. If possible, each major application (Windows NT Server, SMS, SQL Server) should have its own physical disk.

At least 24 MB memory is required.

A site server running only Windows NT Server and SMS should be configured with at least 24 MB. A site server running SQL Server in addition to Windows NT Server and SMS should be configured with at least 32 MB. Additional memory should be allocated to other major applications (such as Microsoft SNA Server or the Windows NT Server Services for Macintosh). In certain cases, up to double the required amount of memory is recommended.

A fast network interface is required.

The site server must communicate with many other servers (some in its own site, some in remote sites).

Optimize Site Design

You should examine the amount of network traffic within each SMS site, and between SMS sites, because the structure of the SMS hierarchy has a significant impact on performance. Poor system performance or excessive network traffic may indicate site design problems. Some possible site design problems are:

- Inadequate bandwidth between sites.
- A single SMS site that should be multiple sites.
- Multiple SMS sites that might perform better as a single site.
- A single domain (perhaps split across multiple sites) that should be split into multiple domains.
- Too many SMS domains or SMS logon servers in a site.
- Too many secondary sites under a primary site.
- Too many or too few package distribution servers per site.
- Clients not reliably mapping to a specific site or SMS domain.
- Clients unable to reliably connect to their SMS logon servers or distribution servers.

Optimize SQL Server Performance

Many SMS services and components make extensive use of SQL Server. In order for SMS to perform well, the computer running SQL Server must be configured for optimum performance. In addition, there should be a fast interface between the SQL Server and the services and components using the SQL Server.

Each instance of the SMS Administrator uses SQL Server. In addition, the following SMS services use SQL Server:

- SMS Executive
- Hierarchy Manager

The following threads (running in the SMS Executive) use SQL Server:

- Alerter
- Applications Manager
- Data Loader
- Scheduler
- SNMP Trap Filter and Receiver

Adjust Server Load

If any SMS servers are performing poorly, see if they are overloaded with other tasks. To do this, determine all other services running on the server, such as logon processing, application sharing, file and print, and so on. Check to see if any of these services can be moved to other servers.

If SMS servers are running SQL Server, serving as package source or package distribution servers, or running SMS sender components, consider moving these functions to other servers. Note that, by default, the site server is used as a distribution server; you can select the distribution servers to be used in a site in the Site Properties dialog box.

Optimize Site Properties Settings

You should optimize the site properties settings for all SMS sites. Site performance is most affected by the service response interval, which is set in the Site Properties dialog box. Setting it to Very Fast causes services to poll more frequently, and increases the load on the SMS system. Setting the service response interval to Slow retards service polling, and causes a much lighter system load. You should set the service response interval so that it runs as often as needed, without overloading the system.

Other site properties settings that can affect system performance are:

- Setting the inventory frequency too high (default is once every seven days).
- Setting the Package Command Manager (PCM) polling interval too high (default is once every 60 minutes).
- Running inventory on clients that use a slow network.

Plan and Monitor Jobs Efficiently

You can use the flexibility built into SMS to schedule and manage jobs efficiently. Schedule jobs to occur during off-hours or on weekends. Use outbox scheduling to ensure data is not sent between sites during busy times. Do not force mandatory installations for large groups at peak times, or even at the same time. Do not recompress or resend packages that have been sent but were not modified.

Optimize Use of Logging

Logging provides very useful troubleshooting data, but significantly degrades system performance. You can use the SMS Service Manager to enable or disable tracing for each SMS service. If you enable logging, you should also use the SMS Service Manager to set the trace file log size. Be sure the file is large enough to collect at least 24 hours worth of data in each log file.

SMS allows you to enable logging for SQL Server as well as for the SMS services. To enable SMS logging for SQL Server, use the following registry key to change the values for SQLEnabled and Enabled from 0 to 1:

HKEY_LOCAL_MACHINE\SOFTWARE\MICROSOFT\SMS\TRACING

You must restart all SMS services and tools for this change to take effect. SQL Server logging is extremely resource-intensive. In general, you should not enable SQL Server logging unless you are actively working on a SQL Server problem.

Control User Group MIF File Collection

If you have a large number of user groups, especially in trusted domains, make sure your site is not generating too many user group MIF files. If you detect a performance problem relating to user group MIF files, use the Set Global User Groups (SETGUG.EXE) tool to turn off or slow down the user group MIF file interval.

SMS collects all global user groups for all SMS domains in each site. User groups are reported at pre-set intervals, as well as each time the Site Configuration Manager starts, even if there are no status changes. User group MIF files include information for every user group that SMS finds in the site—in every SMS domain, and in all trusted domains. In a large SMS hierarchy, especially one with many trusted domains, each user group can be reported many times (once for each site that has access to it through a trust relationship).

User groups are mainly used with program groups, although they can be used with alerts and queries. In most cases, you can reduce the collection frequency. This reduces the load at all sites, and on every server that forwards MIF files.

If you have many MIF files backing up in the DELTAMIF.COL directory, look at some of the bigger files. If they are bigger than 50K and are user group MIF files, you should probably reduce the frequency for user group MIF file collection.

Optimize File Collection and Software Inventory

For file collection, SMS collects all versions of a file. For instance, if you enable file collection and specify CONFIG.SYS, SMS collects every copy of CONFIG.SYS on each client.

Because SMS does not delete collected files, you must do this manually with the SMS Database Manager. For more information, see "Remove Unused Files from the Site Server" later in this chapter.

If you enable software inventory, avoid creating too many software inventory rules. Monitor the time SMS inventory takes to run on typical clients in your sites. If too much time is devoted to software inventory, you can:

- Remove the package rules.
- Disable software inventory.
- Use Software Audit instead of software inventory. Audits are run as Package Command Manager jobs, and can be scheduled to run at a specified time. Software Audit can also be used to target specific computers.

Remove Unused Files from the Site Server

In some cases, you can significantly increase the performance of an SMS site just by removing old, unused files from the site server. Many SMS processes scan all files in a directory each time the directory is accessed. If there are many unused files on a site server, those files will waste disk space and bog down the SMS services. Removing these old files will increase overall performance (stop the SMS services on the site server before removing the files).

You should check for unused files in the following directories:

- SITE.SRV\INVENTRY.BOX\HISTORY

  When records are deleted from the database, the history files in this directory are not deleted. These files are updated each time an inventory record is updates, so if a file is older than several months, the file is probably not being used any more. Search for files with old dates and determine if the files correspond to current records in the inventory; if not, delete the files.

- SITE.SRV\MAINCFG.BOX\PCMDOM.BOX

  Each computer in a site has a package instruction file in this directory (if a package has ever been sent to the computer). These files are not deleted when a computer is deleted from the database. After a simple maintenance job is sent to all computers in a site, any instruction files dated before that job are for computers no longer in use by that database. Sort these files by date and delete the old instruction files.

  After this is done, the same task will need to be done on each SMS logon server in the LOGON.SRV\PCMINS.BOX directory. Delete the files on the logon servers after you have deleted the files on the site server. This ensures that old instructions files are not replicated to the logon servers as you work.

- SITE.SRV\DATALOAD.BOX\FILES.COL

  When you enable file collection in SMS, the collected files are placed in this directory. These files should be deleted with the SMS Database Manager. For more information, see the SMS version 1.2 *Administrator's Guide*, Chapter 15.

Prevent Resyncs

Resyncs occur when inventory information reported to the database does not match information already in the database. The Inventory Data Loader creates a system job to send a resync request to the specified computer. The **resync** command is written to the master inventory command file (RESYNC.CFG) for the computer's SMS domain. This file is then replicated to all SMS logon servers in the SMS domain. When the computer reads the resync request, it generates a full inventory MIF file, which is sent to the database.

Use SMS Database Manager to prevent resyncs by periodically checking for duplicate computers in the database. Delete older duplicates, and fix any problems that may cause duplicate computers to appear. Do not delete all duplicates because this will cause even more resyncs.

Resyncs send system jobs *down* the hierarchy, while resync MIF files and events MIF files are sent *up* the hierarchy. This can overload SMS, especially in a large SMS hierarchy. In addition, the RESYNC.CFG file can grow quite large, which can slow down log ons. If you experience a lot of resyncs in a site, and the resync file grows larger than 50K, you can delete the resync file. The source for the RESYNC.CFG is:

SITE.SRV\MAINCFG.BOX\INVDOpSM.BOX\DOMAIN_X.000\RESYNC.CFG

The next time a resync occurs, SMS will create a new resync file.

Optimize Alerts

Do not set up too many alerts, especially those running complex queries, and do not run alerts too frequently. Alerts that run complex queries can be quite SQL Server intensive.

C H A P T E R   7

Troubleshooting

Microsoft Systems Management Server (SMS) provides a number of techniques for monitoring and troubleshooting the system. The primary troubleshooting techniques are:

- Using the tools provided in the *Microsoft BackOffice Resource Kit* to actively troubleshoot SMS services and applications.

- Using the tools (such as remote control and Network Monitor) provided with SMS version 1.2 to actively troubleshoot computers on the network.

- Checking the status of SMS jobs in the Jobs windows of the SMS Administrator.

- Checking the events in the Events window and in the Windows NT event log.

- Checking the status of the files that are created, modified, copied, and deleted during normal system operation.

- Checking the trace logs for the SMS services and components.

Because jobs are the primary way in which administrators accomplish tasks in SMS, this chapter focuses almost exclusively on troubleshooting jobs. However, all of the information and techniques described in this chapter also apply to troubleshooting other system o`perations, such as client installation or inventory collection.

For more information about	See
Using the tools provided with this resource kit to troubleshoot SMS.	The online documentation (SMSTOOLS.HLP) provided with the *Microsoft BackOffice Resource Kit*.
Using the tools provided in SMS to troubleshoot the system.	SMS version 1.2 *Concepts and Planning*, Chapter 7.

(continued)

For more information about	See
Using job status to troubleshoot the system.	"Monitoring Jobs" later in this chapter.
Using events to troubleshoot the system.	"Using Events" later in this chapter.
Using system flow to troubleshoot the system.	"Using System Flow" later in this chapter.
Using the trace logs to troubleshoot the system.	"Using Trace Logs" later in this chapter.

Monitoring Jobs

After creating a job, you can view the progress and status of the job. For each job, you can view its status at each target site and at each target computer in each target site. Job status can be used to monitor and troubleshoot jobs.

Overall Job Status

In the Jobs window, each job displays its overall status. The overall status is also displayed in the Job Status dialog box.

To view the overall status for a job, in the SMS Administrator, open the Jobs window. The Jobs window displays an overview of the current status of each job for all target sites.

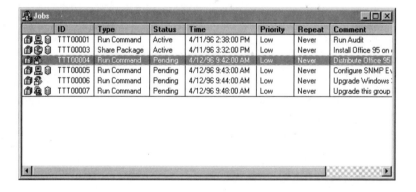

There are seven Overall Status states:

Pending
Indicates that the job has not started and that the Scheduler is waiting to activate the job. When a job has this Overall Status, you can delete the job and prevent it from starting. You can also modify the job's properties before it starts.

Active
Indicates that the Scheduler has started the job and that SMS is currently carrying out the job without errors. The job may be complete or may still be in progress at the target sites or computers.

Retrying
Indicates that the job has failed at some target sites or target computers; however, SMS is still attempting to complete the job at those sites or computers. The job may be complete or may still be in progress at other target sites or computers.

Complete
Indicates that the job successfully completed its tasks on all target computers at all target sites. When a job has this Overall Status, you can delete the job from the Jobs window because the system does no further processing on the job.

For Run Command On Workstation Jobs, Overall Status is Complete when every client targeted in the job has successfully received the package and run the job. For Share Package On Server jobs, Overall Status is complete when the package has been successfully distributed to all specified distribution servers.

Canceling
Indicates that the job is being canceled at all target sites. When a job has this Overall Status, you cannot delete the job from the Jobs window.

Canceled
Indicates that the job was successfully canceled at all target sites. When a job has this Overall Status, you can delete the job from the Jobs window because SMS does no further processing on the job.

Failed
Indicates that the job has failed at some or all target sites or target computers and that SMS has stopped trying to complete the job. The job may have completed successfully at some target sites or computers. You can note the job ID and check the event log to determine why the job failed.

Job Status

The job status dialog box shows the progress of the job at all target sites.

▶ **To view job status at each target site**

1. In the SMS Administrator, open the Jobs window, select the job, and from the File menu, choose Properties.

2. In the Job Properties dialog box, choose Status.

   The Job Status dialog box appears.

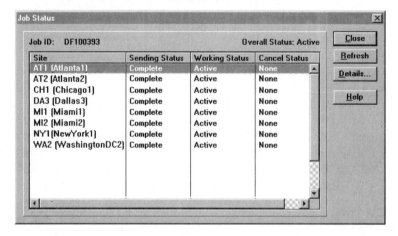

For each target site, Job Status displays an Overall Status, a Sending Status, a Working Status, and a Cancel Status. You can use the detailed status states to help troubleshoot jobs. Overall Status is described in "Overall Job Status" earlier in this chapter. The other three types of job status are described in the following sections.

Sending Status

For each target site, the Sending Status indicates the status for sending the job's package and instructions to the target site. There are seven Sending Status states:

None

Indicates that a sender has not processed the job's send request (the Scheduler has not created a *.SRQ file yet).

Pending
Indicates that the send request for the job has been placed in a sender outbox; however, the sender has not started to send the job package and instructions to the target site. The sender may not have detected the send request for the job yet. It is also possible that the sender has started or even finished sending, but that the Scheduler has not yet processed the sender feedback.

Active
Indicates that a sender is in the process of sending the job package and instructions to the target site (without errors)—but has not completed.

Retrying
Indicates that the sender has failed at an attempt to send the job to the target site; however, the sender is still attempting to send the job to the site. You can note the job ID and check the event log to determine why the job failed.

Complete
Indicates that the sender successfully sent the job package and instructions to the target site.

Canceled
Indicates that the job was successfully canceled before it was sent to the target site.

Failed
Indicates that the sender has failed to send the job to the target sites and that it has stopped trying to send the job to the site.

Working Status

For each target site, the Working Status indicates the job's progress at the target site. There are six Working Status states:

Pending
Indicates that the site has not yet received the job package and instructions.

Active
Indicates that the site has received the package and is in the process of carrying out the job at the site (without errors)—but has not completed.

Retrying
Indicates that the job has failed at one or more target computers in the site; however, the site components are still attempting to complete the job on the target computers.

Complete

Indicates that the job successfully completed on all target computers in the site.

Canceled

Indicates that the job was successfully canceled at all computers in the site.

Failed

Indicates that the job has failed at some or all target computers in the site and that the site components have stopped trying to complete the job. The job may have completed successfully at some target computers. You can note the job ID and check the event log to determine why the job failed.

Cancel Status

For each target site, the Cancel Status indicates how SMS has progressed in canceling the job. This status defaults to none and does not change unless you explicitly cancel the job. There are six Cancel Status states:

None

Indicates that the job has not been canceled.

Pending

Indicates that the site has not received the instructions to cancel the job yet.

Active

Indicates that the site has received the instructions to cancel the job and is in the process of canceling the job at the site (without errors)—but has not completed the cancellation.

Retrying

Indicates that the system has failed to cancel the job on some target computers at the site; however, the site components are still attempting to cancel the job on those target computers.

Complete

Indicates that the job was successfully canceled on all target computers in the site.

Failed

Indicates that the system has failed to cancel the job on some target computers in the site and that the site components have stopped trying to cancel the job. The job may have completed successfully on some target computers. You can note the job ID and check the event log to determine why the job failed.

Job Status Details

Using the Job Status Details dialog box, you can view a job's status for all target computers in an individual target site.

▶ **To view a job's status for all the target computers in a target site**

1. In the SMS Administrator, open the Jobs window, select the job, and from the File menu, choose Properties. In the Job Properties dialog box, choose Status.

   The Job Status dialog box for the job appears.

2. In the box, select the site whose target computers you want to view.

3. Choose Details.

   The Job Status Details dialog box appears.

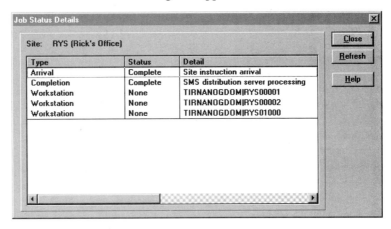

For each target computer, Job Status Details displays the following information:

Type

There are four types of details:

Arrival

Indicates that the package instructions have been received by the destination site.

Workstation

Specifies the target computer for the job's package command (for Run Command On Workstation jobs only).

Server

Specifies the distribution server where the package source directory is installed and made available to the target clients.

Completion

Specifies that the package has been received by all specified distribution servers.

Status

Provides the job status for the target computer. There are seven types of status:

Pending

Indicates that the computer has not yet received the job instructions.

Active

Indicates that the computer has received the job instructions and is in the process of carrying out the job—but has not completed.

Retrying

Indicates that the job has failed at the computer; however, the site components are still attempting to complete the job on the target computer.

Complete

Indicates that the job successfully completed on the computer. For a Run Command On Workstation job, this status indicates that the package command line successfully completed on the client.

Canceled

Indicates that the job was successfully canceled on the computer.

None

For a Run Command On Workstation job, this status indicates that no success or failure has been reported yet (the job has not been run).

Failed

Indicates that the job has failed on the computer and that the site components have stopped trying to complete the job. For a Run Command On Workstation job, this status indicates that the package command line may have failed on the client.

Detail

For a Run Command On Workstation job, the Detail field contains the SMS domain name and the SMS ID for the target computer.

For a Share Package On Server job, Detail contains either an arrival notification string (for example, "JOB ARRIVAL/COMPLETE 11/05/96") or the name of the distribution server.

For a Remove Package From Server job, Detail contains an arrival notification string.

Common Causes for Job Problems

SMS is designed so that a Run Command On Workstations job does not show a status of complete unless all possible target computers have run the package command. Because many Run Command On Workstations jobs are optional, and are distributed to a large number of computers, these jobs typically never complete. This does not indicate that an error has occurred. It just means that not all target computers have run the command.

The following sections describe some other common reasons why jobs might show a failed or incomplete status.

Scheduler Problems

The following are some common reasons why the Scheduler might not begin processing a job:

The Scheduler is sleeping.
The Scheduler runs on a polling interval. When you create a job, the Scheduler won't begin processing the job until its next polling cycle. The frequency of polling cycles is determined by the Service Response speed set in the Site Properties dialog box. Increasing the Service Response speed to a higher frequency might improve the Scheduler processing time.

The Scheduler is busy.
The Scheduler may not get to a job immediately upon beginning its polling cycle. This is because the Scheduler performs many tasks, and some of the tasks (such as compressing packages) may take a great deal of time. Since the Scheduler is single-threaded, it cannot activate any jobs while performing these tasks.

The scheduled job start time has not yet arrived.
When the Scheduler runs, it compares the date and time specified by Start After with the current time on the computer running SQL Server (*not* on the site server). The Scheduler will not start the job until the time on the SQL Server matches the job Start After time.

The Scheduler cannot access the SQL Server.
When you create a job, the job details are stored in the SQL Server database. In order to activate a job, the Scheduler must be able to access the database. If the SQL Server is down, or the Scheduler cannot access the computer running the database, then the Scheduler will not start the job.

The Scheduler is not running.

Under normal circumstances, the Scheduler should always be running on the site server (or on a helper server). The Scheduler is a component in the SMS Executive. You (or another administrator) can stop the SMS Executive, or even the Scheduler component itself (although this is not recommended). If you think that someone may have stopped the SMS Executive, use the SMS Service Manager to check that the SMS Executive is running. To verify that the Scheduler is running, look at the last entry in the Scheduler log file (SMS\LOGS\SCHED.LOG). The time stamp on the last entry should be fairly recent (minutes to hours old, depending on how fast the services are running and what the Scheduler is doing). If the Scheduler is not running, use the SMS Service Manager to start it.

The following are some common reasons why the Scheduler might not complete processing a job:

Scheduler cannot access the source directory.

This error will occur if the Scheduler does not have permission to access the package source directory. The Scheduler uses the SMS Service Account to access the package.

Source directory does not exist or does not contain any files.

This error will occur when the package source directory does not exist or does not contain any files. You must create the package source directory prior to creating the job, and the directory must contain at least one file.

Incorrect path specified.

If you use drive letters when specifying the location of the package source, you must specify the path relative to the computer running the Scheduler. For instance, if you use a specification such as D:\EXCEL, this is interpreted as drive D of the computer that the Scheduler is running on, not drive D of the computer running the SMS Administrator. Also remember, if `you move Scheduler to a helper server, the path means drive D on the helper server.

Site server is out of disk space.

The Scheduler needs to make a compressed copy of the package to send. The compressed version of the package is always created on the root of the SMS installation drive. This cannot be changed. If the drive does not have enough disk space for the compressed package, the job will fail. You can verify that the package has been compressed by looking for it in the SMS\SITE.SRV\SENDER.BOX\TOSEND directory. The compressed package file name uses the package ID (not the job ID).

Sender outbox closed.

If you used the Site Properties dialog box to close a sender outbox, the Scheduler will not assign the job to a sender until the outbox is open.

Addresses aren't defined for the target site.

If any of the target sites for a job do not have an address defined in SMS, the Scheduler will cause the job to fail.

Sender Problems

The following are some common reasons why a sender might not complete processing a job:

Maximum number of sends already in progress.

By default, no more than five jobs can be sent by a single sender, and no more than three jobs can be simultaneously sent to a single site. You can change these defaults using the SMS Sender Manager. For more information, see the SMS version 1.2 *Administrator's Guide.*

A higher priority job is activated.

SMS gives priority to jobs with the highest priority specified in the Job Schedule dialog box. For instance, if there are three sends in progress to a site, and another higher priority job is activated, the Scheduler will suspend one of the lower priority jobs and start the higher priority job. The lower priority job will be resumed after the higher priority job completes.

Sender can't connect to target site server.

Network connectivity problems can prevent a sender from connecting to a remote server. An unreliable network connection can delay a job, or even cause it to fail.

Insufficient disk space on the target site server.

The sender must transfer the entire package and instruction files to the remote site server. The send will fail if the server does not have adequate disk space.

Sender account or password is invalid at target site.

The sender uses the account and password entered in the Address Properties dialog box. The account and password must be valid on the target site server. There can be multiple addresses for one site, so be sure to check the account name for all addresses in the site. To check an account and password, try to manually connect to the server using the following Windows NT command:

net use *destserver***\ipc$ * /user:[***DomainName***\\]***UserName***

For instance, for the user BethS in domain Home1 to connect to a server named FarAway:

net use \\\\FarAway\ipc$ * /user:Home1\BethS

Incomplete account specified in trusted domain environment.
If your organization uses a Windows NT trusted domain model, be sure to specify the domain name when you specify the SMS service account and the site address account. For instance, instead of just specifying the account (for example, SENDACCT), specify the domain and account (for example, BIGDOMAIN\SENDACCT). This ensures that the sender will use the account from the correct domain, even if the same account name exists in other domains.

Despooler Problems

The following are some common reasons why the Despooler might not complete processing a job:

Insufficient disk space on the site or helper server.
The Despooler uses a temporary directory to decompress the package. If the computer that the Despooler is running on does not have enough disk space, then the Despooler cannot complete the job.

Insufficient disk space on the distribution servers.
The Despooler will not be able to complete the job if any of the distribution servers do not have adequate disk space for the decompressed package.

Account or password is invalid on the target distribution servers.
The Despooler distributes the package to the distribution servers using the service account and password specified in the Account dialog box. This account must be valid on all distribution servers in order for the Despooler to complete the job.

Distribution servers do not support package properties.
Distribution will fail if the servers do not support the type of package being distributed. For instance, if your source directory contains Macintosh files, your distribution server must have Windows NT Services for Macintosh installed. Likewise, distribution to a NetWare server will not succeed if the package files use long file names.

Note If the Despooler successfully distributes the package to some servers (but fails on other servers), it will still create the workstation instruction files for the clients. However, it will only include the successful servers in the instruction files, so clients will only access the package from those servers. If distribution to additional servers succeeds later, those servers will be added to the instruction files.

Troubleshooting Jobs

As described in "Monitoring Jobs" earlier in this chapter, you monitor jobs by checking the job status and status details displayed in the Jobs window, the Jobs Status dialog box, and the Jobs Status Details dialog box. If you observe a problem with a job, you can troubleshoot the job by checking the following:

- Events in the Events window and in the Windows NT event log.
- Status of the files that are created, modified, copied, and deleted during the job process.
- Trace logs for the services that manage the job process.

The following sections describe using events, system flow, files, and trace logs to troubleshoot a job.

Using Events

If an SMS service or component encounters an error while processing a job, it reports an SMS system event to both the Windows NT event log and the SMS event database. You should frequently check the SMS Administrator Events window for errors or warnings. If possible, fix conditions that are generating warnings as well as those generating error conditions. Periodically delete old or duplicate events (if appropriate) to minimize the number of events in the event log. The following dialog box shows the Events window in the SMS Administrator:

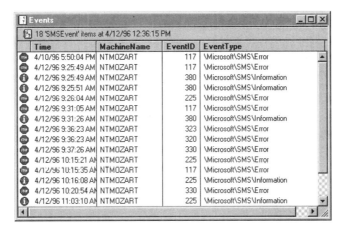

Event Attributes

Event attributes are reported in the Event Detail window for each event. The Event Detail window for event number 225 follows:

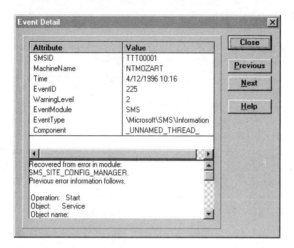

Events in the Event Detail window have the following attributes:

SMSID
The SMS ID for the computer where the event occurred.

MachineName
The network name of the computer where the event occurred.

Time
The date and time when the event occurred. Time is displayed according to the date and time settings on the computer where the error occurred.

EventID
The identification number that specifies the type of event.

WarningLevel
A number that specifies the severity of the event:

WarningLevel	Severity
0	Success
1	Informational
2	Warning
3	Error

EventModule
> The source of the event. This is the text displayed as the Source for the event in the Windows NT Application Log. For most SMS events, the source is SMS. It is also the registry key used to find the location of the DLL that contains the message strings used to display the event's details within the Windows NT Event Viewer.

EventType
> A string that identifies the type of event.

Component
> The name of the service or program that logged the event. For the SMS Executive service, Component may display the SMS Executive thread that logged the event.

Note For Run Command On Workstation jobs, if the job fails to run at a client, the failing component is reported as the Despooler, not as Package Command Manager.

Depending on the type of event and the component that reported the event, the event may also display one of the following attributes:

JobID
> If an event affects the processing of a job, this attribute specifies the job ID of the job that was affected.

JobDestination
> If an event affects the processing of a job, this attribute is the specific destination site (within the Job Target for the job) that was affected.

PackageID
> If an event affects the processing of a job, this attribute is the package ID for the job's package.

RequestID
> If an event affects the sending of a job, this attribute specifies the send request that was affected.

Viewing Events

By default, the Events window displays the main attributes for each event. You can also choose how the events and attributes are displayed in the Events window:

- To choose the attributes that are displayed for each event, from the View menu, choose Partial Details.
- To filter the events so that only the events that meet the criteria you want are displayed in the Events window, from the View menu, choose Filter.
- To sort the events, from the View menu, choose Sort.

You can also change the attributes that are displayed in the Events windows by modifying the default query result format for the SMSEvents architecture, which is used to determine the attributes displayed in the Events window.

You can view events individually by opening the Event Detail dialog box for the event whose details you want to view. The Event Detail dialog box displays the main attributes of the event and provides a full description of the event.

Using Events in Queries and Alerts

Events logged as event MIF files are stored as objects with the Event architecture in the database. As with other objects stored in the database (such as computers and user groups), you can create and run queries against the Event architecture to find the events you want to view. You can also run an Ad Hoc query from the Events window by double-clicking the window panel on the Events window.

As with any other query, you can use a query on events to trigger an alert. For example, you could have a query that searches for events with a value of 3 for WarningLevel. You could then specify that query in an alert. When the alert condition evaluates to true, the alert action is triggered. The alert can send a message, run a command, or log an SMS event.

▶ **To use queries to find events that are related to a specific job**

1. In the SMS Administrator, open the Jobs window and find the job ID for the job you want to query.
2. Open the Queries window and, from the File menu, choose New to create a new query.
3. In the Query Name and Comment boxes, type a query name and comment, respectively.
4. In the Architecture box, select the SMSEvent.
5. Choose Add And.
6. In the Query Expression Properties dialog box, select the line with attribute JobID.
7. Enter the value of the job ID for the job. (Make sure that the Expression Operator is set to is.)
8. Save the query.
9. Run the query.

The events relating to the job are displayed in the Query Results window.

Using this query, you could also create an alert that triggers an action when any events containing the job ID are found in the SMS Event database.

For more information about using events and alerts, see the SMS version 1.2 *Administrator's Guide*.

Using System Flow

A Run Command On Workstation job runs a command defined for a package at specified clients. You can use a Run Command On Workstation job to install a package or to run a command on individual clients. After the job is created, it is added to the site database.

To troubleshoot a job using system flow, you monitor the files that are created, modified, copied, and deleted during the job process. In order to know which files should be created or modified, you need to reference the system flow descriptions in Chapter 3, "System Flow." The following section describes the basic system flow for a Run Command On Workstation job, and then lists the files and directories to check to make sure that the process has completed successfully, or to find where the process has stalled.

System Flow for a Run Command On Workstations Job

The basic system flow for a Run Command On Workstations job is as follows:

1. The job is created and stored in the SMS database.

2. The Scheduler monitors the database for new jobs. When it is time to process a job, the Scheduler compresses the job package and determines the sites and clients that should receive the job. It then creates the send request files and the despooler instruction files needed to complete the job at the target sites.

3. The sender sends the compressed package and instruction files to all target sites. The sender starts processing the send request file as soon as the Scheduler places the file in its directory. (The sender does not use polling; it receives a Windows NT message whenever a file is placed in its directory.)

   If for any reason sending is interrupted, when it resumes it continues from where it left off. If the connection cannot be reestablished, the sender reports this to the Scheduler. The Scheduler postpones the send and tries again later. The Scheduler tries repeatedly to send the job over several days before reporting the job as failed.

4. The Despooler decompresses the package and places it on the specified distribution servers. The Despooler also uses the job's despooler instruction file to create workstation instruction files (WIFs) for each target client.

   Normally, the Despooler does not use polling cycles; it receives notification from Windows NT whenever a file is placed in its directory. It then wakes up and begins processing the file. It also wakes up periodically to retry any failed jobs.

   While the Despooler is processing the instruction files, it sends job status MIF files back to the site where the job originated. As soon as the Despooler successfully decompresses the package, it sends a site arrival MIF file. After it has successfully distributed the package to a distribution server, the Despooler sends a server MIF file. When the package has been completely distributed, it sends a completion MIF file.

5. The Maintenance Manager replicates the WIFs from the site server to the SMS logon servers. The Maintenance Manager also sends package location MIF files back to the site where the job originated. Like the Scheduler, the Maintenance Manager runs on a polling cycle that is controlled by the Service Response speed that is set in the Site Properties dialog box.

▶ **To verify that the Scheduler has processed the job properly**

1. Look for the compressed package file and the despooler instruction files, which the Scheduler places in the SITE.SRV\SENDER.BOX\TOSEND directory in the SMS root directory after the job's Start After time elapses.

   The file name for the compressed package is *packageid*.W* where *packageid* is the eight character package ID for the package used by the job.

   The file name for the despooler instruction file is *instructionid*.I*, where *instructionid* is the five character unique ID in the job ID followed by the site code for the target site. The despooler instruction files contain instructions for completing the job at each target site. The Scheduler creates a despooler instruction file for each target site.

2. Look for the send request (*.SRQ) files on the site server.

    The Scheduler creates a send request file for each target site specified for the job. A send request file contains instructions for sending the compressed package and the despooler instruction file to the target site.

    Initially, the *.SRQ file is placed in the appropriate outbox directory (SITE.SRV\SENDER.BOX\ REQUESTS*sender*.000 where *sender*.000 is the specific sender's outbox directory name, such as LAN_DEFA.000, SNA_BATC.000, or RAS_ISDN.000) for the type of sender being used to send the job to the target site. For example, if a package is sent to the target site using the LAN Sender, the SRQ file would be placed in the LAN_DEFA.000 directory of the REQUESTS directory.

▶ **To verify that the sender has processed the job properly**

1. Look for the sender status (*.SRS) file.

    The sender monitors its outbox for a valid send request. When it detects a send request, it renames it to *.SRS to indicate the send is in progress and to report status.

2. At the receiving site, look in the SITE.SRV\DESPOOLR.BOX\RECEIVE directory for the compressed package file and the despooler instruction file.

    The sender connects to the target site and transfers the compressed package file and the despooler instruction file from the SITE.SRV\SENDER.BOX \TOSEND directory on the site server to the SITE.SRV\DESPOOLR.BOX \RECEIVE directory on the target site server. The Despooler renames the compressed package to *.PCK. When the instruction file is being transferred, it is named *.TMP; once the package and instruction file are received and verified, the instruction file is renamed to *.INS.

▶ **To verify that the Despooler has processed the job properly**

1. Monitor the SITE.SRV\ DESPOOLR.BOX\STORE directory on the site server for the target site.

   The Despooler monitors the SITE.SRV\DESPOOLR.BOX\RECEIVE directory for instruction files and then processes the files. The Despooler moves the compressed package to the SITE.SRV\ DESPOOLR.BOX\STORE directory. Workstation packages are saved as *packageID*.WKS (shared packages are saved as *packageID*.SRV).

2. Check for a temporary decompressed copy of the package.

   The Despooler recreates the original package by decompressing the .WKS (or .SRV) file at the specified servers. The Despooler decompresses the package directory into a temporary directory located on the local drive's root directory with the most space.

3. Confirm that the Despooler has distributed the package to the distribution servers in the site.

   On computers running Windows NT and LAN Manager, the Despooler creates an SMS_PKG*x* share on each distribution server, where *x* is the drive where the package is placed. Then the Despooler creates a subdirectory and places the package in that subdirectory.

   On NetWare servers, the package is placed beneath the LOGON.SRV \PCMPKG.SRC directory on the volume containing the SMS logon server components. The name of this subdirectory is the package ID name.

   For more information about how the Despooler places packages on distribution servers, see Chapter 3, "System Flow."

4. Check WIFs in the master domain box on the site server.

   For a Run Command On Workstation job, the Despooler uses the job's despooler instruction file to create a WIF for each target client in the site's domains. WIFs contain package installation instructions for individual clients. For each domain in the site, WIFs are placed in a domain master box. The domain master box directory is SITE.SRV\ MAINCFG.BOX\PCMDOM.BOX*domain_name*.000. The WIFs are named with the client SMS ID, and an extension of INS (*SMS_ID*.INS).

▶ **To verify that the Maintenance Manager has processed the job properly**

- Confirm that the Maintenance Manager has replicated the WIFs from the site server to the SMS logon servers.

  The Maintenance Manager replicates the WIFs from the SITE.SRV \MAINCFG.BOX\PCMDOM.BOX*domain_name*.000 directories on the site server to the LOGON.SRV\PCMINS.BOX directory on all the SMS logon servers in the target SMS domains.

When all of these processes have completed, the package should be available to the appropriate SMS clients.

Using Trace Logs

SMS employs a number of services to accomplish its tasks. Most SMS services (such as the Hierarchy Manager) consist of a single service component managing one basic task. However, one service (the SMS Executive) consists of a number of service components managing a number of different tasks. Many of the services (including the two already mentioned) are limited to a single copy per site; however, some services and components can support multiple copies running in a site (for instance, you may have multiple senders within a site, and services like the Client Configuration Manager run on every SMS logon server running Windows NT Server).

When tuning or troubleshooting an SMS system, it is extremely important to understand the services and how they are performing. A key indicator is the service trace logs. These logs record the specific actions each service takes, and any errors that are encountered. The log files are ASCII text files that can be viewed with a text editor. Viewing the log files can help you monitor the system and diagnose problems.

Services or components installed on multiple servers (such as senders, Client Configuration Manager, Inventory Agent, and Package Command Manager) read the trace log configuration from the registry of the site server. For example, the Inventory Agent for Windows NT installed on an SMS logon server uses the tracing setting specified for the Inventory Agent on the site server.

The size of the log files is determined by the Trace Log Maximum Size setting, and the amount of data logged. The Trace Log Maximum Size setting determines the maximum size of the trace file. When enough data has been logged so that the file reaches the maximum size, the service renames the current file and starts a new log file. The backup log file has the same name as the active log file, except that the extension for the backup log file has a trailing underscore. For example, the primary log file for the Despooler is called DESPOOL.LOG; the backup log file is called DESPOOL.LO_. If a backup log file already exists, the component overwrites that backup log file when it backs up the log file again.

Because the service keeps a backup log file, the actual amount of data logged can be up to twice the size of the maximum value you set. For example, if you set the Trace Log Maximum Size to 1 MB, you can have up to 2 MB of logged data— 1 MB for the active log file and 1 MB for the backup log file. Therefore, when you plan the amount of disk space taken by a component for trace logging, you should plan for twice the size of the Trace Log Maximum Size setting.

Default Services, Registry Keys, and Log File Names

The default log files for SMS services and components are defined in the following table.

Service/component	Registry key	Log file name
Alerter	SMS_ALERTER	ALERTER.LOG
Applications Manager	SMS_APPLICATIONS_MANAGER	APPMAN.LOG
Bootstrap	SMS_BOOTSTRAP	BOOT.LOG
Client Configuration Manager	SMS_CLIENT_CONFIG_MANAGER	CLICFG.LOG
Despooler	SMS_DESPOOLER	DESPOOL.LOG
Hierarchy Manager	SMS_HIERARCHY_MANAGER	HMAN.LOG
Inventory Agent	SMS_INVENTORY_AGENT_NT	INVAGENT.LOG
Inventory Data Loader	SMS_INVENTORY_DATA_LOADER	DATALODR.LOG
Inventory Processor	SMS_INVENTORY_PROCESSOR	INVPROC.LOG
LAN Sender	SMS_LAN_SENDER	LANSEND.LOG

(continued)

Service/component	Registry key	Log file name
Maintenance Manager	SMS_MAINTENANCE_MANAGER	MAINTMAN.LOG
Package Command Manager	SMS_PACKAGE_COMMAND_MANAGER_NT	PACMAN.LOG
RAS Sender (Asynchronous)	SMS_ASYNC_RAS_SENDER	RASASYNC.LOG
RAS Sender (ISDN)	SMS_ISDN_RAS_SENDER	RASISDN.LOG
RAS Sender (X.25)	SMS_X25_RAS_SENDER	RASX25.LOG
Scheduler	SMS_SCHEDULER	SCHED.LOG
Site Configuration Manager	SMS_SITE_CONFIG_MANAGER	SCMAN.LOG
Site Reporter	SMS_SITE_REPORTER	SITEREPT.LOG
SMS Executive	SMS_EXECUTIVE	SMSEXEC.LOG
SMS Administrator	SMS_USER_INTERFACE	UI.LOG
SNA Sender (BATCH)	SMS_BATCH_SNA_SENDER	SNABATCH.LOG
SNA Sender (INTER)	SMS_INTER_SNA_SENDER	SNAINTER.LOG
SNA Receiver	SMS_SNA_RECEIVER	SNARECV.LOG
SNMP Trap Receiver	SMS_TRAP_FILTER	TRAPFLTR.LOG

Controlling Service Tracing

By default, tracing is turned on for both primary and secondary sites. All services
are enabled for tracing, and the default trace log file size is set to a maximum of
128K. There are two ways to modify tracing properties:

- Use the SMS Service Manager to turn tracing on or off for each service or for
  each component in the SMS Executive.

Note Using the SMS Service Manager to change the state of SMS Executive
changes the state of all components within SMS Executive. For example,
stopping SMS Executive stops all components within SMS Executive. You
should not stop or start individual components in SMS Executive; stop or start
SMS Executive itself.

- Use the Windows NT Registry Editor to edit the values for the service keys
  beneath the HKEY_LOCAL_MACHINE\SOFTWARE\Microsoft\SMS
  \TRACING key. To force a service to use its TRACING key entry, you must
  stop and restart the service. You can use the SMS Service Manager to stop and
  restart the services.

The SMS Service Manager is documented in the SMS version 1.2 *Administrator's
Guide*. Controlling tracing using the registry is described in the following section.

Controlling Tracing for all Services and Components in a Site

The TRACING key has two values (Enabled and SQL Enabled) and subkeys for all SMS services and components. (The subkeys are used to set tracing for individual services and components, and are discussed in the following section.)

The Enabled value in the TRACING key lets you turn on tracing for the site.

The SQL Enabled value enables SMS components and services that access SQL Server to log SQL Server actions to the trace logs of those components and services.

▷ **To control tracing for all services and components in the site**

1. On the site server, start the Windows NT Registry Editor (**regedt32**).

2. Open the HKEY_LOCAL_MACHINE\SOFTWARE\Microsoft\SMS \TRACING key.

3. To turn on tracing for the site, set the Enabled value in the TRACING key to **1**. To turn tracing off, set the key to **0**. To turn on tracing for SQL Server, set the SQLEnabled value in the TRACING key to **1**. To turn tracing off, set the key to **0**.

Controlling Tracing for Individual Services and Components in a Site

If you want to control the tracing for each service and component individually, you can do this by setting the subkeys under the TRACING key in the registry.

▷ **To control tracing for individual services and components**

1. On the site server, start the Windows NT Registry Editor (**regedt32**).

2. Open the HKEY_LOCAL_MACHINE\SOFTWARE\Microsoft\SMS \TRACING key.

3. Select the service or component for which you want to set a different tracing option (for example, SMS_ALERTER).

4. Set the Enabled value for the service or component's subkey below the TRACING key.

   Set the value to **1** to enable tracing and **0** to disable tracing. For services, the subkey name corresponds to the service name. For components within the SMS Executive service, the subkey name corresponds to the component name. (The SMS_USER_INTERFACE key is for the SMS Administrator.)

Setting the Trace Log Path and File Name

All of the trace files for the SMS services and components are assigned a default path and file name. However, you can specify different trace log paths and file names for each service and component. You can also specify that all services and components use the same trace log file and file name. For more information about the default service and component file names, see "Default Services, Registry Keys, and Log File Names" earlier in this chapter.

The path is a relative path to the drive where the component or service is running. When a service reads the registry to get the path and file name of its trace log file, it adds the drive letter for the drive where the service is running. For example, if the trace log path for the Maintenance Manager is SMS\LOGS \MAINTMAN.LOG and Maintenance Manager runs from drive D, the trace log path is D:\SMS\LOGS\MAINTMAN.LOG.

If the directories in the path do not exist, the component creates the directories. If the file name is specified without a path, the service or component uses the first directory in its path. (This is not recommended since it makes the trace log files difficult to find.)

When specifying a trace log file name, you can use a UNC path; however, this is not recommended, especially for components and services that are installed on multiple computers in a site such as senders, the Inventory Agent, and the Package Command Manager. If you specify a UNC name, all of the copies of the services and components in a site write to the same trace log file. In addition, using a UNC path can cause excessive network traffic.

▶ **To set the path and name of the trace log file**

1. On the site server, start the Windows NT Registry Editor (**regedt32**).

2. Open the HKEY_LOCAL_MACHINE\SOFTWARE\Microsoft\SMS \TRACING key.

3. Select the service or component for which you want to set a different tracing option.

4. In the TraceFilename key, set the value for the path and file name.

Setting the Trace Log File Size

You can set the maximum size of the trace log file for individual services or components. To set the maximum file size for a component's log file, you add a MaxFileSize value in the component's tracing key. The value must have a data type of **REG_DWORD**. The data for the value specifies the size of the log file in bytes. If no MaxFileSize value exists, the log file size is the default (128K). For troubleshooting purposes it is often useful to increase the log file size sufficiently such that the logs can hold a full 24 hours worth of data.

▶ **To set the trace log file size**

1. On the site server, start the Windows NT Registry Editor (**regedt32**).

2. Open the HKEY_LOCAL_MACHINE\SOFTWARE\Microsoft\SMS \TRACING key.

3. Select the service or component for which you want to set a different tracing option.

4. From the Edit menu, choose Add Value.

   The Add Value dialog box appears.

5. In the Value Name box, type MaxFileSize.

6. In the Data Type box, select REG_DWORD.

7. In the DWORD Editor dialog box, in the radix field, choose Decimal, and then enter the file size for the log file.

The service will keep a backup copy of the log file, so the log files will actually require twice the amount of disk space specified.

Controlling Tracing for a Component Running as an Executable

You can set up tracing for a component of SMS Executive running as an executable instead of as a service (you may want to do this for diagnosing problems in SMS Executive). The executable will display its tracing output directly to the computer display.

▶ **To control tracing for a component running as an executable**

1. On the site server, start the Windows NT Registry Editor (**regedt32**).

2. Open the HKEY_LOCAL_MACHINE\SOFTWARE\Microsoft\SMS \TRACING key.

3. Select the component that is running as an executable. Set the Enabled value in the TRACING key to **2**. To turn tracing off, set the key to **0**.

Using Trace Logs to Troubleshoot Jobs

The log file for a component has the file name and location specified by the component's key beneath the TRACING key. You can use an ASCII text editor or word processor to view the trace log for a component. You can also use tracing tools provided in this resource kit. For more information about tracing tools, see SMSTOOLS.HLP.

Each line (a line is a string, terminated with an end of line character) in the log file is an action reported by the component. Each line begins with a description of the action. The description ends with two dollar signs ($$). After the description, the component name is enclosed within angle brackets. The component name is followed by the date and time within angle brackets. The date and time is followed by the thread ID within angle brackets.

An example of the data in a trace log for the Scheduler follows:

```
        Sending completed (0 bytes/sec).~    $$<SMS_SCHEDULER><Mon Jul 18
22:28:57 1996~><thread=C1>
MEMORY USAGE:  45103 bytes in 1595 allocations.~    $$<SMS_SCHEDULER><Mon
Jul 18 22:28:58 1996~><thread=C1>
========  Sleeping for 300 seconds  =========~    $$<SMS_SCHEDULER><Mon
Jul 18 22:28:59 1996~><thread=C1>
========  Processing cycle ( 07/18/96 22:33:59 )  ========~
$$<SMS_SCHEDULER><Mon Jul 18 22:33:59 1996~><thread=C1>
UPDATING JOB T100000B~    $$<SMS_SCHEDULER><Mon Jul 18 22:34:01
1996~><thread=C1>
<JOB T100000B>~    $$<SMS_SCHEDULER><Mon Jul 18 22:34:01
1996~><thread=C1>
      Updating status of "Run Command at Workstation" job.~
$$<SMS_SCHEDULER><Mon Jul 18 22:34:01 1996~><thread=C1>
Updating status for request T10000B for destination T10.~
$$<SMS_SCHEDULER><Mon Jul 18 22:34:08 1996~><thread=C1>
Updating status for request T10000B for destination T10.~
$$<SMS_SCHEDULER><Mon Jul 18 22:34:08 1996~><thread=C1>
   <JOB STATUS - ACTIVE>    $$<SMS_SCHEDULER><Mon Jul 18 22:34:08
1996~><thread=C1>
  <SEND STATUS - COMPLETE>    $$<SMS_SCHEDULER><Mon Jul 18 22:34:08
1996~><thread=C1>
  <WORK STATUS - ACTIVE>~    $$<SMS_SCHEDULER><Mon Jul 18 22:34:08
1996~><thread=C1>
UPDATING JOB T1000014~    $$<SMS_SCHEDULER><Mon Jul 18 22:34:08
1996~><thread=C1>
<JOB T1000014>~    $$<SMS_SCHEDULER><Mon Jul 18 22:34:08
1996~><thread=C1>
```

Mapping Job Type and Status in the Log Files

In some of the log files, the Job Type and Status attributes are written as numbers. The following table lists the numbers that correspond to the displayed job type or status in the Job Status dialog box.

Numeric value	Job type	Status
1	Arrival	Pending
2	Workstation	Active
3	Server	Canceled
4	Completed	Complete
5	Reserved	Failed
6	Reserved	Retrying

Reading the Scheduler Log

The Scheduler reports its actions to the SCHED.LOG file. Entries in the SCHED.LOG are reported by job ID.

The following sample log file trace shows that the Scheduler is busy creating (compressing) the package file:

```
Creating package file '\\SMS
SITE\SMS_SHRd\site.srv\Sender.box\tosend\DPW00002.W00'.~
$$<SMS_SCHEDULER><Sun Oct 20 15:48:32 1995~><thread=7D>
```

When the Scheduler submits a job to a sender, it assigns a send request number for the send request. In order to determine the send request number, search for the job ID in the SCHED.LOG file (the job ID is displayed in the Jobs window). Then look for the text Send Request associated with the job ID.

For example, the following trace shows that job DPW000AE has the send request number 30008DPW:

```
~====   Send requests found in outbox \\SMS
SITE\SMS_SHRd\site.srv\schedule.box.~~   $$<SMS_SCHEDULER><Fri Oct 20
19:32:33 1995~><thread=92>
Send Request 30008DPW~    Job:       DPW000AE DestSite:  DPW~
State:     Pending  Status:              Action:   None~   Total
size: 00397693  Remaining: 00397693  Heartbeat: 15:49~   Start:
12:00    Finish:   12:00     Retry:        ~
$$<SMS_SCHEDULER><Fri Oct 20 19:32:33 1995~><thread=92>
Send Request 30009DPW~    Job:       DPW000AF DestSite:  DPW~
State:     Pending  Status:              Action:   None~   Total
size: 00397694  Remaining: 00397694  Heartbeat: 19:32~   Start:
12:00    Finish:   12:00     Retry:        ~
$$<SMS_SCHEDULER><Fri Oct 20 19:32:33 1995~><thread=92>
```

Reading the Sender Log

After you have determined that the Scheduler has submitted the send request to a sender, look in the appropriate sender log for the send request number. For instance, if the send request was submitted to a LAN Sender, look in the LANSEND.LOG file and search for the send request number.

In the following example, the send request number is 30008DPW.

```
Found send request.  ID: 30008DPW, Dest Site: DPW~
$$<SMS_LAN_SENDER><Fri Oct 20 19:34:46 1995~><thread=A3>
~We have 0 active connections   $$<SMS_LAN_SENDER><Fri Oct 20 19:34:46
1995~><thread=A3>
Checking for site-specific sending capacity.  Used 0 out of 1.~
$$<SMS_LAN_SENDER><Fri Oct 20 19:34:46 1995~><thread=A3>
~We have 0 active connections   $$<SMS_LAN_SENDER><Fri Oct 20 19:35:47
1995~><thread=A3>
~Created sending thread (Thread ID = 110)   $$<SMS_LAN_SENDER><Fri Oct
20 19:35:47 1995~><thread=A3>
```

This example shows that the sender has found the send request, and created a sending thread (thread ID = 110) to send the job. Before it created the thread, it verified that it had threads available, and that there were no connections to the destination site.

To continue monitoring the send status, you must use the thread number at the end of each log entry. If multiple threads are active, the messages from the different threads may be intermingled in the log file.

The following example shows a trace log with two active threads. The file name is the package ID (not the job ID nor the send request number). The file type begins with a W (W01 in the following example) to indicate a Run Command On Workstation job. An S is used to indicate a Share Package On Server job.

```
~Wrote 133871 bytes to
d:\dpw692\SITE.SRV\despoolr.box\receive\30008DPW.PCK
$$<SMS_LAN_SENDER><Fri Oct 20 19:35:50 1995~><thread=110>
~We have 1 active connections   $$<SMS_LAN_SENDER><Fri Oct 20 19:36:20
1995~><thread=A3>
~Sending completed [D:\dpw692\site.srv\Sender.box\tosend\DPW00002.W01]
$$<SMS_LAN_SENDER><Fri Oct 20 19:36:20 1995~><thread=110>
Checking for sending capacity.  Used 1 out of 1.~
$$<SMS_LAN_SENDER><Fri Oct 20 19:36:20 1995~><thread=A3>
```

Reading the Despooler Log

After you have determined that the sender has completed sending the package and the job instructions to a target site, you can look in the despooler log (DESPOOL.LOG) to see if the Despooler has started processing the instruction file.

The following trace shows the Despooler processing the instruction file for job DPW000AE. The instruction file has the send request number as the instruction file name (30008DPW.INS). The Despooler also reports the job ID and package ID.

```
~Found ready instruction 30008dpw.ins   $$<SMS_DESPOOLER><Fri Oct 20
20:14:42 1995~><thread=A4>
~Executing instruction of type Microsoft|SMS|WorkstationInstall
$$<SMS_DESPOOLER><Fri Oct 20 20:14:42 1995~><thread=A4>
~Successfully read the instruction file   $$<SMS_DESPOOLER><Fri Oct 20
20:14:42 1995~><thread=A4>
~Start processing Workstation job, Job ID = DPW000AE, Package ID =
DPW00002   $$<SMS_DESPOOLER><Fri Oct 20 20:14:42 1995~><thread=A4>
```

The following trace shows the Despooler determining where to decompress the package, and doing the decompression. The Despooler completely recreates the directory structure of the original source tree.

```
~The package file doesn't require a NTFS drive to decompress to.
$$<SMS_DESPOOLER><Fri Oct 20 20:14:43 1995~><thread=A4>
~D drive has the most free space, we'll use it for temp storage.
$$<SMS_DESPOOLER><Fri Oct 20 20:14:43 1995~><thread=A4>
~Decompressing package W_DPW00002 to D:\_S M0000.TMP
$$<SMS_DESPOOLER><Fri Oct 20 20:14:43 1995~><thread=A4>
```

After the package has been decompressed, the Despooler distributes the package to the specified distribution servers. The following example shows the Despooler creating the package share on a distribution server, and then copying the package files to the server.

```
~D drive on server \\SMS SITE is the suitable drive with most free
space.    $$<SMS_DESPOOLER><Fri Oct 20 20:14:58 1995~><thread=A4>
~Creating share SMS_PKGD on server \\SMS SITE with path D:\SMS_PKGD
$$<SMS_DESPOOLER><Fri Oct 20 20:14:59 1995~><thread=A4>
~Setting permissions on \\SMS SITE\SMS_PKGD\DPW00002 for package
W_DPW00002    $$<SMS_DESPOOLER><Fri Oct 20 20:14:59 1995~><thread=A4>
~Finished setting permission on \\SMS SITE\SMS_PKGD\DPW00002
$$<SMS_DESPOOLER><Fri Oct 20 20:15:00 1995~><thread=A4>
~Copying package from D:\_S M0000.TMP to \\SMS SITE\SMS_PKGD\DPW00002
$$<SMS_DESPOOLER><Fri Oct 20 20:15:00 1995~><thread=A4>
~Copying D:\_S M0000.TMP\itg.dir to d:\SMS_PKGd\DPW00002\itg.dir, OK
$$<SMS_DESPOOLER><Fri Oct 20 20:15:03 1995~><thread=A4>
~Copying D:\_S M0000.TMP\itg2.dir to d:\SMS_PKGd\DPW00002\itg2.dir, OK
$$<SMS_DESPOOLER><Fri Oct 20 20:15:05 1995~><thread=A4>
~Package W_DPW00002 is installed on server \\SMS SITE, register it in
the registry    $$<SMS_DESPOOLER><Fri Oct 20 20:15:06 1995~><thread=A4>
```

If the Despooler has to distribute the package to multiple servers, it copies the files from the temporary directory to the other servers. Then the Despooler creates the WIFs for the clients (the Package Command Manager on the clients reads these instruction files). In the trace logs, the WIFs are called WINST files.

```
~Ready to create WINST instructions.    $$<SMS_DESPOOLER><Fri Oct 20
20:15:06 1995~><thread=A4>
~Found WINST package server SMS SITE    $$<SMS_DESPOOLER><Fri Oct 20
20:15:06 1995~><thread=A4>
~Setting the WINST instruction file, the package path is \\SMS
SITE\SMS_PKGD\DPW00002\, the server type is 2, the zone is
$$<SMS_DESPOOLER><Fri Oct 20 20:15:06 1995~><thread=A4>
~Setting winst instructions for domain DWDOM    $$<SMS_DESPOOLER><Fri Oct
20 20:15:06 1995~><thread=A4>
~Setting WINST data for machine BVT00001 in domain DWDOM
$$<SMS_DESPOOLER><Fri Oct 20 20:15:07 1995~><thread=A4>
~Setting WINST data for machine BVT00002 in domain DWDOM
$$<SMS_DESPOOLER><Fri Oct 20 20:15:07 1995~><thread=A4>
~Setting WINST data for machine BVT00003 in domain DWDOM
$$<SMS_DESPOOLER><Fri Oct 20 20:15:08 1995~><thread=A4>
~Setting WINST data for machine DPW05000 in domain DWDOM
$$<SMS_DESPOOLER><Fri Oct 20 20:15:08 1995~><thread=A4>
```

After the Despooler distributes the package files to all distribution servers, it deletes the temporary directory it created earlier.

```
~ Deleting D:\_S M0000.TMP...    $$<SMS_DESPOOLER><Fri Oct 20 20:15:08
1995~><thread=A4>
~Deleted D:\_S M0000.TMP    $$<SMS_DESPOOLER><Fri Oct 20 20:15:08
1995~><thread=A4>
~Despooler successfully executed one instruction.
$$<SMS_DESPOOLER><Fri Oct 20 20:15:08 1995~><thread=A4>
```

Reading the Maintenance Manager Log

The Maintenance Manager copies the WIFs to all SMS logon servers. After this is done, the Package Command Manager (running on the clients) can offer the new job to clients.

The following trace shows the Maintenance Manager copying the WIFs to the four SMS logon servers in the DWDOM domain.

```
~Working on logon server SMS SITE    $$<SMS_MAINTENANCE_MANAGER><Fri Oct
20 20:51:35 1995~><thread=D6>
~Replicating WINST instructions    $$<SMS_MAINTENANCE_MANAGER><Fri Oct 20
20:51:35 1995~><thread=D6>
~Copying
d:\dpw692\site.srv\maincfg.box\pcmdom.box\DWDOM.000\BVT00001.INS to
d:\dpw692\logon.srv\pcmins.box\BVT00001.INS, OK
$$<SMS_MAINTENANCE_MANAGER><Fri Oct 20 20:51:35 1995~><thread=D6>
~Copying
d:\dpw692\site.srv\maincfg.box\pcmdom.box\DWDOM.000\BVT00002.INS to
d:\dpw692\logon.srv\pcmins.box\BVT00002.INS, OK
$$<SMS_MAINTENANCE_MANAGER><Fri Oct 20 20:51:36 1995~><thread=D6>
~Copying
d:\dpw692\site.srv\maincfg.box\pcmdom.box\DWDOM.000\BVT00003.INS to
d:\dpw692\logon.srv\pcmins.box\BVT00003.INS, OK
$$<SMS_MAINTENANCE_MANAGER><Fri Oct 20 20:51:36 1995~><thread=D6>
~Copying
d:\dpw692\site.srv\maincfg.box\pcmdom.box\DWDOM.000\DPW05000.INS to
d:\dpw692\logon.srv\pcmins.box\DPW05000.INS, OK
$$<SMS_MAINTENANCE_MANAGER><Fri Oct 20 20:51:36 1995~><thread=D6>
```

Glossary

A

ad hoc query A query created for immediate execution. Ad Hoc queries are not stored in the SMS system database, do not affect any queries in the database, and are not displayed in the Queries window. You can create an Ad Hoc query from scratch or by modifying an existing query.

address Specific information for connecting to a target site so that instructions and data can be sent to that site.

alert A set of actions that depend on the results of a specified query. An alert defines how the SMS system should detect a specific condition, using a query, and what actions it should take when that condition is detected. For example, an alert can log an SMS event, run a command from the computer where the Alerter is installed, and send a message to a computer or user on the local network. *See also* Alerter.

Alerter An SMS component (within the SMS Executive service) that processes alerts by evaluating alert conditions and triggering alert actions when the conditions are true. The Alerter also monitors the database for new alerts and any changes to existing alerts. *See also* alert.

APPCTL A program that is part of the Program Group Control feature on SMS clients. This SMS program creates the assigned program groups in the client's Program Manager.

Applications Manager An SMS component (within the SMS Executive service) that communicates package and program group configuration information from the site database to the other components at that site and to the sites beneath it.

Applications Manager database A set of configuration files used by the Program Group Control feature at Windows-based SMS clients. The Applications Manager is installed on all SMS logon servers. At Windows-based clients, the APPCTL program connects to an SMS logon server and collects all program groups assigned to the user logged on at that client. Then it builds the program groups in the Program Manager.

APPSTART An SMS program that is part of the Program Group Control feature on SMS clients. APPSTART lets users start and run SMS network applications that are assigned to them. When a user launches an assigned SMS network application, APPSTART automatically makes the connection to the appropriate server and, along with APPCTL, sets up the proper execution environment for the application.

architecture A structure for recording inventory for a specific type of object. An architecture defines the structure for a set of objects. Each object is composed of groups that contain attributes. *See also* attribute and object.

attribute A property of a group. Each attribute is assigned a value. The set of attribute values for a group comprises the inventory for the component.

audited software   A set of software items that you define. Each software item is defined by the set of files (and their attributes) that you want to use to identify that item. At clients, the user can run the Software Audit program, which scans for these items and reports the items that were found.

B

bottleneck   A single component that degrades system performance. *Bottleneck* is also used to describe the condition in which the limitations in one component prevent the whole system from operating faster.

A bottleneck results in low rates of use on components, sustained queues for one or more services, and slow response time.

C

central site   The primary site that stores system-wide information and manages all sites, with any number of subsites beneath it. The central site is a primary site where all other sites in the SMS system report their inventory and events. When you build a site hierarchy, child sites report their inventory to their parent sites, the parent sites report their inventory and their child sites' inventory to their parent sites, and so on up to the central site. At the central site, you can manage software and view the inventory for any computer in any site in the SMS system. The central site is a primary site that has no sites above it.

child site   A site that has a parent site. A child site can be a primary site that has been attached to another primary site. A child site can also be a secondary site (a secondary site is always the child site of the primary site that created the secondary site).

clause (query)   In a query, the combination of an expression (or subclause) and its adjacent logical operator. *See also* subclause.

client   A computer connected to a network and running network client software.

Client Monitor   A program that monitors changes on the SMS logon servers that must be copied to clients, and copies inventory files from the client to the SMS logon server.

command (package command)   A command line in Run Command On Workstation jobs that runs a program on target clients. A command can be used to install a package (such as an application like Microsoft Excel) or to just run a program (such as a virus scan utility).

community   An administrative relationship between SNMP entities.

conventional memory   The lower 640K (or less) of main memory. The remaining portion of main memory, up to 1 MB, is called upper memory. Beyond 1 MB, an MS-DOS–based computer's memory is either expanded memory or extended memory. The memory map does not map beyond upper memory.

CRC-CCITT   A standard algorithm that calculates the sum of all values stored at a specific set of bytes and compares the sum to a specified value. Unlike CHECKSUM, CRC-CCITT takes into account the sequence of the summed bytes, making it a more reliable tool for identifying files.

current site   The primary site whose database you have logged in to with the SMS Administrator. In the Sites window of the SMS Administrator, the current site is represented as a primary site with a globe.

D

database server A computer running Microsoft SQL Server on which the SMS site database for a site is installed.

default servers machine group A special machine group used for processing jobs at target sites. The default servers machine group specifies the servers where package source directories are installed:

- If Default Servers is selected as the target for distribution servers.

- If a target site does not contain any of the servers specified by Put On New Distribution Servers.

At each site, the SMS system creates the default servers machine group. By default, the default servers machine group contains only the site server.

Delta-MIF A binary file with information stored in the Management Information Format standard and used by the SMS services to add information to the site database.

Despooler An SMS component (within the SMS Executive) that watches for despooler instruction files and compressed packages created by the Scheduler (the instructions and packages can come from the local site or from another site). The Despooler reads the instruction file and uses the instructions to decompress and handle the package files. For example, it decompresses inventory files so they can be processed by the Inventory Data Loader, which then updates the database.

distribution *See* package distribution.

distribution server A server on which the source directory of a sent package is stored and made available at a site. They are called distribution servers because they have a distributed copy of the package's source directory.

For Run Command On Workstation jobs, a distribution server is a computer on which the source directory of a sent package is stored and made available to the target clients.

For Share Package On Server jobs, a distribution server is a computer on which the source directory of a sent package is stored and shared. The shared package on the distribution server can be used for running the SMS network applications contained in the package. Distribution servers are the servers from which the users at clients run SMS network applications.

domain For Windows NT and LAN Manager networks, a domain is an administrative unit based on a database of security and user account information shared by a set of servers. For servers running LAN Manager and Windows NT Server, a domain supplies centralized security and user account information for a group of servers. When a user at a client running LAN Manager or Windows NT logs on to a domain, that client participates in that domain while that user is logged on.

For NetWare networks, a domain is based on a group of NetWare servers on a LAN. The servers in a NetWare domain are specified when the domain is added to a site.

E

expression (query) An instruction to search for objects that have a specified relationship to a specified value for a specified attribute.

An expression compares a specified value against a specific attribute, using an operator (such as is equal to or is like). An expression is made up of an attribute, an operator, and a value.

G

group (query) A set of expressions that are explicitly held together with parentheses. By making a set of expressions a group, you ensure that the group's expressions are treated as a single entity. Groups have a higher operator precedence than the logical operators (AND and OR). You can use groups to help make complex queries easier to read.

H

helper servers SMS Logon servers running SMS components that have been moved from the site server (Scheduler, Despooler, and Inventory Data Loader) or simply installed to those servers (the sender components).

Hierarchy Manager An SMS service that monitors the site database for changes to the configuration of that site or its direct secondary sites. If the Hierarchy Manager detects a change in a site's proposed configuration, it creates a site control file (which contains all proposed configurations for a site) and sends it to the site. The Hierarchy Manager exists only in primary sites.

hit count (query result) The number of objects that the SMS system has found in the site database, according to the criteria specified by a query.

I

identification group A collection of attributes that uniquely identify a computer.

installation Creation of a Run Command On Workstation job. A Run Command On Workstation job enables you to run a package command line at target clients. The command line can start an executable file, batch file, or Microsoft Test script to install the package or simply to run a command.

installation script A file of script commands that a shell program (for example, Microsoft Test) uses to automate a setup program.

instance (inventory/query) A single occurrence of a group in the inventory for an object.

Some groups (such as Disk Drives and Software Packages) can have multiple instances on a single client. For example, a client can have multiple instances of the group Software Packages—one for each package installed (such as a Microsoft Excel version 4.0 package, a Microsoft Word version 2.0 package, and so on).

Other groups logically or physically can have only a single instance (such as the Identification and Mouse).

inventory The information that SMS collects for each computer on the network. The inventory includes hardware (CPU, BIOS, drive information, and so on), software (specified packages), and collected files.

Inventory Agent A component that scans a computer for hardware and software inventory and reports the inventory to the SMS system.

On clients, the Inventory Agent is a program that is run from SMS logon servers. When a user runs the SMSLS batch file, the Inventory Agent is executed from within the SMSLS batch file.

On computers running Windows NT Server and LAN Manager, the Inventory Agent is a service (Inventory Agent for Windows NT and Inventory Agent for OS/2) that reports inventory every 24 hours. For NetWare servers, the Maintenance Manager performs inventory on NetWare logon servers.

Inventory Data Loader An SMS component (within the SMS Executive service) that monitors the SMS system for Delta-MIFs (which store information about computer inventory, job status, and events) used to update the database.

inventory frequency The interval at which the Inventory Agent scans a computer for inventory. Each site has settings for inventory frequency. A site's inventory frequency settings apply to all clients in the site.

The inventory frequency is the time between the last scan and the current time when the Inventory Agent is invoked, either from a logon script or explicitly from the command line. The Inventory Agent scans for two types of inventory: hardware and software. You can set the frequency independently for both hardware and software scanning.

Inventory Processor An SMS component (within the SMS Executive service) that collects all the RAW files created by the Inventory Agent and creates a history file for each computer (an image of the last RAW file). When new RAW files are ready, it compares them with the history files and writes changes to inventory files called Delta-MIFs. The Inventory Processor also converts MIF files in the ISVMIF directory into Delta-MIFs.

inventory rule The set of files used to identify the package. To detect each file, specify its attributes (such as file date, file size, CRC, and so on). The SMS inventory system uses this criteria to identify a software package on individual computers and to include it in the computer inventory.

J

job An object that stores instructions for actions that the system performs. For example, you can define a Run Command On Workstation job to install a package on clients or SMS can create a job to maintain part of the system.

L

LAN Sender *See* sender.

logical operator Connector between two expressions, two subclauses, or a combination of an expression and a subclause. A logical operator defines the relationship between two adjacent expressions or subclauses.

There are two logical operators: AND and OR. AND takes precedence over OR.

logon server *See* SMS logon server.

M

machine group An alias for a group of computers. A machine group is a list of the computers. You use a machine group as a shortcut for referring to multiple computers—instead of having to refer to each computer in a group individually, you can include them in a machine group and use the machine group name.

Machine groups can be used to specify the job targets for Run Command On Workstation jobs and used to specify distribution servers for Share Package On Server jobs.

Maintenance Manager An SMS component (within the SMS Executive service) that installs and maintains the SMS components on the SMS logon servers at a site. It replicates client components and configuration information to SMS logon servers within the site and collects inventory and status information.

Management Information Format A standard for accessing desktop computer components (hardware and software) across multiple platforms. This interface was designed by the Desktop Management Task Force.

mandatory package A package command that must be run by the user from the Package Command Manager at an SMS client before the user can continue working on their computer.

MIF file A management information format (MIF) file is an ASCII text file that contains information about a computer component. A MIF file is a description of the component that is available to other applications through a standard management interface.

MIF files can be ASCII text or binary (formerly called a *delta MIF* file). Binary MIF files are used by SMS services to add information to a site database.

ISVMIF files are generated by independent software vendors (ISVs) to report objects such as computers that have custom architectures. IDMIF files contain inventory information. NOIDMIF files report inventory information that contains groups with no ID or architecture.

N

named pipes An interprocess communication (IPC) method used to transfer data between separate processes, usually on separate computers. You can set permissions on named pipes.

network application *See* SMS network application.

Network Monitor An SMS utility used to capture, edit, transmit, and display frames from the LAN.

O

object An item (whose structure is defined by its architecture) stored in the site database. For example, a Macintosh computer is an object with the Personal Computer architecture.

optional package A package command that can be run by the user at any time (or not at all) from the Package Command Manager on an SMS client.

outboxes Directories where SMS services can put send request files, which contain instructions for transferring data and instructions to other sites. There is a separate outbox for each type of sender.

P

package An SMS object that contains diverse information about software so that the software can be identified and installed.

A package is an object that defines software to the SMS system. When you create a package, you define the files that comprise the software, and the package's configuration and identification information. After you create a package, you can use the SMS system to install the package on clients, share the package so that it can be run from network servers, or maintain inventory on the package.

package command A command line (within a package) that runs a program or runs an installation script that installs an application. A package can have multiple package commands defined. When you use a package in a Run Command On Workstation job, you choose the specific package command that you want to run at the job's target computers.

Package Command Manager An SMS program that runs package commands on SMS clients. The Package Command Manager lets users see the packages that are available and control the installation of optional packages. Mandatory packages are automatically installed by the Package Command Manager.

There is a different version of the Package Command Manager for each supported operating system. On SMS logon servers running Windows NT Server, the Package Command Manager is installed as a service.

package definition file (PDF) An ASCII text file that contains pre-defined Workstations, Sharing, and Inventory property settings for a package. When you create a new package, you can use the Import command from the Package Properties dialog box to define the properties for the package, using a PDF. By importing a PDF, SMS uses the PDF's property definitions to enter the package properties for you. SMS includes PDFs for some of the more popular applications (such as Microsoft Excel).

package distribution An action that is performed with a package. Distribution means placing a package on servers and making the package available from a shared directory.

For Run Command On Workstation jobs, distribution installs the package's Workstation source directory on the specified distribution servers at the target sites, shares the directories on the network, and makes them available to the Package Command Manager.

For Share Package On Server jobs, distribution installs the package's Sharing source directory on the specified servers, shares the directories on the network, and makes them available to users with the specified permissions. The package can be used as just a shared directory or as an SMS network application.

package source directory A shared directory that contains a package's source files. For each package, one source directory can be specified for Workstations properties and another source directory for Sharing properties.

parent site A primary site to which another site has been attached (that is, a primary site that has child sites beneath it in the site hierarchy). A parent site can have primary or secondary sites attached to it.

PDF *See* package definition file (PDF).

pragma statement A line in a MIF file or event configuration file that indicates how the information relates to the information in a site database. *See also* MIF file.

primary site A site that has its own SQL Server database to store the system, package, inventory, and status information for the site itself and the sites beneath it in the site hierarchy. It also has administrative tools that enable you to directly manage the site and the sites beneath it in the site hierarchy.

A primary site must be installed from the Microsoft Systems Management Server version 1.2 compact disc. When a primary site is initially installed, it is a standalone central site. Once a primary site is installed, you can use the SMS Administrator to integrate the new site (and any of its subsites) in the hierarchy of another SMS system.

program group (SMS program group)
A collection of program items within the Program Manager. You create program groups using program items defined by the Sharing properties of packages. From the packages, you choose the program items to include in the program group. You then assign program groups to LAN Manager user groups, NetWare user groups, and Windows NT global groups. Wherever the users in these groups log on, their assigned program groups appear in the Program Manager on the local computer. By choosing a program item, these users start the SMS network application for that item.

Program Group Control　A set of programs (APPCTL and APPSTART) on computers running Windows version 3.1 and Windows NT that enable users to run SMS network applications. The Program Group Control feature sets up and starts the SMS network applications so that the applications can be run over the network from distribution servers.

program item (package)　An object composed of an icon and the command line for running an SMS network application. A program item also contains other details about how the SMS network application should be started (such as running the application minimized). Program items are displayed to the user as icons contained within a program group that is assigned to a user group in which that user is a member. The user can use the program items to start SMS network applications. You define a package's program items in the package's Sharing properties.

promiscuous mode　A state in which a network adapter card detects all the frames that pass over the network.

Q

query　An SMS object that contains the criteria used to find objects in the site database. A query defines and stores the criteria used to identify the objects you want to find. By running a query, you search the inventory for the objects that match the query's criteria. The results are displayed in a Query Results window.

query criteria　The set of instructions used to search for the objects you want to find. When you run a query, the SMS system finds the objects that satisfy the query's criteria and displays them in a Query Results window.

query result format　An object that stores the format used to display the results of a query. A query result format enables you to select which attributes to display for the list of objects returned in the Query Results window. A format is specific to a single architecture. For example, a query format defined for an Employee architecture cannot be used to display computers, which may have a Personal Computer architecture.

Query Results window　A window that displays the results of a query using the specified query result format. A Query Results window displays all the objects that match the query's criteria.

You can modify the query and run it again by choosing the query bar. Note that any modifications you make to the query from a Query Results window do not affect the original query (which is stored in the database).

R

RAS Sender *See* sender.

RAW file A binary inventory file that is processed by the Inventory Processor into a binary MIF file.

relational operator (query) Part of an expression (such as is equal to or is like) that defines how the specified value should be compared with the actual value stored for the specified attribute. *See also* expression (query).

remote control agent A program (either USERTSR.EXE or USERIPX.EXE) that enables you to use the remote troubleshooting utilities to diagnose or control a client.

remote site A site other than the current one.

remote troubleshooting utilities Tools that allow you to directly control and monitor remote clients running MS-DOS, Windows version 3.1, and Windows for Workgroups version 3.11.

Remove Package From Server job A job that removes a package installed on servers.

A Remove Package From Server job can remove the compressed package stored on the site server and the package source directory installed on specific distribution servers.

repeating job A job with its Repeat option set to a time interval. (You set the Repeat option in the Job Schedule dialog box.) The SMS system measures the interval starting from the Start After time. For example, a job with a Repeat setting of Daily and a Start After setting of 8/1/93 10:00 P.M. will have its second repeat job activated after 8/2/93 10:00 P.M., the third at 8/3/93 10:00 P.M., and so on.

Run Command On Workstation job A job that runs a package command at target clients.

A Run Command On Workstation job sends the source directory specified by the package's Workstations properties to target sites (and places them on specified distribution servers) and makes the package command available at target clients. At each target client, the user can run the package command by selecting the package command.

S

Scheduler An SMS component (within the SMS Executive service) that detects pending jobs and creates auxiliary files that allow jobs to be processed. This includes jobs initiated by a user, such as a Run Command On Workstations job, as well as system jobs.

secondary site A site that has no SQL Server database to store its system, package, inventory, and status information. Instead, it forwards inventory and status information to its primary site for processing and storage. It also does not have administrative tools for direct administration of the site—you must administer a secondary site through one of its parent sites (a primary site above the secondary site).

You install a secondary site by using the SMS Administrator at the primary site under which the new secondary site will be placed. A secondary site can only be created and configured from an immediate primary site. A secondary site cannot have subsites beneath it.

send An action that is performed by a job when handling a package. Sending is the method used by the SMS system to transfer data and instructions for jobs between sites (limited sending also occurs within a site). When a job is activated by the Scheduler, the Scheduler compresses the data or instructions needed to complete the job and writes a send request for a sender to transfer the data or instructions. The sender transfers the data or instructions to the target site, where the Despooler handles or routes the data or instructions to the SMS services required to complete the job at that site.

send request file A file with instructions that the sender uses to connect to a specified site and to transfer the specified data to the site.

sender An SMS component (within the SMS Executive service) that is used by the SMS system to send instructions and data from one site to another (such as reporting inventory information or installing software on clients at another site). There are three types of senders: LAN Sender, RAS Sender, and SNA Sender. The RAS Sender and SNA Sender are divided into subtypes to support different means of communication.

SMS supplies three RAS Senders: MS_ASYNC_RAS_SENDER, MS_ISDN_RAS _SENDER, and MS_X25_RAS_SENDER. SMS supplies two SNA Senders: MS_BATCH_SNA _SENDER and MS_INTER_SNA_SENDER.

Share Package On Server job A job that places files on servers and shares them, enabling users access to the files at each target site. A Share Package On Server job installs the package's Sharing source directory on target servers and shares that directory using the specified share and permissions.

This job can be to simply distribute and share a directory at a set of servers in a site, giving users access to a copy of the source directory files. Or it can be used to install the package so that the applications it contains can be set up as SMS network applications, letting assigned users run the package's programs over the network.

site An SMS object that logically groups a set of domains into an administrative unit for managing computers. Every site has a site server.

When you configure a site, you select the domains that you want to include in the site.

There are two types of sites: primary sites and secondary sites.

When you set up an SMS system for your organization, you must have a primary site that serves as the central site.

site code A three-character code that the SMS system uses to identify a site. Used as part of the addressing information for communicating between sites, the code for any site must be unique across the SMS system.

Site Configuration Manager An SMS service that installs and maintains the SMS services at the site server and the SMS logon servers in the site. The Site Configuration Manager monitors all the SMS services on the site server and all the SMS logon servers to ensure that those servers are active and the SMS services are started.

site control file An ASCII text file that contains the configuration for a site.

When a site is first created or the site properties are modified, the Hierarchy Manager creates a site control file with the proposed configuration for the site. The Site Configuration Manager reads this file to configure the site.

A site control file is also used by the Site Configuration Manager to report the current site configuration to the Hierarchy Manager, which uses the file to update the site configuration information stored in the site database.

site database   A Microsoft SQL Server database that stores system information (configuration and status) and the software and hardware inventory at a primary site. Every primary site must have a site database.

site group   An alias for a group of sites—that is, a shortcut for referring to multiple sites. Instead of referring to each site individually, you can include them in a site group and use the site group name. You can use a site group to limit a job to the sites in the site group. You can also use a site group to narrow down a query.

Site Reporter   At child sites, an SMS component (within the SMS Executive service) that detects a queue of Delta-MIFs containing inventory, job status, or event information, and creates a mini-job to send these files on to the parent site. The Site Reporter exists in both primary and secondary sites.

site server   A computer that contains the SMS components needed to monitor and manage the site, its domains, and its computers. Each site must have a site server.

SMS Administrator   The program used to administer the SMS system.

SMS client   A computer included in the SMS computer inventory. An SMS client is included in the computer inventory, receives packages for installation, and can run SMS network applications. In addition, the SMS system assigns the client an ID that is unique across the whole SMS system.

SMS logon server   A server added to the computer inventory of a site. An SMS logon server supports SMS configuration, inventory collection, package installation, and SMS network applications for the SMS clients in its domain. A site server is automatically added as an SMS logon server.

SMS network application   A computer program defined within a package and run over the network by individual users at clients. In the SMS system, SMS network applications are defined as program items within a package. You can assemble program items from any package into program groups. These program groups are then assigned to LAN Manager user groups, Windows NT Server global groups, or NetWare user groups. Wherever these users log on, they will see a program group that contains their assigned SMS network applications in the Program Manager on the local client.

SMS system database   *See* site database.

SNA Receiver   An SMS service that processes instructions and data sent by an SNA Sender. When you install an SNA Sender on a computer, the SNA Receiver is automatically installed with it.

SNA Sender   *See* sender.

subclause (query)   A set of expressions that can be logically treated as a single expression. You can explicitly specify that a subclause is a group. A group is surrounded by parentheses.

subsite   A site beneath another site in the site hierarchy.

system database   *See* site database.

system job   A job that transfers system instructions to other sites. System jobs are used to maintain a site or report event, status, or inventory data to other sites.

T

target clients The computers where a package is installed by a Run Command On Workstation job. The target clients can be specified as a machine group, as the result of a query at the job's start time, or as all clients in the whole corporation, site, or SMS domain.

target sites The sites where a job sends a package or performs an action. For example, when you create a Run Command On Workstation job, the target sites are the sites where the target clients are located.

trigger A condition that sets off an alert when the condition is true. *See also* alert.

W

workgroup A logical grouping of computers for browsing network resources. Windows NT, Windows for Workgroups, and Microsoft Workgroup Add-on for MS-DOS support workgroups.

Index

How to **build**
groupware applications
in **less than** a **day.**

With this results-oriented step-by-step guide and Microsoft® Exchange, you can do it. In fact, with this volume, even nonprogrammers can learn to quickly create professional-quality mail-enabled and groupware applications. And Visual Basic® programmers can give those applications more power. The secret for customizing Microsoft Exchange is in three built-in components—public folders, the Exchange Forms Designer, and Visual Basic for Applications. This book shows you how to put them to work. Get BUILDING MICROSOFT EXCHANGE APPLICATIONS. And start saving time.

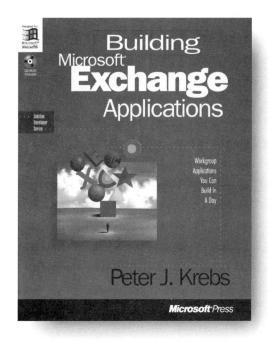

U.S.A.	$39.95
Canada	$54.95

ISBN 1-57231-334-X

Microsoft Press

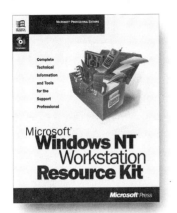

How to become a **Microsoft® SQL Server™** version 6.5 **maven.**

And how to prepare yourself for the Microsoft Certified Professional exams.

Learn to install, configure, implement, administer, and troubleshoot Microsoft SQL Server version 6.5 on a corporate network, an intranet, or an Internet site. This two-volume self-paced workbook with its companion CD-ROM will train you to support SQL Server in your organization. What's more, it will help you to prepare for the Microsoft Certified Professional exams for Microsoft SQL Server. In short, to become an expert—especially a Microsoft Certified Professional—this is the kit you need.

Included on the companion CD:

- Microsoft SQL Server version 6.5 (training version)
- Microsoft Internet Explorer
- Lesson files that work with the tutorial
- Animated demonstrations

U.S.A.	**$199.95**
Canada	$275.95

ISBN 1-55615-930-7

Microsoft® Press